CAMP Z

CAMP Z

THE SECRET LIFE OF RUDOLF HESS

STEPHEN McGINTY

HarperCollins Publishers Ltd

Camp Z

Published by HarperCollins Publishers Ltd
First published in Great Britain in 2011 by Quercus

First Canadian edition

HarperCollins Publishers Ltd
2 Bloor Street East, 20th Floor
Toronto, Ontario, Canada
M4W 1A8

www.harpercollins.ca

Library and Archives Canada Cataloguing in Publication
information is available upon request

ISBN 978-1-44340-659-8

Printed and bound in the United States
RRD 9 8 7 6 5 4 3 2 1

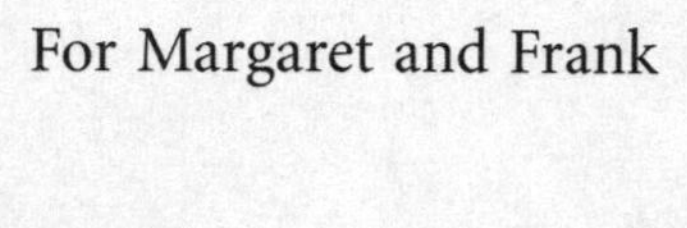

For Margaret and Frank

To Lori, 'She was high society in a low Hollywood dive.'

The psychiatrist suddenly found himself a participant in the inner history of world events.

Henry V. Dicks

The Hess episode was comedy from beginning to the end.

Sir Ivone Kirkpatrick

Contents

Author's Notes xiii
1: Arrival 1
2: Genesis 14
3: Flight 41
4: Hitler 55
5: House of Secrets 64
6: A Psychiatrist in the Rain 93
7: A Lord Comes Calling 112
8: Whistling in the Dark 150
9: Into the Darkness 158
10: Jagged Thoughts and Treacherous Suspicions 176
11: The Man in the Homburg Hat 207
12: The Black Art 235
13: The King and I 256
14: Departure 286
Epilogue 307
Acknowledgements 323
Index 325

Author's Notes

To write a book on Rudolf Hess is to tread a well-worn path and to benefit from the Herculean labour of those for whom his flight on 10 May, 1941 remains a life-long fascination. I am deeply indebted to a number of authors whose pioneering work on different strands of the case I have been able to draw upon. The relationship between Rudolf Hess and Albrecht Haushofer was thoroughly explored by Lord James Douglas Hamilton, the son of Hess's intended target, in his book *The Truth About Rudolf Hess* (Mainstream Publishing, 1993). He can also be credited for bringing Albrecht Haushofer's moving poetry to a wider audience. The background to, and huge risks taken, by Frank Foley in permitting the escape of so many German Jews is brilliantly detailed in *Foley: The Spy Who Saved 10,000 Jews* (Hodder & Stoughton, 1999) by Michael Smith. Following the publication of his biography Michael Smith uncovered an entry in Foley's wife's diary that indicates the likelihood that Frank Foley and MI6 at least examined the possibility of responding to Albrecht Haushofer's letter, with the officer heading to Portugal, before the plan was abandoned. The historical insight into Russia's concerns about Rudolf Hess and suspicions over Britain's future use of him was the result of the pioneering work of Gabriel Gorodetsky in his tremendous book, *Grand Delusion: Stalin and the German Invasion of Russia*, (Yale University Press, 1999) which mined the then newly open Russian archives to tell both sides of how Britain tried to 'Run the Bolshevik Hare' and gave another insight into why the Soviet Union refused all arguments about Hess's possible release.

The man who first shone a torch onto what went on at 'Camp Z' was the historian David Irving in his book *Hess: The Missing Years 1941–1945* (1987) and it was Mr Irving who first discovered, in the Federal Records Center in America, the eighteen notebooks in which the RAMC orderlies jotted their observations of the deputy Führer following his attempted suicide until his departure to Nuremberg.

Another invaluable book was *The Case of Rudolf Hess: A Problem in Diagnosis and Forensic Psychiatry* by J. R. Rees, (William Heinemann, 1947) which tells the story of Hess's captivity from the viewpoint of the men, including Henry V. Dicks who were charged with his psychological care while at 'Camp Z'. A fascinating text, it also includes a 33 page statement from Rudolf Hess, detailing his own experiences and delusions during his stay in Britain.

For details on the flight of Rudolf Hess, I would point readers to *The Flight of Rudolf Hess: Myths and Reality* by Roy Conyers Nesbit and Georges Van Acker (The History Press Ltd, 2007), while an excellent overview of the entire story can be found *Flight From Reality: Rudolf Hess and His Mission to Scotland*, 1941 edited by David Stafford (Pimlico, 2002), a collection of essays written for a historical conference at Edinburgh University, published to coincide with the 60th anniversary of his flight.

The primary basis of this book were the documents found in Britain's public records offices.

At the Imperial War Museum I was able to draw upon Lieutenant Colonel A. Malcolm Scott's 'Camp Z diary 1941–1942' (IWM69/66/1).

At the Public Records Office at Kew Gardens in London I was able to access the following files:

FO 1093/1 Conversations between Hess and various officials, May–June 1941

FO 1093/2 Translations of Hess's correspondence, August–December, 1941

FO 1093/3 Translation of Hess's correspondence, December 1941–December 1942

FO 1093/4 Translation of Hess correspondence, Feb 1942–Dec 1943

FO 1093/5 Correspondence between War Office and PoW reception station, June 1941–Oct 1945.

FO 1093/6 Exploitation of Hess for Propaganda

FO 1093/7 Memo by O'Neill on Propaganda use of Hess, 1941

FO 1093/8 General Correspondence on Camp Z 1941-1944

FO 1093/10–14 Conversations between Hess and various officials, 1941

FO 1093/14 Letters between War Office and Camp Z 1941

FO 1093/15 Letters between War Office and Camp Z 1942

FO 1093/16 Letters with Swiss Legation

KV 2/34 MI5 Documents relating to Hess, 12 May 1941–20 May 1941

KV 2/35–38 MI5 files relating to Hess

PREM 3/219/1 Hess's effect on the USA, June 1941

PREM 3/219/2 Hess medical report, Aug 1941

PREM 3/219/4 Hess: Public statements, May 1941

PREM 3/219/5 Hess's interview with Dr Guthrie (Lord Simon)

PREM 3/219/6 Soviet attitude to Hess and report by Lord Privy Seal, Oct–Nov 1942

At the House of Lords, I was able to make full use of Lord Beaverbrooks's papers, which include letters and a full transcript of his conversation with Hess.

Over the years all those fascinated by the Hess case have lived in hope of a new deluge of public documents. During the research for my book, my own Holy Grail was the dozens if not hundreds of secret recordings, that had taken place at Camp Z using the hidden microphones. Sadly I was unable to uncover them, and now that Professor Keith Jeffery has published *MI6: The History of the Secret Intelligence Service 1909–1949* (Bloomsbury, 2010), the official history, for which he was allowed to rummage where no other historian had set foot, and where he found no trace of the transcripts or records, it can only be assumed that like so much of MI6's paperwork, the transcripts and recordings were destroyed as soon as they were no longer required for active operations. However, should any reader know differently, I would be delighted to hear from them.

1

Arrival

At five o'clock on the afternoon of 20 May 1941 a dark green army ambulance, marked with the distinctive Red Cross on a white circle, drove along the rural lanes of Surrey. Two hours earlier it had departed the portcullis gate of the Tower of London and headed south through a city which, ten days before, had sustained the heaviest night of bombing during the Blitz. On that same evening, as wave after wave of German bombers dropped their payload over the capital, four hundred miles north a lone Messerschmitt had flown across Scotland on a mission that would beguile a world at war.

Earlier in the day, a reconnaissance team had determined the swiftest route for the ambulance's journey, and the roads on which it travelled were clear. But the windscreen still framed evidence of the destructive power of thousands of tonnes of high explosives as the vehicle passed houses reduced to rubble sculptures and streets rendered into flattened fields of brick.

At the wheel was a Scots Guardsman, accompanied on the passenger seat by a colleague while, leading the way in a nondescript car, was an escort of three members of the Coldstream Guards, their Tommy guns discreetly wrapped in rugs and each armed with a pistol.

In the back of the ambulance, rocking gently side to side, were two men in military uniform. While one wore the sand-coloured tunic of a doctor in the British Royal Army Medical Corps, his companion wore apparel of an entirely different hue, design and nationality. He was a distinctive figure in his polished black leather boots, puffed-out navy blue breeches, blue shirt, tightly knotted blue tie, and his fitted tunic jacket on the bright polished buttons of which were decoratively carried the distinctive eagle of the Luftwaffe.

Preparations for the ambulance's arrival had begun a few days earlier. At 3.30 p.m. on Friday, 16 May 1941, Major Malcolm Scott received a telephone call at Donaldson's school camp in Edinburgh with curt instructions to hand over command to a new appointment who would be arriving the next day. He was then to report to Colonel Norman Coates at Hoban House in London at twelve noon on Sunday. After spending Saturday briefing his successor and nervously awaiting the auditor's approval of the camp accounts, Major Scott caught the night train to London, which clanked out of Waverley Station at 10 p.m.

He was not alone in being shunted from one job to another. On that same Saturday, Colonel Swinton, the commanding officer of the training battalion of the Scots Guards, was enjoying the sunshine and the role of honoured spectator at the regimental sports day at their base in Pirbright. There, the Brigade Major arrived 'in great secrecy after luncheon and a conference was held in the middle of the croquet lawn'. Swinton was to pick a team of men to secure the grounds of Mytchett Place against a covert enemy attack. Work was to begin immediately.

The following morning, in the office of Colonel Coates, Scott received a temporary promotion and his new orders. These were marked: 'Operation Order No: 1 Most Secret', and detailed as follows:

> Major A.M. Scott:
>
> These are your orders:-
>
> 1. You will proceed to Camp 'Z' at 12.00 hours on Sunday May 18th instant to take Command.
> 2. This camp is a special one and will be guarded by a contin-

gent of Coldstream and Scots Guards from Pirbright.

3. You will be responsible for the custody of the prisoner at 'Z' and for the security of the camp. You will be responsible also for the health and comfort of the prisoner. Food, books, writing materials, and recreation are to be provided for him. He is not to have newspapers nor wireless.
4. He is not to have any contacts with the outside world whatsoever.
5. He is not to have any visitors except those prescribed by the Foreign Office, who will present Military Permit A.F.A.17 with the stamp of the D.D.P.W on the left, signed by Sir Alexander Cadogan, Permanent Under-Secretary at the Foreign Office and on the right, the Foreign Office stamp. No matter who the visitor may be he must not be allowed inside the perimeter of your camp unless he produces this authority.
6. The prisoner will not be allowed to send any letters whatsoever from your camp without first having been submitted to D.P.W.
7. All correspondence addressed to the prisoner, arriving at your Camp will be submitted in the first instance to D.P.W.
8. A small car is being attached to the camp for the purposes of contact.
9. You are accorded the local rank of Lieut. Colonel whilst employed as Commandant of Z Camp, but it will be clearly understood that when this special duty is completed you will revert to your personal rank.
10. Further orders will be issued to you in writing from time to time, and these orders will formulate your authority.

Signed: N. Coates. (D.D.P.W)

After Scott had read his new orders and noted that, according to the first, he was already late, he and Colonel Coates travelled by car to the camp.

*

The precise origins of Mytchett Place are unclear, but it is thought that it was built in 1779 – on the site of an earlier farmhouse – by a builder named John Hollest as a home for his mother-in-law, Mary Leigh Willis. The small dwelling was originally christened Mytchett House and held the name for sixteen years until the death of Mrs Willis in 1795, when the male ego exerted itself and it became known as the Hollest Place, after its creator who moved in with his wife.

Yet while John Hollest may have built the house, its later renovation and striking gardens were the work of different hands. Thomas Allason, whose principal job was as permanent surveyor to the Alliance Fire Office, was much influenced by the style of the ancient Greeks whose antiquities he had studied on a visit to the country in 1814. While his day job of advising on repairing fire damage brought him into frequent contact with the cream of society (families such as the Rothschilds, Montefiores and Ricardos), he established his private reputation with his work for the Earl of Shrewsbury. He designed various extensions to Alton Towers, but it was the layout of the gardens where his genius was most clearly exhibited. He also redecorated Blenheim Palace, in one of whose many commodious lavatories Winston Churchill was later born.

The Hollest family, like many, was unable to avoid the touch of tragedy. Mary Leigh Hollest died in 1820, followed nineteen years later by her husband, John in 1839. The estate and house were bequeathed to their eldest son, John Leigh Hollest who, four years later and for reasons unknown, changed his name by deed poll to John Leigh Williams.

As was the custom for younger sons who lacked the inheritance of land, George Hollest sought refuge and a comfortable living in the Church. Unfortunately, it was neither as safe nor reliable a sinecure as one might have expected. Instead, as the rector of Firmley, George became the victim of a notorious Victorian murder in 1850. He was shot in the stomach by a marble bullet on disturbing two burglars, after whom – unaware of the extent of his injuries – he then gave chase, A day and a half later, having endured great pain, he forgave his killers and died.

The case became a *cause célèbre*, with letters to *The Times* bemoaning the absence of police in rural parts, thus prompting the formation of the Surrey Constabulary. As one correspondent wrote: 'What is the country coming to if a village parson cannot sleep safely in his bed through lack of proper policing, while the taxes are being spent on warships that couldn't withstand the first shot from an enemy ship?'

In 1847, three years before the murder, John Leigh Williams as he now was leased Mytchett Lodge to a Mr R.R. Bayley, whose wife remained in residence until 1862. The house and surrounding land was passed into the hands of Captain Hastings David Sands in 1860 who initially permitted Mrs Bayley to remain as tenant, and, following his death in 1867 his wife, Georgina Elizabeth, took up residence for a time while also setting about mortgaging sections of the land.

After six decades of being passed from owners to tenants who left it untouched, Mytchett Place, as it would soon be known, was purchased in 1880 by George James Murray who set about a radical transformation of the property. Murray, who had been educated in Dresden, studied law at Gray's Inn, and joined the London legal partnership of Whitehead, Barlow and Radcliffe, rising through the ranks to run the firm, viewed the property not as a farmhouse but, as the gazetteer of the Property Services Agency would later describe it, 'a purely gentleman's residence'. To this end, Murray added a porch of pink marbled columns, front hall, study, billiard room, kitchens, two new bedrooms and a tower. The renovations were in the Italian stucco style then popular with the Victorians, with the windows consisting of large areas of glass set in a simple wooden frame. After his death, his widow continued to live in the house which was now in the care of a trust.

By 1910 the War Office already had its eye on the house and its estate, but was first required to persuade the Treasury of its worth. In a letter dated 9 January 1911, they indignantly refuted the suggestion that the sole aim of the purchase was to provide the major general in charge of administration with elegant accommodation. That, they insisted, would merely be an 'incidental' benefit. The principal reason was that Mytchett Place was now centrally located near the army training areas of Pirbright Common, Deepcut Barracks, Blackdown and Bisley, as well as the important military properties at Aldershot.

The War Office's memo argued that the purchase of the estate would provide adequate space for 'modern tactical formations' requiring training in 'large combined movements', which were a necessity for the London Territorial Troops, and would also prevent a bottleneck in troop movements and the frequent and annoying accusations of trespass by neighbouring landowners. Furthermore, the estate offered the potential to generate income from trees that could be cut down and sold, and the 'extensive farm buildings' could be utilised as practice in the art of fortifying homes against the prospect of enemy invasion 'so important in modern warfare'.

The prudent barricades of the Treasury had no defence against such a well-aimed fusillade of facts and argument. On 25 March 1912, at a price of £16,500, the War Office took possession of the keys to Mytchett Place. Sir Frank S. Robb, a veteran of the Sudan and Khartoum, and then Military Secretary to the Chief of General Staff at the War Office, was responsible for appointments; he was also the first of eleven senior officers to enjoy the billiards room.

The Second World War turned the house into an important centre of military activity, but one whose sinister atmosphere had a repellent effect on guests. Ghosts were said by staff to creep through the corridors. On 10 September 1939, King George VI and Queen Elizabeth took tea at Mytchett Place after inspecting the troops at Aldershot. He declined a second cup and departed almost immediately.

The area did not escape Germany's bombs. At one a.m. on Saturday, 3 August 1940, a trail of bombs were dropped from Frimley Green to Mytchett Place, which was one of the sixty homes that lost tiles and suffered broken windows in the assault. Although the bomb craters measured ten feet wide by four deep, there was no loss of human life: casualties mercifully were restricted to a single cow and a pony.

When Major, now Lieutenant Colonel, Scott and Colonel Coates arrived at Mytchett Place, or Camp Z as it was now designated, they were greeted by a flurry of activity. Ditches had been dug, wire fences erected, and a van-load of heavy antique furniture arrived courtesy of the Ministry for Works. Amid the organised chaos Scott met his senior officers, Swinton and Sutton. As Swinton recorded, it was 'all very hush-hush. Forbidden to enter the house till Coates had gone.' Coates returned to London after making the necessary introductions, while Scott spent the night at Pirbright where he met the other officers under his command.

The following morning Scott arrived at ten o'clock to oversee the final preparations. An advance party of guards from Pirbright Barracks came in the morning, with the remainder of the guards and officers on site by four p.m. 'Feverish activity,' noted Sutton, 'much wire erected. Sgt Jeffreys and 24 picked men arrived.' As dusk fell Scott drafted the first Camp Orders.

At 2.45 p.m. on 20 May, three men from the Secret Intelligence Service, MI6, arrived at the camp in generic army uniforms and equipped with duffel bags and suitcases. Two of them also carried false names: Colonel Wallace was, in fact, Thomas Kendrick, a South African who had served in Field Intelligence Security during the First World War. He had risen to become Head of Station in Vienna until August 1938 when he was arrested by the Gestapo just as he was preparing to leave for England on holiday. He was interrogated for three days, then released and ordered out of the country. An assistant and two female secretaries also had to be whisked away and every secret document incinerated. A handsome man with a roguish charm, Kendrick/Wallace had previously been described by his former boss in Vienna as having 'decidedly leftish views', as well as so strong an eye for the ladies that he was 'constantly catching VD and having to have medical treatment'. For now he had been seconded from the Combined Services Interrogation Centre.

Meanwhile, to find the true identity of Captain Barnes required not one but two names be peeled back. He was not Barnes, but Richard Arnold Baker. However, this was his stepfather's name, which Baker had adopted by deed poll as war approached. He was, in reality, an anglicised Prussian aristocrat, born Werner Gaunt von Blumenthal in Berlin, into a family descended from the Emperor Charlemagne – unfortunately from the wrong side of the blanket.

In command of the trio, and the only one not using a pseudonym, was Major Frank Foley who, with his owl-rimmed spectacles, receding silver hair and round, creased but kindly face, resembled more the benevolent priest he had once longed to be, rather than the seasoned secret agent he had become. A philosophy student who had studied in France and Germany, he had been caught in Hamburg at the outbreak of the First World War, but escaped back to Britain through the Netherlands. Wounded on the Western Front in March 1918, he was transferred to the Intelligence Corps and posted, after the November Armistice, to the British Occupation Force in Cologne.

It was, however, as Head of Station in Berlin from 1923 until the outbreak of war in 1939, where Foley had best served his country. He had also served humanity, helping thousands of Jews to escape the coming Holocaust by securing false papers for them. From Berlin he had been switched to Oslo with a view to meeting former contacts permitted to travel outside Germany, as well as to recruit neutral residents who could then visit the Reich. While there, he succeeded in putting Britain's Government Code & Cypher School in touch with Norwegian cryptographers who had already cracked German diplomatic codes and were then hard at work on Russian naval and military ciphers.

The German invasion of Norway forced Foley to follow the Norwegian High Command north to Lillehammer, where he provided the necessary wireless communications to allow their Commander-in-Chief, General Ruge, to make an appeal to the British Government. Finally Foley and his secretary, Margaret Reid, retreated while under attack from German bombers, eventually sailing from Molde on Norway's West Coast to Scotland.

Back in London, he was made Head of A Section at MI6, in overall charge of operations in Scandinavia, Holland, Belgium and with the Free French. Considered MI6's top German expert, he had been informed almost immediately after their forthcoming guest's arrival in the country. Foley knew he was in for a long haul so, while his colleagues wandered over the house, he picked out the most comfortable bedroom before checking all the necessary 'wiring' was securely in place.

At 3.45 p.m. Major General Hunter and Colonel Coates arrived and began an immediate inspection of the new security arrangements. The 'baggage', as they informed the men, was now on route.

The convoy from the Tower of London led by Lieutenant Colonel Swinton, had assembled at 09.30 hours at Pirbright before splitting up into two teams – team Wolseley with four Scots Guards and team Lincoln with Henry Winch and three Coldstream Guards. Swinton was surprised that so small a number of men was responsible for so important a mission, later writing, 'Appalled to hear that we alone were responsible for the baggage and the police knew nothing.' The plan was formulated in the middle of Stanhope Park, where they gathered eight chairs in a circle. Henry Winch was charged with carrying out a reconnaissance of the route, after which they were all instructed to report to Tower Wharf at 2.30 p.m. With time to spare, Swinton then went off for a haircut, followed by lunch at the Tower.

Inside the ambulance an atmosphere of apprehension began to build – one that would only have increased had the passenger been able to see the country roads give way to an imposing entrance, protected by armed guards who raised the defensive gate.

The outer perimeter was marked by a barbed-wire fence, around which soldiers patrolled. The single entrance was buttressed by slit trenches and earthen-work barriers. As the ambulance progressed along the gravel drive, it passed a second inner barrier of barbed wire on top of which were fitted powerful electric spotlights and alarm bells strung at intervals of 50 yards. The sentries who marched alongside were careful to avoid the numerous weapon pits concealed along the perimeter.

After travelling 200 yards up a gentle camber, the ambulance pulled up outside a once elegant country house that now bore the necessary camouflage of war. The windows were taped against the threat of bomb-splintered glass and a sentry box stood at the entrance. The Scots Guards opened the ambulance's rear doors and the passenger stepped down, crunching the gravel under his well-polished jackboots. In the bright light of late afternoon, he looked up at the house of striped breeze block with the three-storey square tower that rose above the structure like a funnel over a landlocked ship.

The front porch of the house was propped up by two pink marble columns with a black marble base; above the white stone step, worn down by generations of shoe leather, hung a single cast iron light. The dark, heavy oak door swung open and the prisoner walked into the oak-panelled hall, whose black and white tiled floor was set in a pattern of diminishing diamonds with a floral star at the centre. He was greeted by General Hunter, who then escorted him up the dark oak staircase which dominated the hall. He counted thirteen steps to the first landing, then ten more to the top, where he stopped under a domed plaster ceiling at the centre of which was a skylight, now covered in canvas lest any light might escape. In front him stood a guard behind an L-shaped grille that separated the top landing and stairs from a small suite of rooms into which he was led.

The first room was a small bedroom with four rectangular windows and a fireplace screened by a metal guard. Simply furnished with a single steel-framed bed made up with white sheets and a heavy woollen blanket, there was also a small bedside table, wardrobe and a chest of drawers. A door in the left-hand wall led through to a larger sitting room, neatly furnished with a coal fire, two lightly worn armchairs, a floral print sofa and, towards the curved windows, a chair and writing desk equipped with drawers, on top of which sat a leather-backed blotting pad.

Although early, with the room still bathed in sunlight, he stripped off his uniform, hung it neatly in the wardrobe provided and changed into the English-style pyjamas provided. Then, suitably attired, he climbed into bed. It was from such a recumbent position, though propped up against the pillows, that he was introduced by General Hunter to the men who would be looking after him during his stay in the house. First he was introduced to Lieutenant Colonel Scott, then Colonel 'Wallace', Captain 'Barnes' and finally Major Foley. He shook hands and scrutinised each in turn, noting to himself that Captain Barnes's uniform appeared much too big and ill-fitting to be his own.

General Hunter explained that while Lieutenant Colonel Scott was in charge of the camp he was responsible to him and would forward any requests accordingly. The prisoner said he was quite comfortable but that he wished immediately to meet with the Duke of Hamilton and Ivone Kirkpatrick. Hunter said his request would be passed on.

At eight p.m. he was served dinner in his room. Three hours

later, Second Lieutenant William Malone of the Scots Guards took up his position, sitting in the locked grille cage outside the bedroom door.

The prisoner's name was famous around the world. For now, however, on all official government communications, memos, transcriptions and reports, he was to be referred to either by a single letter – Z – the junkyard end of the alphabet, or by the benign Englishness of 'Jonathan'. In the village of Mytchett, less than one mile away down a sloping bray of sycamore trees and green fields, they had another name for the new guest in the big house: 'The Squire of Mytchett Green'.

That evening in London the head of MI6, Sir Stewart Menzies – known and referred to as 'C' – dictated a memo to Winston Churchill. *Report NO.1*, as it was headed, read:

> Jonathan is very depressed, and wished to be left alone. We are of the opinion that this might be the psychological moment when he might change his attitude if his wish concerning visits by the Duke and Kirkpatrick is complied with. Speed might be highly productive. Doctor says he is moody, 'like a spoilt child'. His present mood should, if possible, be exploited.

The previous night, according to reports still unconfirmed to this day, searchlights near Luton Hoo had picked up two parachutists, SS men in plain clothes, in whose possession was said to be a map, circled in several places that included that of the home in Scotland of the Duke of Hamilton. The target of the men who were arrested, interrogated and then hanged was believed to be Jonathan, who had secrets the German High Command now wanted silenced.

In bed and unaware of what was unfolding all around him, Jonathan's sighs slowly transformed into snores. The sound waves from each nocturnal shudder radiated out and struck a small black concealed disk. It was a hidden microphone, one of dozens secreted around the house, connected to a network of cables that ran through the coving, skirting boards and rafters to a small back room where a man in headphones sat and listened.

2

Genesis

On the first night that Rudolf Hess, the Deputy Führer of the Third Reich, spent at Mytchett Place a gunshot was fired outside the perimeter fence. At 1.15 a.m. the commander of the guard dispatched the officer on duty at the front lodge to investigate. He returned forty-five minutes later, explaining that it had been discharged at least six hundred yards away, and the 'All Clear' was issued at 2.02 a.m.

Hess did not sleep well. The crack of gunfire had sharpened a growing anxiety, triggered by the barbed wire fences, the steel grilles over the window and in the outer corridor, and the presence of armed guards, that he was in the hands of men who would do him harm. He had expected to visit an elegant country house on his mission to Britain, but this was not the one.

Breakfast was served in the living room promptly at eight o'clock, but Hess examined it suspiciously and ate very little. At ten o'clock he was joined by the doctor, Gibson Graham, who had accompanied him on the previous day's ambulance ride and had catered to his medical needs since his arrival in Britain eleven days earlier. The pair had developed a rapport, and no sooner had Graham sat down than Hess began questioning his treatment. Why the fences and grilles? If he was now in the hands of the Secret Service then he would not survive long; they would 'murder him in some manner', more than likely as 'a suicide by poison in some food'.

Hess explained that he had come as an emissary of peace, but was now in the hands of warmongers who were deliberately preventing him from reaching out to those who could unite their two countries. Dr Graham was quick to reassure him that there would be no such plot against his life and, over the next two hours, asked him a series of questions on which he had been previously briefed by Major Foley. Afterwards he wrote a detailed report, possibly unaware that the listening devices concealed around the room should have been picking up every word. (The system had been temperamental, as Foley reported to C: 'We hope the conversation has been recorded. If it has, it will be sent to you in due course.')

The report, sent at 12.20 p.m., read as follows:

1. During the Olympic Games, Professor Haushofer and the Duke of Hamilton became friendly. The Professor conceived the idea that the Duke admired some things in Germany, especially in connection with Athletics.
2. Jonathan had absolutely no doubt in his own mind that Germany can win this war. There is no oil shortage; she has more aircraft than she knows what to do with; submarines are being made in every part of the country, even in Czechoslovakia. They can be taken down the larger rivers. There is no shortage of essential metals; food supply has been arranged.
3. The Führer has no wish to destroy the British Empire, but if we persist in fighting he will be forced to launch a terrible air offensive against her, such as we have never experienced. It will result in the killing of hundreds of thousands of people.
4. He came here on his own responsibility, and without the knowledge of the Führer. He came here because he was horrified at the thought of this useless slaughter.
5. Up till his departure, he was in the Führer's confidence.
6. Professor Haushofer, also convinced of the futility of the

slaughter and under the impression that there was a large body of opinion in England desirous of peace, suggested that if he, Jonathan, could reach Hamilton and, through him, the King, His Majesty would take him under his personal protection and initiate peace negotiations.

7. These negotiations could not be undertaken with the present Government. He believed that events are developing in the United Kingdom which will soon result in a change of government. Thus, his mission is one of extreme urgency, as negotiations must begin before the new government has settled its policy. Has no idea of the composition of the new government, or of the nature of the impending crisis which would bring about the change.
8. The mass attack on England is not, repeat not, imminent, but there is a time limit, in which he Jonathan can be useful.
9. He is in a high state of depression at the possible failure of his mission, and has hinted that it might be better for him to die (suicide). He is convinced that he is in the hands of a clique who are preventing him from daily access to the King, and that the only way for him to secure access to the King is through the Duke of Hamilton.
10. We suggest that, with a view of disabusing his mind that he is being deliberately sabotaged, and, with the object of giving him a correct picture of the political state of England, the Duke should, if possible come to-day or, if that is out of the question, that he should be informed forthwith of the date of his arrival.

The present impasse is likely to continue until he has seen the Duke again, who is the only person in whom he appears to have complete confidence.

This was not the first time Rudolf Hess had been imprisoned, but back in 1924 it had been with the man he grew to worship and for whose admiration and respect he had embarked on the most bizarre episode of the Second World War.

Rudolf Walter Richard Hess was thirty years old when he joined Adolf Hitler in Landsberg Prison in Munich. It was there that he used his skills as a trained stenographer to jot down then type up the political thoughts that would become *Mein Kampf* (*My Struggle*). There is an argument that certain political concepts espoused in the manifesto, such as *Lebensraum* (the 'living space') required by a greater Germany, were more the thoughts of Hess than Hitler, but as an acolyte he would never have tilted the spotlight away from his high priest. Rudolf Hess knew his role was to serve the man he believed that destiny had appointed to lead Germany. The five months they spent in a prison cell served to bind them ever tighter.

Hess was born in Egypt on 26 April 1894, the eldest son of Fritz Hess and his wife Klara. The family (Rudolf, his younger brother Alfred and, later, his sister, Margarete, born in 1908), lived in a comfortable, three-storey villa in Ibrahimieh, an eastern suburb of Alexandria, surrounded by lush gardens, their domestic needs tended to by servants. Fritz Hess enjoyed considerable success as a merchant, expanding the trading firm set up by his father and, like many Germans living abroad, was anxious that his children should appreciate that, although they were living in Egypt, their hearts belonged to their native country. Young Rudolf attended the German Protestant School in Alexandria, and had the benefit of an Egyptian tutor in the evenings, while each summer the family departed for the cooler climate of their home in Reicholdsgrun, six miles outside their home town of Wunsiedel, north-west of Nuremberg.

At the age of fourteen, Rudolf was sent to the Evangelical School in Bad Godesberg, where he proved a keen student of science and mathematics. The expectation was that, as the eldest son, he would accede to the family business. In preparation, he rounded off his academic career by attending the École Superieur de Commerce in Switzerland for one year, after which he began an apprenticeship with a firm in Hamburg so as to gain a better understanding of the domestic market.

But all thoughts of ledgers and logbooks dissolved in the summer of 1914. While on a few days break at Reicholdsgrun in August, Hess, then twenty years old, broke the news of his enlistment to his father.

The First World War brought an education of a different kind. In the trenches and above the battlefields, Rudolf Hess learned how to fight and how to fly, and he was educated in the pain of bullet wounds and the passion of camaraderie. As a private in the 7th Bavarian Field Artillery Regiment he fought through the Battle of Ypres, won the Iron Cross Second Class for bravery and, after promotion to Lance-Sergeant, took part in the Battle of Verdun. His first wounds were shell splinters to his left hand and upper arm. On Christmas Day, 1916, he was posted to the 18th Bavarian Reserve Infantry Regiment and appointed platoon leader of the 10th Company.

In July 1917 he was again struck by a shell splinter, and in August was shot while storming a hill in the Carpathian mountains of Romania. The bullet entered the front of his chest near the left armpit, leaving what was later described as a 'pea-sized' hole. During his convalescence he made a formal application to train as a pilot. The German air force, like those of other nations, was in its infancy, but Hess had long been captivated by the notion of flight and, as he wrote on his application form, was diligent in his studies: 'I am familiar with the engines of motor bicycles and motor cars. So far as possible, I have prepared myself by reading technical books about flying.'

After passing the aptitude and medical tests he began the three-month training course in March 1918. His first solo flight ended when he crashed into a meadow. It was not until October that he officially joined Jagdstaffel 35B, a Bavarian fighter squadron based at Givry in Belgium, and though he took to the air there was no time to engage in aerial jousts with the enemy prior to the signing of the Armistice Treaty on 11 November 1918. The war was over. Germany had lost.

The pain of defeat was doubled for Hess. Not only was his fighter squadron disbanded – he received his discharge on 13 December – but his father's business in Alexandria had been taken over by the British, forcing his family to return to Germany in straitened financial circumstances. Like many soldiers, Hess could not quite understand the reasons behind his nation's capitulation to the Allies, and while the humiliation and penury to be imposed on Germany by the Versailles Treaty had not yet been unveiled, he seethed with anger and frustration.

He found an outlet for his feelings in the Thule Society, founded the previous year by Baron Rudolf von Sebottendorff, as a means of elevating the Aryan race and beating down both Jews and Communists, who were viewed as the principle cause of the nation's defeat. The organisation's principal goal was the overthrow of the Soviet Republic of Bavaria, set up by the Spartacus League, a militant Communist organisation whose ambition was to conquer Germany and strengthen ties with the USSR. In the violent confrontations at the time Hess became an accomplished street fighter, handy with a wooden club, although he wounded his leg in the pitched battles that broke out on 30 April 1919, after the Spartakists kidnapped seven members of the Thule Society (as well as an innocent Jewish professor who was a mere bystander) then executed them. It required troops to quell the violence and overthrow the 'Red Guards'.

Hess, meanwhile, also joined the Freikorps, the cluster of paramilitary organisations set up with the support of the Minister of Defence as an organised means of combating Communist activity.

But as well as battling on the streets, Hess also began hitting the books. Since soldiers were exempt from sitting entrance exams and eligible to attend any course they pleased, he began taking classes in economics and history at Munich University. It was here that he became enamoured with Karl Haushofer, a retired major general (he became a professor in 1933) and a charismatic figure despite his cold eyes, a walrus moustache, and a penchant for tweed three-piece suits. Haushofer believed that what Germany required in order to cope with its high population density was 'living space'; the nation should push out into neighbouring countries, collect their rich resources and co-opt land for German dwellings. Small nations, according to Haushofer's thesis, were proof of political regression at a time when the future lay in the hands of a small group of powerful nations and their empires. In his plan, this 'Greater Germany' would then be surrounded by a fat girdle of subdued former nation states which would then act as a buffer zone against any future attacks. Hess and Haushofer had first met in the summer of 1919 when Hess had been invited by a mutual friend to dine at Haushofer's house, and where he was introduced to his sixteen-year-old son, Albrecht. At Munich University Hess became Haushofer's personal assistant, with the academic describing him as 'my favourite pupil', though admittedly one whose 'heart and idealism were greater than his intellect'.

For Rudolf Hess, 1920 was a year when minds and hearts met. After the beginning of his relationship with Haushofer he met, in short succession, his future wife and his future leader. At the time Hess lived at a boarding house in Schwabing, Munich's student quarter, and one afternoon he was leaping up the stairs in his field-grey Freikorps uniform when he noticed a young lady waiting on the landing for her new room to be prepared. He stopped, clicked his heels, bowed deeply, then continued to bound up the stairs.

Ilse Prohl was the daughter of a surgeon-general in Berlin. After the death of her father and her mother's remarriage she moved from Berlin to Lake Ammer, near Munich. She had arrived in the city to study and came to occupy an adjacent room to Hess. The first thing she noticed about her husband-to-be was the bushiness of his eyebrows – that, and his deep-set eyes. He initially struck her as aloof, but when he did invite her on a date it was to listen to an electrifying young speaker whose name had escaped him. 'A man – I've heard a man, he's unknown, I've forgotten his name. But if anyone can free us from Versailles, then it's this man. This unknown man will restore our honour.'

Together the couple went to the Sterneckerbrau and listened as Adolf Hitler denounced Germany's defeat, the armistice and the Versailles Treaty as the fault of Jews and Bolsheviks. Hess was mesmerised. He joined the National Socialist German Workers' Party (NSDAP) in June 1920, then carried his commitment into the classroom. When the University announced an essay competition, he answered the question posed – 'What must the man be like who will lead Germany back to the heights?' – with an eloquent pen portrait of Hitler, for which he won first prize. In November 1921 he invited Hitler to speak at the University, and when Marxists tried to blow up the Hofbrauhaus where the NSDAP held their meetings, it was Hess who protected Hitler, receiving a series of violent blows to the head in the process. He was among the first to join the *Sturmabteilung* (SA), or Storm troopers, as the party's paramilitary force was named, but was not the most adept at co-coordinating a military operation.

By 1923, following the occupation by French and Belgian troops of the Ruhr, Germany's industrial heartland, the national economy had collapsed; hyper-inflation had taken hold but among the few beneficiaries of the crisis was the NSDAP. When Hitler launched his attempted putsch in Munich on 8 November, Hess was by his side. While the intention was to hold the regional government hostage, then declare a new government led by Hitler and General Erich Ludendorff, it did not go according to plan. Hess's role was to round up a group of 'enemies of the people', take them in a waiting car to a house near Lake Tegern then guard them. Unfortunately, when he stepped out to make a phone call, his hostages succeeded in persuading the driver to take them back to

Munich, leaving Hess stranded without transport. It was left to Ilse to bring him a bicycle on which he made good his escape.

The next day the Bavarian State Police fired on marchers, killing sixteen and scattering the remainder. Hess, meanwhile, had sought refuge at Haushofer's home and, with his assistance, fled to Austria. There he learned that both the SA and NSDAP had been banned, while Hitler had been arrested and sentenced to five years' imprisonment (although the judge – who supported his cause – recommended a release after six months). Swayed again by Haushofer, Hess surrendered himself and followed Hitler through the art nouveau façade of Landsberg Prison with its distinctive onion dome towers. During their imprisonment they were visited by Haushofer, who stayed for six hours and brought copies of Friedrich Ratzel's *Political Geography* and Carl Philipp Gottlieb von Clausewitz's *On War*. Hitler was released on 20 December 1924, and Hess ten days later. A tight bond, born of incarceration, now formed between the pair. When in February 1925 Hitler announced the re-formation of the SA and NSDAP, he appointed Rudolf Hess as his private secretary.

For the next fourteen years, until the outbreak of war, the two men were seldom separated. Hess accompanied Hitler on tours across Germany, preparing leaflets and posters and listening to his advice. It was Hitler who urged Hess to marry Ilse Prohl, which he did on 20 December 1927, with Hitler and Haushofer as witnesses, though – to the wits of the party – it was clear to whom Hess was most devoted. Hitler's comfort and needs were his principal concern. Goebbels described Hess as 'the decent, quiet, friendly, reserved, private secretary', but as Hitler rose up the political ladder so Hess's authority and influence were elevated. Yet his job presented him with difficult situations. It was Hess who, in 1931, broke the news to Hitler that Geli, his twenty-three-year-old niece with whom he was besotted, had shot herself.

In 1930, the NSDAP became the second largest party in the

Reichstag. Hess was appointed Political Central Commissioner of the NSDAP and a delegate to the Reichstag in December 1932. When Hitler became Chancellor of Germany on 30 January 1933, he made Hess his deputy, issuing a decree that read, 'I appoint Party Member Rudolf Hess to be my Deputy, and bestow on him plenary powers to take decisions in my name on all matters affecting the leadership of the Party.' By December that year Hess had taken a seat in the Cabinet as minister without portfolio, a position that carried with it a sphere of influence that stretched across Foreign Affairs, the Press, Reconstruction, Finance, Law, Germans living abroad, Education, Building, Technical Matters, Health, Race, Art and Literature. Hess wrote to his parents of his role within the party. He was, he believed, 'a connecting link between the mass movement and the educated classes'.

He was also unafraid of the bloodshed deemed necessary to exert supreme control over the party. The growing strength and belligerence of Ernst Rohm, the leader of the SA, was a challenge to Hitler's leadership and it was Hess who fired the warning shot across his bows in a speech broadcast across Germany on 25 June 1934. '[Hilter] has always been right, and he will always be right. In uncritical loyalty, in devotion to the Führer that does not ask about the whys and wherefores of individual cases, in the silent execution of his orders – that is where the National Socialism of us all lies anchored.' In a stark warning to the SA leadership, Hess insisted, 'Woe to those who break their allegiance in the belief that they are able to serve the revolution by means of a revolt. They are poor in spirit who believe themselves chosen to serve the Führer in revolutionary fashion by agitating from below . . . woe to him who plants his flat feet among the fine threads of the Führer's strategic plans, thinking to force the pace.'

Five days later, during the Night of the Long Knives, Hitler dismissed Rohm and the leadership of the SA, ordering the murder of many and consigning critics to prison. The SA was replaced by the SS (*Schutzstaffel* or Protection Squad) in which Hess was made an *Obergruppenführer*, or General.

Following the death of Hindenburg and the plebiscite of August 1934, which secured Hitler the support of ninety per cent of Germany's voters, it was Hess who fused Hitler to the German people during an impassioned speech at the Nuremberg Rally in September. 'The Party is Hitler!' he declared. 'But Hitler is Germany and Germany is also Hitler! Heil Hitler! Sieg Heil!' And the crowd shouted back: 'Sieg Heil!'

From his office at the Brown House, Munich's Nazi headquarters, Hess sought to infiltrate all aspects of German life while maintaining two different but complementary roles. He was the high priest of the cult of the Führer. Along with Joseph Goebbels, the propaganda minister, Hess was the principal architect of the myth of Hitler as more than a mortal: as a man imbued with almost supernatural powers and sent by Providence. During a speech in Kiel in August 1939, he said, 'However great is the need of our people, so great is the man who was to come and overcome this need. Providence gave him the gifts and powers to take the favourable and unfavourable circumstances that he found and what were developing with time, and to employ them for the attainment of his goal: the salvation of Germany.'

His second role was as 'keeper of the Holy Grail' or, as he saw it, defender of the true values of the Nazi Party. On Hess's forty-fifth birthday he was described in one Nazi paper as *kunder und mahner* (herald and prophet) with the paper informing its readers that he was a man who 'more than any of the movement's other mouthpieces, was the herald of the National Socialist idea and thus the servant of Adolf Hitler's mission'. The people saw in him 'the wakeful prophet, ensuring that National Socialism remains pure and undistorted, that everything that happens in the name of National Socialism is truly National Socialist'.

But Hess was also vain, insisting that at all public events he be treated as second-in-command, and he had a dislike of paper-work, preferring verbal briefings; and even then he left much of the daily routine to his own chief-of-staff, Martin Bormann. The Office of the Deputy of the Führer was a curious organisation, for since Hess had been appointed by Hitler, he believed that the Führer's unrestricted powers now flowed through him. He refused to hand over any organisational chart detailing the extent of his kingdom lest it limit future expansion. He succeeded in strengthening the hierarchical structure of the Party, bringing hundreds of organisations under the control of regional and local Party chiefs.

Over time Hess became known as 'The Good Nazi', a figure with no personal lust for power who nonetheless dedicated himself to solving the day-to-day problems of the population. At the Nuremberg Party Rally he would urge the party faithful to embrace moderation in all things and avoid excessive smoking and drinking, but also to take exercise and to work. A period of ill-health led to a personal fascination with alternative medicine and diets, which he then extended into the political realm. In 1937 he became patron of the Twelfth International Homeopaths' Congress in Berlin and founded the Rudolf Hess Academy for Modern German Medicine, based in Dresden.

War would see a gap grow between Hitler and Hess. Hess was not involved directly in the military or diplomatic preparations for the campaign, or in the economic preparations for rearmament, but at the start of the war his position was enhanced. On 1 September 1939, Hitler announced that in the event of his death Hermann Goering would succeed him, and that Hess would then succeed Goering. Hess also became a member of the Ministerial Council for the Defence of the Reich, an inner cabinet designed to pass laws rapidly but which did not act as a war cabinet. Although still a crucial part of government, and included in major events such as banquets at the Russian embassy with Molotov in 1940 and the signing of the French armistice in June 1940, Hess felt diminished. A request from Hitler, however, served to re-invigorate him.

It was part of Hitler's form of management to quietly entrust to a colleague a specific task which had the potential to end in failure or ignominy. For example, Goering was permitted to appeal to the Chamberlain Government, using his Swedish friend, Birger Dahlerus. Later, in 1943, Ribbentrop was allowed to sue for peace with Russia through his agent Peter Kleist, while Heinrich Himmler was made responsible for the 'Final Solution'. All such orders were given orally, leaving no written record. In late July 1940, after France had been successfully crushed, Hitler summoned Hess to explain his 'wishes'. He had no desire to fight Britain, he told him. Both Britain and France's declarations of war after Germany had invaded Poland to 'free' Danzig was a decision he, Hitler, for all his 'supernatural powers' had not foreseen. ('Who wishes to go to war over Danzig?') Hitler thought he had crushed Britain at Dunkirk, but the British army had escaped, and now the Luftwaffe was in the process of attempting to subdue the nation in the Battle of Britain. On 19 July 1940, Hitler offered peace, but on terms that would make it clear he was the victor. In a broadcast speech he announced that if the British Government sought a settlement he would be both generous and magnanimous. Had he not proven himself just so by permitting France to govern half its nation from Vichy? Hitler believed a deal was possible; after all the same British Parliament had cheered Chamberlain. Churchill proved him wrong by having Lord Halifax, a former appeaser deliver a firm rejection.

Now Hitler tasked Hess with exploring the means to dispose of Winston Churchill. Had Hitler discussed the matter with Ribbentrop, his Foreign Minister, he would have been told that the King was key to achieving such a goal. German intelligence put its faith in the 'peace party', a group of aristocrats who had access to the King and the means to circumvent Churchill. As Hitler said to Hess, 'What do I have to do? Do I have to go over there myself and talk to them?' There is evidence that at the time Hitler had planned a pincer movement in which an internal coup would be balanced by a planned invasion. He had already asked Ribbentrop to organise the abduction of the Duke of Windsor (if he could not be persuaded to come along voluntarily) so that he might be set up in Germany as 'a king across the water' if his brother, King George VI, proved unwilling to capitulate. (In the event, Churchill succeeded in dispatching the Duke to govern the Bahamas.) Meanwhile, British aristocrats, such as Viscount Lascelles, later the Earl of Harewood and a cousin of the King, were segregated in case their connections could be called upon.

The man to whom Hess then turned was Professor Karl Haushofer. Over the years they had remained friends but both birth and circumstance had put him in Hess's debt. Professor Haushofer's wife was half-Jewish, which made her and her three children vulnerable to harsh discrimination under Nazi racial legislation. However, Hess had insisted on issuing the sons with protective letters declaring each an 'Honorary Aryan'. He had also made Albrecht Haushofer, no longer the sixteen-year-old he met at his father's dinner table but now a brilliant scholar, his personal adviser whom he then seconded to the Foreign Office.

On 31 August 1940, Hess and Professor Haushofer spent eight hours talking over the issues of contacting the 'peace party', with the professor hinting that his son might be able to assist. Four days later, on 3 September, Professor Haushofer wrote to Albrecht:

> As you know everything is so prepared for a very hard and severe attack on the island in question that the highest ranking person only has to press a button to set it off. But before this decision, which is perhaps inevitable, the thought once more occurs as to whether there is really no way of stopping something which would have such infinitely momentous consequences. There is a line of reasoning in connection with this which I absolutely must pass on to you, because it was obviously communicated to me

> with this intention. Do you, too, see no way in which such possibilities could be discussed at a third place with a middle man, possibly old Ian Hamilton (General Sir Ian Hamilton, a veteran of the Gallipoli campaign in the First World War who had once lunched with Hitler and Hess), or the other Hamilton?

The 'other Hamilton' to whom Professor Karl Haushofer referred was the Duke of Hamilton whom his son had befriended four years previously. Albrecht, who spoke English like an Englishman and was a keen admirer of the British Empire, had met the Duke, then still the Marquess of Douglas and Clydesdale, in August 1936 at a reception for British MPs during the Olympic Games in Berlin, at which Hess had also been in attendance. At a time when pioneering aviators were renowned, the Marquess was a celebrity for having become the first man to fly over Mount Everest. The pair kept in touch, and when the Marquess went on a skiing holiday to Austria the following January, he visited Albrecht and his father at the family home at Hartschimmelhof, bearing a gift of his book, *The Pilot's Book of Everest.* Four days after the Marquess's departure, Hess arrived and was fascinated both by the book and stories of the man.

On 8 September Hess summoned Albrecht and they spoke for two hours in his office. Albrecht, having first asked permission to speak freely, told Hess that no one of influence in Britain would regard a treaty with Hitler as anything other than a 'worthless piece of paper'. To secure peace required not only the removal of Churchill, but also of Hitler. If Hess was shocked by Albrecht's statement, as he surely must have been, he displayed no sign of it. After the meeting, Albrecht drew up a memo marked Top Secret. headlined ARE THERE STILL POSSIBILITIES OF A GERMAN-ENGLISH PEACE? It read:

> I was immediately asked about the possibilities of making known to persons of importance in England Hitler's serious desire for

> peace . . . The Führer had not wanted to see the Empire destroyed and did not want it even today. Was there not somebody in England who was ready for peace?
>
> First I asked for permission to discuss fundamental things. It was necessary to realise that not only Jews and Freemasons, but practically all Englishmen who mattered, regarded a treaty signed by the Führer as a worthless scrap of paper. To the question as to why this was so, I referred to the ten-year term of our Polish Treaty, to the Non-Aggression Pact with Denmark signed only a year ago, to the 'final' frontier demarcation of Munich. What guarantee did England have that a new treaty would not be broken again at once if it suited us? It must be realised that, even in the Anglo-Saxon world, the Führer was regarded as Satan's representative on earth and had to be fought.'

Towards the end of their discussion, Hess had asked Albrecht to name those who might make suitable contacts: 'As the final possibility I then mentioned that of a personal meeting on neutral soil with the closest of my English friends, the young Duke of Hamilton, who has access at all times to all important persons in London, even to Churchill and the King.' Albrecht pointed out the difficulty in making contact and the improbability of success, and asked for very precise directions from the highest authority before he could act. Hess said he would consider the matter.

'From the whole conversation I had the strong impression that it was not conducted without the prior knowledge of the Führer, and that I probably would not hear any more about the matter unless a new understanding had been reached between him and his deputy.'

The next question was how to contact the Duke. In a coincidence (one that would intrigue historians and conspiracists for seven decades), Professor Haushofer had just received a card from Mrs Violet Roberts, an English friend and the widow of a Cambridge geography professor, in which she expressed regret over the war but hope that their correspondence would still continue. The daughter-in-law of Lord Roberts, who had been Viceroy of India, Mrs Roberts had lost her son, Maxwell, who had worked in the British Embassy in Berlin and was killed in a car crash in 1937. She gave Haushofer a post office box number in Lisbon to which a reply could be sent. The professor told his son, who told Hess.

On 10 September 1940, Hess wrote to Karl Haushofer referring to the professor's letter to his son of 3 September:

> The prerequisite, naturally, is that the enquiry in question and the reply would not go through official channels, for you would not in any case want to cause your friends any trouble. It would be best to have the letter to the old lady, with whom you are acquainted, delivered through a confidential agent of the AO [*Auslandsorganisation*, headed by Hess, which watched over Germans abroad and was associated with the *Abwehr*, the German secret intelligence service] to the address that is known to you. For this purpose Albrecht would have to speak to either Boble or my brother. At the same time the lady would have to be given the address of this agent in L. [London] or if the latter does not live there permanently, of another agent in the AO who does live there permanently, to which the reply can in turn be delivered.
>
> As for the neutral I have in mind, I would like to speak to you orally about it some time. There is no hurry since, in any case, there would first have to be a reply received here from over there. Meanwhile let's both keep our fingers crossed. Should success be the fate of the enterprise, the oracle given to you with regard to the month of August would yet be fulfilled, since the name of the young friend and the old lady friend of your family occurred to you during our quiet walk on the last day of that month.

While Hess was determined to make a peace overture to the British, Albrecht wrote to his parents on 18 September pointing out that it was not as easy as he had imagined to contact a person such as Hamilton, and he did not wish to endanger their friend Mrs Roberts, on whose shoulders would rest the responsibility of conveying the letter from Portugal to Britain. The next day he wrote to Hess, mentioning that he had seen Hess's letter to his father, and again marking his communication Top Secret:

> I have been thinking of the technical route by which a message from me must travel before it can reach the Duke of H. With your help, delivery to Lisbon can of course be assured without difficulty. About the rest of the route we do not know. Foreign Control must be taken into account; the letter must therefore in no case be composed in such a way that it will simply be seized and destroyed or that it will directly endanger the woman transmitting it or the ultimate recipient.
>
> In view of my close personal relations and intimate acquaintance with DH I can write a few lines to him (which should be enclosed with the letter to Mrs R without any indication of place and without a full name – so A would suffice for signature) in such a way that he alone will recognise that behind my wish to see him in Lisbon there is something more serious than a personal whim.

Albrecht Haushofer ended the letter by suggesting that the mission could be better served by contacting, not Hamilton, but Philip Kerr, the 11th Marquess of Lothian and the British Ambassador in Washington, or Sir Samuel Hoare, the British Ambassador to Spain, based in Madrid who would also prove easier to reach. On the same day Albrecht wrote to his parents, saying 'the whole thing is a fool's errand.'

Over the next few days Albrecht prepared a draft of the letter and passed it on to Hess's brother, Alfred, for delivery to Lisbon. It read as follows:

Sept. 23rd.

My dear Douglo,

Even if there is only a slight chance that this letter should reach you in good time, there is a chance, and I am determined to make use of it. First of all, to give you a personal greeting. I am sure you know that my attachment to you remains unaltered and unalterable, whatever the circumstances may be. I have heard of your father's death. I do hope he did not suffer too much – after so long a life of permanent pain. I heard that your brother-in-law Northumberland lost his life near Dunkirk – even modern times must allow us to share grief across all boundaries. But it is not only the story of death that should find its place in this letter. If you remember some of my last communications in July 1939, you – and your friends in high places – may find some significance in the fact that I am able to ask you whether you could find time to have a talk with me somewhere on the outskirts of Europe, perhaps in Portugal. I could reach Lisbon any time (and without any kind of difficulties) within a few days of receiving news from you. Of course I do not know whether you can make your authorities understand so much, that they give you leave.

But at least you may be able to answer my question. Letters will reach me (fairly quickly: they would take some four or five days from Lisbon at the utmost) in the following way: double closed envelope: inside address: Dr A.H. Nothing more! Outside address: Minero Silricola Ltd, Rua do Cais de Santarem 32/1 Lisbon, Portugal. My father and mother add their wishes for your personal welfare to my own . . . Yours ever, 'A'

On the same date Albrecht wrote again to Hess explaining that the letter had now been dispatched. 'In accordance with your last telephone call I got in touch with your brother immediately. Everything went off well, and I can now report that the mission has been accomplished to the extent that the letter you desired was written and dispatched this morning. It is hoped that it will be more efficacious than sober judgment would indicate.'

The hope held out to Hess dissolved in Albrecht's next letter to his father: 'I am convinced, as before, that there is not the slightest prospect of peace; and so I don't have the least faith in the possibility about which you know. However, I also believe that I could not have refused my services any longer. You know that for myself I do not see any possibility of any satisfying activity in the future.'

Six weeks after Albrecht wrote the letter it was intercepted in Britain by the Censor's Department of the Ministry of Information. The original was sent to MI5 on 6 November, and a photostat copy delivered to the Foreign Office. After pondering what to do, on 22 November MI5 sent a letter to Mr Hopkinson, secretary to Sir Alexander Cadogan, head of the Foreign Office, which read: 'A letter dated 23 September 1940, written by somebody named "Dr. A.H.", obviously a German, to the Duke of Hamilton was intercepted by the censor and copies sent to MI5, the Foreign Office and I.R.B. We are pursuing enquiries into this case, but meanwhile I should be grateful to know if you have taken any action. We propose to forward the letter to the Duke of Hamilton provided you do not object.'

Two weeks later, on 4 December, a Foreign Office official replied: 'We don't seem to come into this very much and no doubt the Duke of Hamilton will be tickled to death to receive in December a letter which was addressed to him on September 23rd. I see that Dr A.H. says that "letters will reach me fairly quickly; they would take some 4 or 5 days from Lisbon at the utmost in the following way . . .", but perhaps MI5 does not step in that direction.'

Hopkinson wrote his own letter to MI5 on 7 December. It is clear that MI5 and the Foreign Office were unaware of who was behind it, and the letter ends, 'we have not done anything about it ourselves and we have no objection to the letter being allowed to go on to its destination if you think this worthwhile in view of the length of time which has elapsed since it was written.'

Even more time was to elapse before the letter finally reached its addressee. Almost three months later, on 26 February 1941, Hamilton received a letter from Group Captain F.G. Summers, who asked if he might visit his office at the Air Ministry during his next visit to London. When the pair met in mid-March, Summers asked Hamilton what he had done with the letter from Albrecht Haushofer. Hamilton thought he was referring to a letter he had received in July 1939, in which Albrecht had warned of the forthcoming war and requested that the letter be shown to Lord Halifax, then Foreign Secretary. In the end, Hamilton had also shown it to Churchill, and the then Prime Minister, Neville Chamberlain, before depositing it in a bank vault. When it became clear that each was referring to a separate letter, Summers slid a photostat copy across the desk and Hamilton read the new letter for the first time.

Summers then explained that MI5 having researched Albrecht Haushofer, now felt he might be a figure of significance and that it could be valuable to make contact with him. One month later, at 11.30 a.m. on 25 April, Hamilton attended a second meeting at the Air Ministry with Group Captain D.L. Blackford and Major T.A. Robertson, head of Section B1A at MI5, who ran the inter-service 'XX' (Double Cross) committee. MI5 were keen that Hamilton should travel to Lisbon and secure all the available intelligence Haushofer had to offer. Hamilton, who was reluctant, said he would dutifully go if ordered to do so, only to be told that such delicate operations required volunteers – whose involvement could then be officially denied in the event of failure.

The Duke was offered time to consider the matter and sought counsel from Lord Eustace Percy, a former Foreign Office veteran who had served as a Cabinet minister in the Government of Stanley Baldwin. Percy advised Hamilton to be careful and secure specific caveats before proceeding. Hamilton then wrote back to Blackford, agreeing to go to Lisbon on the condition that both the British Ambassador to Portugal and Sir Alexander Cadogan be informed of the plan. He also pointed out the necessity of securing a plausible explanation for his delay in replying to Albrecht Haushofer's letter: 'I must be able to explain to X why I am answering his letter after a delay of seven months.' He continued: 'It would be dangerous to allow him to believe that the authorities had withheld his letter from me last autumn and had now released it and had asked me to answer it. That would give the impression that the authorities here had "got the wind up" now, and want to talk peace. May I therefore have an explanation of the circumstances in which the letter was withheld from me last autumn?'

Major Robertson would later explain that the reason for the delay in processing Haushofer's letter was simple: it had been lost, temporarily misplaced or wrongly filed during the upheaval following the relocation of B Division to a new address. A second plausible reason for the delay was that Hamilton was the subject of a thorough investigation to re-establish his loyalty, cast in doubt by the letter. Despite Robertson's enthusiasm for the mission during his meeting with Hamilton, he later stated that he was also concerned by the delay and doubted the efficacy of the plan, and, as a result, it was dropped.

On 3 May 1941, Hamilton received an explanatory letter from Group Captain Blackford:

> In my own view, the delay which has occurred makes it extremely difficult to find a watertight excuse for action at the present time, and although quite a good one has been suggested on the lines of an enquiry from you as to why your previous letters have not been answered, it might not carry conviction and so have undesirable political consequences. Incidentally, the delay was in no way due to any fault of Air Intelligence, another department having mislaid the papers. It is Air Commodore Boyle's view that in the present circumstances, a move of any kind suggested could not be made without Cabinet authority, and with this I agree. In the circumstances, will you, therefore, regard the matter as in abeyance.

There is an important footnote to the British side of the letter. On Friday 17 January, Frank Foley, with his secretary Margaret Reid, flew out of Whitchurch aerodrome near Bristol and spent the next two weeks in Lisbon. He arrived back on Saturday 1 February, according to his wife Kay's diary in which she noted the telegram her husband sent to report his safe return. Why did Foley go to Lisbon? According to one MI6 historian it was to explore the possibility of a 'sting operation' in response to the Haushofer letter.

On 4 May 1941, the day after Hamilton had received the order to stand down, Adolf Hitler gave a speech to the Reichstag deputies, stepped back from the rostrum and sat down beside Hess. It was to be the last time they were together. For the past six months Hess had been preparing for a feat of flying and negotiation that he believed would return him to his rightful place as the Führer's most favoured follower, a post now held by Goering. According to Albert Speer, Hitler had said, 'When I talk to Goering, it's like a bath in steel for me. I feel fresh afterwards. The Reichsmarshal has a stimulating way of presenting things. With Hess every conversation becomes an unbearably tormenting strain. He always comes to me with unpleasant matters and won't leave off.' In one of their last conversations, Hess asked Hitler if his attitude towards Britain had changed and he insisted that it had not. On the same day, Hess wrote to his wife, 'I firmly believe that from the flight I am about to make one of these days, I will return and the flight will be crowned with success. However, if not, the goal I have set myself will have been worth the supreme effort. I know that all of you understand me; you will know that I could not have acted otherwise.'

Prior to the outbreak of war between Britain and Germany, Goering had suggested that 'we must fly to Britain and I'll try to explain the position . . .' Hitler told him, 'It will be of no use but if you can, try it.' Word reached the British Government and Lord Halifax recorded in his diary on 21 August 1939:

> C tells us that he had received an approach suggesting that Goering should come to London and if he can be assured that he will be able to see the Prime Minister. It was decided to send an affirmative answer to this curious suggestion, and arrangements were accordingly set in hand for Goering to come over secretly on Wednesday, 23rd. The idea is that he should land at some deserted aerodrome, be picked up in a car and taken direct to Chequers. There the regular household is to be given *congé* [time off] and the telephone is to be disconnected. It looks as though it is going to be a dramatic interlude and, having laid the plans, we await confirmation from Germany.

Goering never made the flight and twelve days later Lord Halifax wrote, 'I did not see that there was any good in Goering coming here.'

What Goering had suggested but failed to carry out, Hess decided he would actually do. Then he would return to Germany clutching the prize of peace with Britain. One part of the appeal was the flight. He felt a kinship with Hamilton on account of their passion for aviation. When Charles Lindbergh made the first solo crossing of the Atlantic in his plane *The Spirit of St Louis* on 20/21 May 1927, Hess had been captivated by the 33-hour flight and had struggled for a year to raise the money to top it by flying the Atlantic east to west and against the prevailing winds. He even wrote to Henry Ford for funds, but received no reply. He gained his private flying licence in 1929; in July 1930 he was given a two-seater monoplane by the Party newspaper, *Volkischer Beobachter*, whose logo was mounted on the side. He spent two hours in the plane buzzing an open air meeting of political rivals on 10 August 1930, at one point flying so low that he was summoned to explain his actions to the Munich police. He won the first national air race round the Zugspitze Mountain in 1934, taking great pride in hoisting the Challenge Cup, and in the congratulatory telegram he received from Lindbergh.

A dream was to nudge Hess's elbow. Karl Haushofer told him

that he had dreamt Hess was walking along the corridors of a British castle, one of whose walls were lined with tapestries, and that he was meant to bring peace between Britain and Germany.

In September 1939, Hess asked Hitler to transfer him to the Luftwaffe so that he might fly at the Front. Hitler refused, and insisted he promise not to fly for the duration of the war, but Hess negotiated the no-fly ban down to one year. He tried a number of airfields in a bid to secure a plane to practise in. Ernst Udet, chief of aircraft supply at Berlin-Tempelhof airfield, agreed to supply one on condition that Hitler sign a permit. Hess then visited factories where Messerschmitts were assembled, but again the chief test pilot said no, explaining that the planes were too dangerous in the hands of a newcomer. Rejection also greeted him at the Arado factory in Warnemunde. Finally, he visited Willy Messerschmitt at Augsburg where the Bf108 touring aircraft and the Bf109 fighter had been built, and where the two-seater Bf110 was currently being tested. In 1932 Hess had helped keep Messerschmitt in his factory at a time when the city had wished to take it over as a base for tramcars. Hess called in the favour, and by October 1940 he had begun training under the instruction of a chief test pilot, Willi Stoer.

Once trained he secured the use of his own plane, a Bf110E-1/N, radio code VJ+OQ, which he had fitted with two huge drop tanks each containing 900 litres of fuel, and a radio compass capable of picking up the transmitting station near Kalundborg in Denmark, which was on the same latitude as Dungavel House, the Duke of Hamilton's residence in Scotland. In order to monitor the weather over the North Sea, Hess had his secretary call the meteorologists at the Central Weather Group each day at 10 a.m., when she was given weather conditions for three locations, 'X', 'Y' and 'Z'. For Hess's purpose the weather on 10 May 1941 was perfect. The Met Office in Hamburg said there would be solid cloud at 500 metres, covering the North Sea with high pressure and perfect weather with light winds over Britain.

Rudolf Hess packed ten Reichsmark notes, the visiting cards of Dr Albrecht Haushofer and Professor Karl Haushofer, a Leica camera, a small electric torch, a safety razor blade and a hypodermic syringe sterilised in alcohol. He also packed twenty-eight medicines in small tin cases, boxes, tubes and bottles – a collection which included methylbenzedrine for preventing sleep; barbiturates for inducing sleep; opiates for dulling pain; atropine tablets to alleviate air sickness, and tablets containing dextrose, kola and lecithin for reducing the effects of fatigue.

On Saturday 10 May, he spent the morning with his son, Wolf Rudiger. They strolled along the banks of the River Isar then visited the Hellabrun Zoo before returning home at noon. He had a lunch appointment with Alfred Rosenberg, one of the founders of the Nazi Party, and together they dined on cold meat and salad. Afterwards Rosenberg drove off to Hitler's retreat at Berchtesgaden. The Hess servants had the day off and Ilse stayed in bed with a head cold.

Rudolf, wearing the new blue Luftwaffe uniform he had ordered from the tailor, brought her a cup of tea. She complimented him on his blue-grey uniform, high boots, blue shirt and dark blue tie. She had asked him for years to wear that particular combination of shirt and tie and he had always refused. When she asked why he was wearing it now he replied, 'To make you happy!' (The unpaid tailor's bill would arrive after his departure.) Ilse later claimed that at the time she was reading *The Pilot's Book of Everest*, and that Hess picked it up, commenting on the author's photograph, 'He's very good-looking.' He told his wife he had received a telephone call ordering him to Berlin, but that he first had to make a detour via Augsburg. When Ilse asked when he would return, he replied Monday evening at the latest. He then kissed her goodbye, said farewell to his son, and left the house by his official car at 3.30 p.m.

The airport was quiet but not deserted when he arrived, and because his flying suit was being repaired he 'borrowed' one from another pilot, Helmut Kaden. Today would be Hess's third attempt to embark on his mission, for on two previous attempts he had been driven back by the weather. As he prepared to climb into the plane Hess handed his assistant Karlheinz Pintsch an envelope containing four letters, for Hitler, Ilse Hess, Willy Messerschmitt and Kaden, in which he apologised for taking his suit, and instructed Pintsch not to open it until at least four hours had passed. Pintsch was aware of the contents and Hess's mission, for in January, during a previous abortive attempt, Hess had returned late, by which time he had opened the letter, but decided to keep Hess's secret.

Once strapped into the cockpit, Hess gave his destination to air traffic control as Norway, and at 17.45 hours German Summer Time, the aircraft took off.

3

Flight

Hess later described the preparations for the flight. 'I had lived those months in a whirl of instruments, cylinder head pressures, jettison fuel containers, auxiliary oil pumps, coolant temperatures, radio beam widths – which didn't even work when the time came – the heights of Scottish mountains and God knows what else.' As he ascended into the evening sky all those hours of secret training were to be put to the test.

The weather for the flight was almost perfect. The meteorological office in Hamburg confirmed the blanket of cloud over the North Sea, while an anticyclone was churning up high pressure and forming clear weather over Britain, with brief showers along the east coast. The moon would rise at 20.45 and the sun would set over Glasgow at 22.00 hours. The moonlight would allow him to spot the Scottish coastline, lakes and rivers.

In a letter to his son which Hess would write from the captivity of Camp Z, he described the smooth take-off and how he had gazed down at the wide sweep of the River Lech. He set a course of 320 degrees towards Bonn but struggled at first to recognise a fixed point, eventually checking his position using a notable railway junction. Darmstadt was on his starboard side, and a little later he watched as the River Main flowed into the Rhine, at which point he made a small adjustment to the automatic pilot.

At the islands Hess turned east for 23 minutes, and although he did not explain why, it may have been to avoid the British radar system. When the 23 minutes had elapsed, he turned onto a heading of 335 degrees for the long journey out over the North Sea. At 8.10 p.m. he flew low over two U-boats, startling them into beginning to dive until the look-outs on the conning towers recognised the plane as friendly. He then climbed to 5,000 feet.

Hess arrived at the 'North Point' at 20.58 hours, then turned to port on a course of 245 degrees towards 'Point B', the small coastal town of Bamburgh in Northumberland, which he had marked on his map.

The radio was tuned to a station at Kalundborg in Denmark, the same latitude as his destination, Dungavel Castle. Unfortunately it had failed to pick up the signal during his first attempt in January, as it lacked sufficient range, and so instead he was advised to first tune into the nearest transmitter, which was Munich, until he reached a suitable range to reach the Danish station.

Although the sun was low in the sky as Hess approached the British coast, it was still too bright for safely entering enemy territory; he flew back and forth for 40 minutes as darkness descended, after which he once again headed west.

His navigation over water for three hours had been perfect. In the fading light he looked down on two British destroyers sailing near Holy Island, as well as a cluster of smaller fishing vessels. He tilted towards the Cheviots in order to avoid the possibility of anti-aircraft fire and saw the mist obscuring the coast. He could see that the moonlight was shining onto the layer of mist and knew it would provide suitable cover for any patrolling plane, so he pushed into a shallow dive and down into the fog. It was a fortunate move: Hess's plane was spotted by British radar at 22.08 hours soon after sunset. The information had been passed to Fighter Command's headquarters at Bentley Priory in Middlesex, where a single coloured counter was placed near Holy Island on the plotting-table map, which now identified him as 'Raid 42'. It was to be a busy night in the room where the girls plotted one of the heaviest bomber raids of the war, the target of whose incendiary bombs included the House of Commons.

After radar contact was made with Hess, two Spitfires from 72 Squadron (then patrolling over the Faroe Islands) were dispatched in swift pursuit. A third Spitfire scrambled from Clinton but returned after 35 minutes having found nothing. There were also three Hurricanes in the air, but piloted by Poles on a training flight.

Meanwhile, Hess, unaware that he had been picked up by radar, was marvelling at the Cheviot Hills, 2,676 feet high, which he described as a 'heavenly, polar-like view'. He flew up one side of the hills and down the other before turning towards St Mary's Loch, near Broad Law in the southern uplands, where he gazed down at farmhands still toiling in the fields and waved to them as he passed.

In preparation Hess had obtained a map of Scotland, pinned it on his bedroom wall, marked the mountains in red ink then committed their position and height to memory. The three topographical maps of north England and southern Scotland were on a scale of 1:250,000 and produced by the British Ordnance Survey for aerial map reading. A red arrow beside the nearby reservoir marked the Duke of Hamilton's home.

He was fortunate in being able to evade the British defences. It was dusk and he had picked a route that was lightly defended. Radar did not operate inland and, although the Royal Observer Corps post spotted the plane and accurately recorded its speed, the RAF did not believe them, incorrectly assuming it was a Dornier bomber flying at a slower rate and adjusting their calculations accordingly. There was also low-lying mist, which made it difficult for a plane above to spot one below, especially against a background of the dark hills over which the German had flown.

Hess arrived at the west coast at 10.55 p.m. and described what would have been the Cumbrae Islands as a 'fairy-like view' with 'steep mountainous islands visible in the moonlight and fading twilight'. As he headed back east he recognised Dungavel from the curve of the railway line and the L-shaped Glengavel Water. He must have been dismayed to spot that the grass and sloping runway was too small for such a plane as his, having been designed for use by small bi-planes. The Messerschmitt's wingspan was 53 feet and powered by two Daimler-Benz engines, which dictated a high landing speed.

Hess had no choice but to bail out, a dangerous move. He climbed to 6,000 feet, then switched off the engine, setting the pitch of the airscrews to zero. One of the engines had overheated and was now creating combustion in the cylinders as it continued to turn over. He patiently waited for the engine to stop then opened the cockpit, which was hinged back against the antenna mast, and unfastened the two side windows which then hung down against the fuselage. But when Hess tried to climb out, the airstream generated by the current speed of 300 m.p.h. pinned him back into the seat. He was trapped, but not without his wits: he suddenly remembered a piece of advice given to him by Robert von Greim, a fighter group commander, who stated that the swiftest way to exit a plane is to put it into a roll and allow gravity to tumble you out.

The wisest move would indeed have been to roll the plane over but, perhaps beginning to panic, Hess pulled back on the stick and began to manoeuvre the aircraft up into a half loop. The centrifugal force drained the blood from his head and induced a blackout. When he came to, the plane was standing on its tail and about to stall. He pulled the ripcord and managed to exit, but smacked his right foot against the tail in the process. The parachute opened and he began floating down through the night sky.

As radar did not operate inland, it had been left to the men and women of the Royal Observatory Corps, armed with binoculars, to keep track of 'Raid 42' as it headed west to the Clyde, turned back, and finally crashed on Bonnyton Moor. As Hess prepared to bail out, a Boulton Paul Defiant from 141 Squadron at Ayr was just a few miles behind him. Hess landed close to Floors

Farm ten miles south of Glasgow's city centre. He suffered a chip fracture of the twelfth dorsal vertebra after hitting the ground hard, was dragged forward by his parachute, and passed out a second time.

After touching down on Scottish soil, Hess was discovered grappling with his parachute by David McLean, a farmer who escorted him to the farmhouse where, once he was settled on a rocking chair in front of a log fire, he was offered a cup of tea. He politely declined, explaining that at this hour he would prefer a glass of water. The plane crash had been spotted by the Home Guard, whose officers arrived to collect him and take him to Major Graham Donald, the Assistant Group Officer of the Royal Observer Corps, at their headquarters. Major Donald listened as Hess stated his name as: Hauptmann Alfred Horn – his brother-in-law's name – and insisted that he had 'a secret and vital message' for the Duke of Hamilton, who he insisted on meeting at once. By now there were fifteen or twenty soldiers in the room who burst out laughing. The translation was carried out by Roman Battaglia, a member of the Polish Consulate who, in an extraordinary scene, asked any question shouted out by the assembled throng. (MI5 would later raise questions about Battaglia's swift appearance, which was suitably explained by the fact that he was staying in a nearby house.) Hess explained that he had seen Hamilton at the Olympic Games in Berlin and that they had a friend in common, though he made no mention of Haushofer.

Major Donald was the first to suspect Hauptmann Horn was not who he claimed to be. When he suggested he might instead be Rudolf Hess, the Deputy Führer shirked the question and gave a 'forced laugh'. Major Donald then called the duty controller and asked him to contact Wing Commander Hamilton and explain that a captured German pilot called Alfred Horn was asking to meet with him. Donald said he added that if Horn meant nothing, then his real name was Rudolf Hess. The second portion of the message was not passed on to Hamilton, who made arrangements to visit Maryhill Barracks, where Hess had been moved. The next morning Hamilton checked the list of all Luftwaffe officers he had met during the Olympics, but found no mention of a 'Horn'.

Hamilton, accompanied by the RAF Interrogation Officer, arrived at Maryhill Barracks at 10 a.m. Perusing the pilot's possessions, which included a large assortment of medications, photographs of a young boy, and a Leica camera, Hamilton examined the two visiting cards: that of Professor Karl Haushofer and of his son, Dr Albrecht Haushofer, which he immediately linked to the recent letter that so interested MI6. Hess was lying in bed, injured from his parachute drop, and asked Hamilton if they could speak alone. Hamilton asked the Interrogation Officer and the duty guard to leave. Hess began by explaining that Haushofer had met Hamilton at the Olympic Games and that the Duke had lunched at his house, adding, 'I do not know if you recognise me, but I am Rudolf Hess.'

Hess then stated he was on a humanitarian mission: Adolf Hitler did not wish to defeat England and wished to stop the war. Hess had been briefed by Albrecht Haushofer that Hamilton was an Englishman who would understand his point of view; he, Hess, had tried to arrange a meeting in Lisbon and attempted on three previous occasions to fly to Dungavel. He had postponed planned attempts when Britain was achieving successes in Libya, lest his mission be mistaken for weakness, but now that Germany had gained the upper hand he was 'glad to come'. Hitler predicted victory within one to three years, and was anxious to avoid unnecessary slaughter. Hess then asked Hamilton to unite leading members of his party, so that together they might agree peace proposals. Hamilton robustly insisted that there was now only one party in the United Kingdom, all dedicated to victory.

Having laid out Hitler's peace terms – supremacy in Europe – Hess requested that Hamilton ask the King to secure his 'parole' on the grounds that he had come unarmed and of his own free will. He also asked that a telegram be sent to his aunt in Zurich stating that Alfred Horn was 'in good health'.

Hamilton's initial impression was that Hess was a man of considerable self-confidence who, while admitting that he had arrived without Hitler's knowledge, declared that he knew the Führer's mind so intimately that any peace negotiation agreeable to Hess would certainly suit Hitler. As Hamilton departed, Hess asked, 'Will you please have me moved out of Glasgow, as I am anxious not to be killed by a German bomb.'

The meeting left Hamilton badly shaken. There was no precedent for finding oneself viewed as a potential Nazi confidant and co-conspirator in the overthrow of a wartime coalition government. He instructed the commanding officer to ensure the prisoner remained under strong guard, visited the crash site to ensure the authenticity of Hess's statements and then returned to the operations room to dictate his report. The question now was how to break the news to the Government. He began by calling Sir Alexander Cadogan, but found himself instead arguing with a civil servant who refused to put him through. Fortunately Jock Colville, the Prime Minister's private secretary, happened to be passing, overheard the call and took over the receiver. Hamilton then insisted that he had to meet urgently with Churchill.

Colville was receptive. The previous night he had slept at 10 Downing Street, unable to leave due to the ferocity of the evening's bombing, and while in a fitful sleep he had dreamt that Goering had flown over to London. It was a scene described in the novel *Flying Visit* by Peter Fleming, which Colville had read a few months before. When Hamilton said that something extraordinary had taken place, but he was unable to divulge exactly what over the telephone, Colville asked, 'Has somebody arrived?' 'Yes', answered Hamilton, who was then instructed to fly directly to Kidlington and go on to Ditchley, where the Prime Minister was spending the weekend at Ditchley Park, the country home of Ronald Tree, an affluent friend.

Hamilton arrived by Hurricane at Kidlington airfield, where the Prime Minister's chauffeur was waiting on the tarmac, the engine already purring. A dinner for Churchill, Brendan Bracken and Sir Archibald Sinclair, the Secretary of State for Air, as well as twenty-five other guests, was drawing to a close when Hamilton arrived and, still wearing his flying jacket, met the Prime Minister.

He asked that they speak in private, and when only Churchill and Sir Archibald Sinclair remained in the room, Hamilton told them that the pilot who had crashed in Scotland the previous evening claimed to be Rudolf Hess. Hamilton felt that Churchill greeted this news with the patronising look of a man addressing a shell-shocked soldier. (Churchill later told Parliament he had not initially believed it.) The Prime Minister then said slowly, 'Do you mean to tell me that the Deputy Führer of Germany is in our hands?' Hamilton explained that that was indeed what the pilot had told him.

Now Churchill, who enjoyed a Hollywood movie after dinner and who had been told that the projector next door had *The Marx Brothers Go West* laced up and ready to roll, then uttered one of the most priceless lines of the Second World War: 'Well, Hess or no Hess, I am going to see the Marx Brothers.' And with that he stomped off, no doubt chewing on an unlit cigar.

It was only after the last gag had been cracked that Churchill called Hamilton back and grilled him from midnight until three a.m. on the story as it had unfolded so far. Hamilton said that to his mind the German was indeed Hess and showed Churchill copies of the two letters Albrecht Haushofer had sent him. He told the Prime Minister that Hess had come to the conclusion that Britain was on the verge of defeat, but that Churchill would not be sympathetic to Hess's view: 'By God I would not,' roared Churchill.

The next morning Churchill and Hamilton returned to 10 Downing Street where Anthony Eden, the Foreign Secretary, was briefed. He insisted that Ivone Kirkpatrick (former British Ambassador in Berlin and a Foreign Office expert on Germany) be dispatched north with Hamilton to carry out an official confirmation.

Kirkpatrick's first meeting with Hess took place shortly after midnight on the morning of 13 May 1941. At one o'clock in the morning he was interrupted by a telephone call from Anthony Eden who was anxious for confirmation of the identity of their new guest. A droll figure, Kirkpatrick said Hess had been speaking for almost an hour, but had said nothing. However, he was certainly the Deputy Führer and, for that first hour, had read from notes a convoluted speech that laid the blame for the current conflict at Britain's feet. Hess had pointed to a book, *England's Foreign Policy under Edward VII*, whose author admitted that from 1904 the nation's policy was to oppose Germany and back France in the certain knowledge that this would lead to conflict with Germany. 'Thus England was responsible for the war in 1914,' as Kirkpatrick later reported.

Hess had then moved through the events of recent years. Hitler was forced to occupy Austria as it was the will of the Austrians; Czechoslovakia fell as a consequence of France's attempt to use it as an air base; the Polish crisis was triggered by England's refusal to permit the Poles to agree to Germany's rational requests. 'The conclusion was clear that England was responsible for the present war,' wrote Kirkpatrick. Hitler, explained Hess, had never intended conflict with Britain and was surprised when Britain declared war and later refused the Führer's offers of peace. When Britain began to bomb Germany in May 1940, Hitler stayed his hand 'so as to spare the world the horror of unrestricted air warfare, and partly out of a sentimental regard for English culture and English monuments'. It was 'only with the greatest reluctance' that he had given the order to bomb England.

Hess averred that Germany's victory was guaranteed by its ability to produce a greater number of aircraft, as well as ships and submarines, and that he had been horrified at the unnecessary killing required to force Britain to capitulate. Thus he had embarked on his mission, without Hitler's permission, to persuade England that the wisest course was to make peace now. It was ill-advised to keep Hitler waiting, for though he was 'a tenderhearted man' he could be impatient. Kirkpatrick was keen to test Hess's knowledge of Hitler's plans regarding Russia, and so asked if that nation was regarded as part of Europe – and thus subject to Hitler's domination – or of Asia.

'Asia,' replied Hess.

Kirkpatrick then commented that, therefore, under the terms of Hess's proposal in which Germany had a free hand in Europe, Russia would not be attacked. 'Herr Hess reacted quickly by remarking that Germany had certain demands to make of Russia which would have to be satisfied, either by negotiation or as the result of war. He added, however, that there was no foundation for the rumours now being spread that Hitler was contemplating an early attack on Russia.'

Both Kirkpatrick and Hamilton, who was sitting in, came to different conclusions about Hess's comment. While Kirkpatrick later wrote in his memoirs, 'I got the impression that Hess was so much out of things that he really did not know', Hamilton, who was unimpressed by Kirkpatrick's manner (he described it as that of a man with better things to do), thought Hess had said more than he should by making any mention of an 'early attack', and so sought to cover his tracks by insisting that Hitler had no plans for such action.

Lying in bed in a sparse room illuminated only by a light bulb and a shade made of old newspaper, Hess added one final point as the two men prepared to leave: he had forgotten, he declared, 'to emphasise that the proposal could only be considered on the understanding that it was negotiated by Germany with any government other than the present British Government. Mr Churchill, who had planned the war since 1938, and his colleagues who had lent themselves to his war policy, were not persons with whom the Führer could negotiate.'

The conversations, or monologues to be precise, had lasted almost three hours and Kirkpatrick closed his report by adding, 'In general, I allowed even the most outrageous remarks to pass unanswered, since I realised that argument would be quite fruitless and would certainly have deprived us of our breakfast.'

Eden instructed Kirkpatrick and Hamilton to conduct a second interview on Wednesday 14 May, during which Hess appeared perturbed that the negotiations he had arrived to undertake had not yet been set up. He did, however, ask for a loan of Jerome K. Jerome's novel *Three Men in A Boat*, his medicines, and a piece of his wrecked plane as a souvenir. The next day Hamilton was ordered back to London while Kirkpatrick carried out a third interview alone, in which Hess attempted to make Kirkpatrick's 'flesh creep' by arguing that America had designs on the British Empire.

After returning to London, Kirkpatrick briefed Churchill who said, 'If Hess had come a year ago and told us what the Germans would do to us, we should have been very frightened, and rightly, so,' but having already endured the Battle of Britain and wave after wave of bombing raids, 'why should we be frightened now?'

Winston Churchill issued his instructions on 14 May that Hess should be equipped with 'special guardians' and treated as a prisoner of war – 'one against whom grave political charges may be preferred. This man is potentially a war criminal, and he and his confederates may well be declared outlaws at the close of the war. In this case his repentance would stand him in good stead.

'In the meantime he should be strictly isolated in a convenient house not too far from London, fitted by C with the necessary appliances, and every endeavour should be made to study his mentality and get anything worthwhile out of him.

'His health and comfort should be ensured; food, books, writing material and recreation being provided for him. He should not have any contacts with the outer world or visitors except as prescribed by the Foreign Office. Special Guardians should be appointed. He should see no newspapers and hear no wireless. He should be treated with dignity as if he were an important general who had fallen into our hands.'

Churchill had decided to inform the British public about the truth behind Hess's flight, but was dissuaded from doing so.

The process had begun on Monday 12 May when the Germans announced Hess's arrival in Britain in a radio statement. Anthony Eden was dining at the time when Churchill called, insisting a statement be released immediately, so the Foreign Secretary rushed round and together they composed a suitable form of words. Yet when Kirkpatrick called the Foreign Office the next morning to report on his interview with Hess, he was told that 'the British Government were embarrassed by the whole affair and did not know exactly how to handle it.'

When Churchill appeared in the House of Commons he declared that he had nothing to add to the official statement, but said, 'obviously a further statement will be made in the near future concerning the flight to this country of this very high and important Nazi leader'. When a fellow MP asked if it would be left to the Ministry of Information to treat the situation with 'skill and imagination', the Prime Minister replied, 'I think this is one of these cases where imagination is somewhat baffled by the facts as they present themselves.'

Harold Nicolson, Parliamentary Secretary to the Ministry of Information, lunched with Churchill on Wednesday 14 May and asked for guidance on how the Ministry should handle Hess's arrival. All Churchill said was, 'We must not make a hero out of him.' Yet that evening Churchill rang Eden at home with a statement he had prepared and now planned to make to the House of Commons the following afternoon. Eden disagreed with

Churchill's open approach, instead insisting that it was wiser to keep the Germans guessing as to what Hess had or had not revealed. In a huff, Churchill demanded that if he did not like the draft he should compose his own. Eden climbed out of bed, went to his desk and did exactly that, which he then read over to Churchill. It was noted down by a secretary and circulated to Lord Beaverbrook, Minister of Air Production, with whom it found favour, and Duff Cooper, Minister of Information, whom it displeased. At such an impasse, Churchill declared that he was either going to use his own statement or make none at all and asked Eden which was it to be? 'No statement,' replied the Foreign Secretary, who was rewarded with 'All right, no statement,' and with that 'the telephone was crashed down'.

Nevertheless, Churchill had the support of Duff Cooper who tried to persuade him that it was crucial to issue a statement clarifying the British Government's position as regarded Hess's arrival. Churchill told him to come over at midnight 'and we shall discuss it again'. Yet when Cooper arrived he discovered that Lord Beaverbrook was also present. If Cooper was the angel on Churchill's right shoulder, advocating openness, Beaverbrook was the Devil on his left, adamant that silence was currently the Government's best servant. This time the Devil was not in the details. When Churchill returned to the subject, he was met by a united front from Beaverbrook and Eden, who reported that, 'The Prime Minister reverted to his projected statement about Hess, this time at the Cabinet, but nobody liked it so that nothing came of it. Lord Beaverbrook told me afterwards that we might have to "strangle the infant" a third time, but fortunately it was not reborn.'

It was a decision regretted by the Ministry of Information. Harold Nicolson took the view that, 'This is bad, since the belief will get around that we are hiding something and we shall be blamed in this Ministry.'

On Friday 16 May, Hess was driven to Glasgow Central Station and under armed escort travelled by train to London where he spent the next four days in the Tower of London. Earlier that day the Duke of Hamilton had lunch with King George VI at Windsor Castle, and while that demonstrates the access Hess had hoped the Duke possessed, it was not a conversation that he would have liked to hear, as evidenced in a letter sent to the King by Hamilton a few days later: 'It is clear that Hess is still an unrepentant Nazi who repeats ad nauseam the usual Nazi "claptrap". While his action seems unlikely to affect the course of the war, his arrival here uninvited has been of considerable advantage to us, if only in the difficulties and discredit in which it has involved the German propaganda machine.'

Hamilton, however, was to endure considerable discomfort over his role in the affair, with questions raised over his loyalty – a dreadful slight for a serving RAF officer. Things were not helped by the fact that Duff Cooper had told the BBC that Hamilton had met Hess at the Berlin Olympics and that Hess had written to him directly in a letter that he had then passed on to the authorities. It was left to the Air Ministry to send a stern letter to the Ministry of Information insisting on a correction. The Duke was later forced to defend himself, successfully, against a libel in a Communist pamphlet that he was a friend of the Deputy Führer. As Hamilton put it to Churchill, 'What do you tell your wife if a prostitute throws her arms around your neck?'

4

Hitler

Albert Speer was working on an architectural drawing, one of the towering new buildings set to rise up in Germanica, as the victorious greater Germany was to be christened at the close of the war, when a horrendous howl echoed around Berchtesgaden. It was the morning of Sunday 11 May, and Adolf Hitler had opened Hess's letter, dutifully delivered by a trembling Pintsch who, minutes later, was arrested. Such was the fate of a bearer of bad news. (The hapless creature was later dispatched to the Eastern Front.) As his scream subsided, Hitler bellowed, 'Bormann immediately! Where is Bormann?'

The letter has been lost, but it was seen by many who noted its contents and was said to have begun, 'My Führer, when you receive this letter I shall be in England. You can imagine that the decision to take this step was not easy for me, since a man of forty has other ties with life than one of twenty . . .' The colour drained from Hitler's face as he read how Hess planned to meet the Duke of Hamilton, and lay out a peace plan that would unite Britain and Germany ahead of the forthcoming invasion of Russia. As well as going into lengthy details of the technical requirements of his flight, Hess noted that among the criteria that made him suitable for such a mission was his childhood in Alexandria, which he described as an English environment. He insisted that he would inform the British Government that his mission should not be read as a sign of weakness, but as one that the nation was invincible and did not have to ask for peace. It should be noted that Hess reportedly concluded the letter by stating that if his Führer did not agree, he could say that he, Hess, was mad. 'And if, my Führer, this project – which I admit has but very small chance of success – ends in failure and the fates decide against me, this can have no detrimental results either for you or for Germany; it will always be possible for you to deny all responsibility. Simply say I was crazy.'

After finishing the letter Hitler immediately telephoned Goering. When the Air Marshal, who was then in residence at his castle at Edelstein, picked up, Hitler shouted, 'Goering, get here immediately. Something dreadful has happened.' As the head of the Gestapo, SS-*Gruppenführer* Mueller coordinated a series of arrests among personnel at Augsburg Airport, as well as among Hess's staff, and began a thorough investigation of his private life, paying particular attention to the astrologists, anthroposophists and nature therapists. Ribbentrop was dispatched to Rome with a view to appeasing Mussolini in case the Italian leader feared Germany was attempting to do a deal behind his back, and then did a deal first, forcing the collapse of the Anti-Comintern Pact signed by Germany, Italy and Japan.

Goering arrived in the evening, accompanied by Luftwaffe General Ernst Udet. Hitler asked what the odds were of Hess reaching Britain. Udet said that, given the limited fuel capacity of the Me110, he would most likely crash into the North Sea, and that he lacked the requisite technical expertise. Hitler disagreed, and began pacing up and down the corridors. His interpreter later said it was 'as if a bomb had hit the Berghof'. But Hitler was, however, clear-headed enough to abolish the position of Deputy Leader, rename his department Party Chancellery and appoint Martin Bormann as its head – subordinate, of course, to himself.

Hitler was worried that Hess would reveal the plans for Barbarossa, the invasion of Russia. He was heard muttering that a fool could cause unimaginable harm and what if the British drugged him and forced him to make a radio statement. The question was how to tell the German people that the nation's second most prominent Nazi had fled to Britain? Usually Goebbels, the master of propaganda, would have been to hand, but he was absent at his country residence and later commented, 'There are situations which even the best propagandist in the world cannot cope with.' Instead, Hitler relied on Dr Otto Dietrich, the Reich head of press who, with contributions from Hitler himself, Goering and Ribbentrop, prepared a vague statement, broadcast on the evening of Monday 12 May, that appeared to take Hess's lead in branding him unbalanced:

> The Party authorities state: Party Member Hess, who had been expressly forbidden by the Führer to use an aeroplane because of a disease which had been becoming worse for years was, in contradiction of this order, able to get hold of a plane recently. Hess started on Saturday 10 May, at about 18.00 hours, from Augsburg on a flight from which he has not yet returned. A letter which he left behind unfortunately showed traces of a mental disturbance which justifies the fear that Hess was the victim of hallucinations. The Führer at once ordered the arrest of Hess's adjutants, who alone knew of his flight and who, in contradiction to the Führer's ban, of which they were aware, did not prevent the flight nor report it at once. The National Socialist Movement has, unfortunately, in these circumstances, to assume that Party Comrade Hess has crashed or met with a similar accident.

The German statement was followed shortly by the British statement of Hess's arrival, broadcast by the BBC at 11.20 p.m. The fact that Hess had not been lost in the sea but was now on British soil forced the German Government to issue a second statement on Tuesday, 13 May:

On the basis of a preliminary examination of the papers which Hess left behind him, it would appear that Hess was living under the hallucination that by undertaking a personal step in connection with the Englishman with whom he was formerly acquainted it might be possible to bring about an understanding between Germany and Britain. As has since been confirmed by a report from London, Hess parachuted from his plane and landed near the place in Scotland which he had selected as his destination; there he was found, apparently in an injured condition.

As is well known in Party circles, Hess has undergone severe physical suffering for some years. Recently he had sought relief to an increasing extent in various methods practised by mesmerists and astrologers, etc. An attempt is being made to determine to what extent these persons are responsible for bringing about the condition of mental distraction which led him to take this step. It is also conceivable that Hess was deliberately lured into a trap by a British party. The whole manner of his action, however, confirms the fact, stated in the first announcement, that he was suffering under hallucinations.

Hess was better acquainted than anyone else with the peace proposals which the Führer has made with such sincerity. Apparently he had deluded himself into thinking that, by some personal sacrifice, he could prevent developments which, in his eyes, could only end with the complete destruction of the British Empire. Judging by his own papers, Hess, whose sphere of activities was confined to the Party, as is generally known, had no idea how to carry out such a step or what result it would have.

The National Socialist Party regrets that this idealist fell prey to tragic hallucinations. The continuation of the war, which Britain forced on the German people, will not be affected at all. As the Führer declared in his last speech, it will be carried on until the men in power in Britain have been overthrown or are ready to make peace.

The statements were hasty, ill-planned and unsuccessful in cloaking the enormity of the scandal in the straitjacket of a madman. Goebbels later wrote, 'It was so absurd that it could be taken for a mystification.' He would have preferred to have made no statement until the situation forced it, and then to suggest that Hess had lost his nerve, which would allow them to use the more understandable (and plausible) cover of weakness rather than madness. The flight of a weak man was more defensible than the current position which was, that a man known for years to be mentally unbalanced, had held such a position of authority. 'It's rightly asked how such an idiot could be the second man after the Führer.'

On 13 May, Hitler called a meeting of the Reichsleiters and Gauleiters at the Berghof. When the sixty to seventy men were assembled, Goering and Bormann entered the room with grim faces. Bormann then read Hess's letter aloud, to growing anger among the gathering. Once his audience was sufficiently stoked, Hitler entered the room and made a speech on the theme of loyalty and betrayal. He explained that Hess, who he insisted was mentally ill and had acted without his knowledge, had betrayed him, and that he now required the loyalty of his most trusted 'old fighters'. He told of the promise Hess had made not to fly, how he had broken the promise by practising in a specially equipped Messerschmitt, and revealed that Hess had spoken to him days before his departure to ask if he still wished to co-operate with England. At the end of his speech, Hitler leaned against a big table positioned near the window and 'was in tears and looked ten years older', according to one witness; while another said, 'I have never seen the Führer so deeply shocked.' As if in need to comfort their stricken leader, the gathered men stood up and went over to the window, silently surrounding Hitler in a semi-circle. It was left to Goering to articulate the strength of their loyalty and their anger and hatred towards Hess.

As Hitler briefed his most senior officers on Hess, Ribbentrop was in Rome speaking to Mussolini and to Ciano, who detailed the meeting in his diary:

> The official version is that Hess, sick in body and mind, was victim of his pacifist hallucinations, and went to England in the hope of facilitating the beginning of peace negotiations. Hence, he is not a traitor; hence, he will not talk; hence, whatever else is said or printed in his name, is false. Ribbentrop's conversation is a beautiful feat of patching things up. The Germans want to cover themselves before Hess speaks and reveals things that might make a great impression in Italy. Mussolini comforted Von Ribbentrop, but afterwards told me that he considers the Hess affair a tremendous blow to the Nazi regime. He added that he was glad of it, because this will have the effect of bringing down German stock, even with the Italians.

When Mussolini met Hitler later, the Führer spoke of Hess and wept.

Goebbels later recorded in his diary, 'What a spectacle for the world: a mentally deranged second man after the Führer.' When he was shown Hess's letter, Goebbels wrote: 'A muddle-headed shambles, schoolboy dilettantism . . . That Churchill would immediately have him arrested hadn't, unfortunately, occurred to him.' The letter was crammed with 'half-baked occultism'.

Germans were bewildered, angered and upset by the news. 'Didn't you already know that we are governed by madmen?' an old gardener said to Schmidt, Hitler's interpreter. The Nazi Party took the brunt of abuse. While Hitler was still wrapped in adulation and the *Wehrmacht* (armed forces) respected, the political party that had brought him to power was now viewed as corrupt and self-serving. Rumours raced across the country. Himmler and Ley were reported to have fled abroad; the Gauleiter of Upper Bavaria, Adolf Wagner, arrested on the Swiss border with 22 million Reichsmarks. None were true but, collectively, they gave an insight into what the public now believed their leaders to be capable of. But many felt sympathy for Hitler, seeing the defection of Hess as yet another burden with which he had to contend.

On 18 May, the diplomat Ulrich von Hassell spoke for many when he noted in his diary that 'The effect of Hess's flight . . . was indescribable, but immeasurably increased by the stupidity of the official communiqué, which could clearly be traced to Hitler's personal explosions of wrath. The first one especially, which implied for months, even for years, he had presented to the people a half or even entirely insane "Deputy" as heir-apparent of the Führer. The background of the flight is not yet clear. The official explanations are, to say the least, incomplete. Hess's sporting and technical performance alone showed that he could not be called crazy.'

Weizsaecker, Secretary of State at the Foreign Office, wrote: 'To hold office meant, in fact, to be above criticism. That is why the fall of Hitler's deputy, Rudolf Hess . . . seemed so fantastic; yesterday he had been a demigod and today he was nothing but a pitiful idiot . . . I was sorry when his old friends attributed to him defects other than defects of intelligence.'

A popular joke at the time had Hess called before Churchill. 'So you're the madman are you?' 'Oh no,' replied Hess. 'Only his deputy.' In imitation of the clipped accents of the BBC, Germans would announce that on Sunday no further German Cabinet members arrived by plane, and a German High Command communiqué stated that Goering and Goebbels remained in German hands. Photographs of Hess were immediately removed from all public places. Books on the NSDAP were reprinted minus his image. He was erased from the Reich's Card Index and those members of its leadership.

The principal beneficiary of Hess's departure was Bormann, who wasted no time in crowing. He wrote to Himmler that his former superior had an inferiority complex, had suffered from impotence (even during the conception of his son) and had made the flight to prove his virility. Goebbels also stated that Hess was impotent due to psychological problems and that the couple had been so desperate over their inability to have a child that they had visited both astrologers and mystics. They also drank potions prior to the successful conception, after which Hess had replicated the dance performed in birth celebrations by South American Indians. After the child was born, said Goebbels, Hess instructed every Gauleiter to send a portion of soil from their area so that it could be placed under the crib and his son could live on Germanic soil. Goebbels, who represented the metropolis of Berlin, pondered sending a flagstone before opting instead for manure from his garden. Hitler was also supposed to have said, 'One can be prepared for anything, except the aberrations of a lunatic.'

Albrecht Haushofer was brought to Berchtesgaden on Monday 12 May and instructed, under armed guard, to write a report for Hitler entitled *English Connections and the Possibility of Utilising Them.* After Hitler – still unaware of Hess's fate – finished reading the report, he instructed that Haushofer be interrogated by Gestapo chief Heinrich Mueller at the Prince Albrecht Strasse Gestapo Prison in Berlin. On 7 July 1941, Haushofer wrote to his parents from prison: '. . . I know exactly that at present I am a small beetle which has been turned on its back by an unexpected and unforeseeable gust of wind, and which realises that it cannot rise to its feet by its own strength – and now, with some knowledge of two-legged creatures, does not entertain great illusions regarding its future . . . I suppose you are now going to the Alpine pasture. My regards to the mountains! Sometime I shall, no doubt, see them again.' Mueller and his superior, Reinhard Heydrich, had been unable to prove any serious charge against Haushofer but recommended his continued detention. However, Hitler ordered his release and in July he was set free, though he remained under the watch of the Gestapo.

*

In the first few days after Hess's departure Hitler met with General Walter Schellenberg of the *Sicherheitsdienst* (SD) – the secret service – to evaluate the potential damage the deputy Führer could cause if he was to reveal his secrets. It was considerable. The General dismissed reports of Hess's derangement, writing: '. . . Nor was his intellect so deranged that he would be incapable of giving a clear account of our [German] plans.' When Schellenberg met Hitler in Berlin to discuss the potential damage, he assured him that Hess's 'fanatical devotion' would stop him from disclosing 'details of our strategic planning . . . though he was certainly in a position to do so'.

5

House of Secrets

On Sunday morning, 25 May 1941, Rudolf Hess sat on the terrace of Mytchett Place in the company of his new 'guardians', Foley, 'Wallace' and 'Barnes', and watched as the night's rain steadily dripped off the trees. His mood was 'gloomy and morose' and he spoke little. In the distance he could see the commissioned officers of both the Scots and Coldstream Guards lined up, then paraded through their paces by Lieutenant Colonel Scott, who was keen to exert his authority and bond both units together, and whose shouts of 'a-ten-shuuuun' carried across the summer's air and back to the house. Hess pretended not to be impressed but, determined not to be outdone, chose to give a display of German martial superiority. He stood up, stamped his feet, then goose-stepped along the gravel path and past the roses and gladioli, before administering a neat about turn and marching back, his feet pointed and flung high. It was, according to Scott, a 'ludicrous exhibition', but one designed to demonstrate that he 'was equal to the occasion'.

While he was out, a search of his room had revealed some scraps of paper, on one of which was written, 'Our people need our own land. (with the exception of the colonies) . . . space for the young generation. F [was this von Fritsch, or Führer?] had always had aspirations towards World Domination . . . The Support of E [England] through the ruling circle in the United States. Should England succumb after a long war, we would not acquire any of her own territory. If we achieved World Conquest we would . . . The United States would have her Dollar position. England would not give in too soon. Anxious Consultations.' The memo about Hess's note which was sent to C ended 'part of an essay?'

It had been a difficult week. On Wednesday Foley and Barnes had questioned Hess about the German construction of submarines, and submarine warfare, but it had not gone well. On Friday 23 May, the log reported: 'O845 "Z" came down to breakfast. He went into the garden with his companions but only stayed there a few minutes and then went up to his room with Capt. Barnes. It is now noticed that Z will talk very freely with the doctor and seems to trust him but all other officers are treated with suspicion. Z walked in the garden both in the morning and the afternoon. He appears to have quite got over the injury to his ankle – walked with a firm step and did not find it necessary, as heretofore, to wear a slipper on his right foot. He stayed in his sitting room after tea but had a stroll in the garden with the doctor after dinner. Z is still apprehensive that the guard officers are out to murder him.'

During their daily walks and long conversations, Dr Gibson Graham began to build up a picture of his patient. Hess was careful about his diet, avoiding eggs, jams, and fried foods, and drinking only the weakest of tea. This, he explained, was to avoid a recurrence of previous ill-health: in the past he had suffered 'gall bladder trouble, colitism, renal trouble and also cardiac pains'. Together they discussed the efficacy or not of unorthodox medical practitioners, with Hess placing his trust in individuals who could deliver an accurate diagnosis by merely looking at a patient. He was an early supporter of chiropractors and extolled the work of the Swedish explorer Sven Hedin, who had returned from Tibet with herbs which, once distilled, delivered a certain cure for gall bladder disease. With pride, Hess explained that he knew Mr Hedin personally. The thorough medical check-up revealed that Hess had no serious organic disease, but there were a few pus cells in his urine which occurred in clumps. Hess explained that he had a history of prostatitis or, as Graham noted, 'gonorrheal infection'. He was given the Khan test for syphilis, which proved negative.

If his physical health was sound, Graham raised questions about his mental well-being. It was clear that arrival at Camp Z had caused Hess 'intense agitation' and he was convinced that he was now surrounded by 'sinister forces' who 'desired his death'. Was this such an irrational response from a German keenly aware of the circumstances in which individuals disappeared in his home nation? Perhaps not, but what Graham noted was the inconsistency of his patient's suspicions. At first, the target of Hess's worst fears were his 'companions', but the anxiety had quickly spread to his guards.

Hess had explained to Graham in general terms why he was 'seeking the chivalry of the King'. It was a simple desire for peace, not, he was anxious to point out, because of any doubts over Germany's imminent victory, but because of his detestation of the needless slaughter of hundreds of thousands of 'innocent English people'. Graham was told of the dream Haushofer had had, that on three occasions he had seen him in an aeroplane travelling to an unknown destination:

> From such cloudy material the concept took shadowy form of flying to this country, seeking the Duke of Hamilton and then the King in order to be on hand with peace proposals when a new government arose in this country. Why a new government should arise he could not say, but he seems convinced of this; nor did he know its composition. The present British Government would try and prevent peace proposals taking shape; moreover, his government could not deal with them, only with their successors. He apparently sees nothing incongruous in a member of a hostile government running away to its enemy in order to initiate peace proposals which he has not been given the power to conduct.

A point which struck Graham was Hess's inability, or refusal, to appreciate the reality of his position: that he was a captive of the enemy. 'Hess stated that, if his mission fails, he should be returned freely to his government and not exchanged or placed in a prisoner of war camp. He shows little appreciation of his position.'

Graham wrote: 'To sum up, one gets the impression, in the absence of concrete evidence to the contrary, of an intelligent man of no great character or driving force who has been dominated and hypnotised by his master. He has swallowed whole his party doctrines, but has no conception of the thought and tide of opinion in other countries. He is conceited, introspective and neurotic. In addition there is evidence of delusions and lack of judgment. He reasons, at times logically, on obviously unsound premises.' Graham noted that, 'It would be extremely interesting to obtain the opinion of a skilled psychiatrist on these mental traits,' then put forward what he described as 'tentative personal conclusions':

1. Loss of party confidence (but not immediate danger of eclipse) due to development of lack of judgment and balance.
2. Desperate and dramatic event required to rehabilitate and save himself: Peace proposals conducted and initiated by himself; flight to Britain, etc.
3. The whole plan is vague and shadowy, but even if this is so he is convinced of success since Professor Haushofer (his prophet) has pointed the way by (a) mentioning a specific name (Hamilton) and (b) on three occasions dreaming of Hess in an aeroplane.
4. A man afraid for his life but determined in his confused way to gain again the respect and love of his Führer and so confound his enemies.
5. He is still a Nazi and reverences his Führer. He is determined to give away no essential information, but one wonders how much detail is in his possession.

6. From time to time he has waves of acute fear for the failure of his mission due to the non-appearance of the Duke of Hamilton.

Graham filed his report on Hess in the evening of Friday 23 May. After tea the following evening, the pair met in the drawing room and talked at length in front of a crackling fire in the hearth. Hess said that he had made a promise to Hitler that he would not commit suicide, but his manner gave the doctor cause for concern. Afterwards he told Scott that 'Z is clearly decreasing in stature and he estimates his worth at not more than £2 a week.' After his acrobatic march on Sunday morning, Hess's mood fell with the rain that tumbled down all day Monday and, apart from meals, he spent the day reading in his room. In what little conversation could be prised from him, Colonel 'Wallace' detected a growing realisation that England 'was very different from what he had been led to believe'.

For the past fortnight Professor H.H. Dale at the Medical Research Council had been analysing the collection of Hess's drugs. His finished report stated:

> The general impression given by inspection of this collection of drugs is that of a rather large and varied collection, mostly conventional, and all harmless in the quantities present. The presence of Pervitin tablets, and of tablets of barbiturate to overcome the sleep-preventing effect of Pervitin when opportunity for sleep presents itself, is in accordance with previous reports of drugs carried by German troops. For the rest, there are small doses of opiates, which might be used either as intestinal sedatives, or to dull pain in case of wounding, and small doses of atropine, which might be used to alleviate air sickness. Other tablets, containing dextrose, kola, lecithin, etc, are probably designed to stave off exhaustion or mitigate the sense of fatigue. There is, in addition,

> a collection of pillules and solutions, suggesting homeopathic medication. Altogether a very harmless collection; but some of the components seem to have got badly distributed, having strayed in some cases into several boxes with different labels, corresponding in no case to the nature of the tablets in question.

In Whitehall, Anthony Eden had a private meeting with Lord Simon, the Lord Chancellor, who, although a minister, was not a member of the War Cabinet. Eden had a favour to ask. Would Simon agree to interview Rudolf Hess on behalf of the Government? While Churchill's Government had no intention of negotiating with the Deputy Führer, it did believe that more could be extracted from him, and one way was by means of a *faux* meeting. The reason Simon had been chosen was two-fold: firstly, he had already met Hess in March 1935, and secondly – and most importantly – for the manner of the subterfuge, he was considered a prominent appeaser, whose appearance would therefore be taken favourably by Hess. Simon's concern was exactly that point – if word leaked of the meeting, his reputation would be ruined. He asked for time to consider the matter and a written request as a form of personal insurance. When the idea of a *faux* 'negotiation' was raised and Simon's name put forward, Churchill roared with laughter, declaring him 'the very man'.

In a letter marked 'most secret' Lord Simon wrote back to Eden in order to articulate specific points:

'I take it that the proposed interview with H. is for the purpose of giving him a favourable opportunity of talking freely about his "mission" and of seeing whatever, in the course of unburdening himself, he is led to give [of] any useful information as to enemy strengths and intentions. If the PM and you think that I would be the suitable choice for this piece of "intelligence" work, I am certainly ready to undertake it and to do my best.'

Concerned lest he be portrayed once again as an appeaser, Simon was adamant that he state whose orders he was carrying out: 'I should have to say that I came with the Government's approval. I cannot regard the prospects of a useful outcome as bright, but I do not see that any harm would be done if I draw a blank, for I assume that I can be assured that in no circumstances would the interview be known outside.'

The next day Eden wrote to Churchill: 'I saw Simon yesterday, and I think he will be willing to undertake the work of which we spoke. He has asked for 24 hours to consider the matter. We are agreed that he should make it plain that the Government knows of the interview, but that it would be unwise of him to indicate close collaboration with you and me – rather the reverse. Simon will be fully briefed before he goes for the interview, and I propose to write him a letter saying that you and I would be glad if he would undertake this task. All this will be kept most secret, and only Cadogan and I in this office are aware of the project.'

Eden later wrote back to Simon, agreeing with his 'description of your mission' and stating, 'I agree that you must say that you have come with the govt's approval, though I hope that it would not be necessary to emphasise this too much, since the man dreams of a change of govt!' The principal question Churchill wanted answered was why Hess 'so earnestly desire[d] a patched-up peace now?'

On the evening of Monday 26 May, while Hess was complaining that his food was over-seasoned, one of the flagships of the German navy had been struck a fatal blow. The battleship *Bismarck*, fast and well-armoured, had already sunk HMS *Hood*. She was a few hundred miles off Brest in Brittany, awaiting the imminent protection of U-boats and fighter planes, when she was struck by fourteen Swordfish 'stringbags' fired by HMS *Ark Royal* at nine p.m. As one of the torpedoes struck beneath the *Bismarck*'s stern, disabling her steering gear, the vast vessel began to turn in futile circles. Just before midnight the captain, Admiral Lutjens, sent the message, 'Ship incapable of manoeuvring. Will fight to the last shell. Long live the Führer.' For thirteen hours, the *Bismarck* was pounded by the sixteen- and fourteen-inch guns of the Royal Navy's *King George V* and *Rodney* battleships respectively, until she was reduced to a blazing hulk. At 10.36 a.m. on Tuesday 27 May, the torpedoes of the cruiser *Dorsetshire* finished the task: the *Bismarck*'s bows rose up, the vessel turned on its side, then sank.

When briefed on the Royal Navy's success at delivering a blow to the pride of the German navy, Foley made a calculated decision to use the *Bismarck*'s fate as a tool to break down Hess's resolve. He was aware of the risk, given Hess's fragile mental state of the past few days, but decided to introduce the matter into conversation during lunch on Wednesday 28 May. At one o'clock, after spending the morning walking in the garden, Hess took his seat for lunch in the officer's mess. His mood, described as 'better' by Scott, was not to last. The doctor noted: 'For tactical reasons, which had been carefully weighed in advance, he was quietly told during the general conversation of the sinking of the *Bismarck*. He showed immediate anxiety and looked ill. He drank a glass of water and then asked where she had been struck and whether there had been any survivors.'

As the *Bismarck* sank, the *Dorsetshire* and other British ships stood by in readiness to pick up survivors, but were forced to depart when news reached them of U-boats in the vicinity. It was later discovered that just 110 out of the 2,200 men on board were saved.

At lunch, Hess immediately after hearing the news began to complain of feeling unwell and left the table. 'He then brought a physical ill to account for his agitation, and complaining of a pain in his back went to bed.' When the doctor examined him that afternoon, he could find nothing wrong. Two hours later, Hess rose, stating that his back was better. Dr Graham suggested that they dine together in Hess's room that evening, but this made him nervous. Instead, he requested that they dine in the mess as usual, but from a common pot, from which he then selected with great care but with an excellent appetite. It was clear the sinking of the *Bismarck* had shaken him badly.

Hess did, however, have a need which could be met: as Scott noted, 'Z's one request today was for a hairnet!' Scott believed the decision to reveal the fate of the *Bismarck* had been the wrong move. In a report to Colonel Coates at Hobart House, he wrote, 'I think there is no doubt that the borderline between mental instability and insanity was reached at lunch yesterday when the attendants mentioned casually to him the sinking of the *Bismarck*. In my opinion this was a mistake in view of the very difficult mental state he was in at the time.'

Silent and morose during dinner, Hess retired to bed at 10 p.m. An hour later he requested a sedative from Graham. As the doctor prepared the drink, Hess spoke of his confusion and worries. Graham reassured him: 'I talked to him, explaining how worry, grief, thwarted hopes, failure and suchlike, upset one, and could produce his symptoms.'

Earlier in the evening Hess had talked with his guard, Malone. He had previously described him as a 'sort of Gestapo man', one he treated with caution, but they had since bonded over a shared interest in skiing, which Malone had introduced in a desperate attempt to melt a frigid silence. Before the doctor's arrival, Hess had enjoyed an unforced conversation and showed Malone photographs of his son.

At 2.20 a.m. Hess got up and came to the duty officer's room where Malone was sitting reading. 'I cannot sleep. Could you get me some whisky – just a small one?' Although taken aback by such a request from a man noted for his aversion to alcohol, Malone decided to fetch a whisky, which he drowned with water. After slugging it down Hess asked, 'The whisky was not too small? It had been enough?' Malone assured him that this was so, then asked if he would like a dose of the sleeping mixture, which was kept in the duty officer's room, but Hess refused and returned to bed.

Twenty minutes later he was back at the office door, in a state Malone recorded as 'nervously distressed' and with a request to speak to him. Malone said of course, and listened as Hess, 'speaking in a stage whisper which never rose above a murmur', explained the reason for his arrival in Britain and the necessity of meeting with the Duke of Hamilton. He asked Malone to contact the Duke on his behalf so that Hamilton could then arrange an audience with the King. Hess was clear that if Malone did so he would not only receive the thanks of the Monarch but he would be carrying out a great service to humanity. Malone was frank, saying it was impossible and that 'this sort of thing put the Duke of Hamilton in a most unfortunate position'.

To Hess no one was in a more 'unfortunate position' than himself. Was Malone aware that he was now in the hands of the Secret Service who, at the behest of a 'clique' of warmongers, had hidden him here in Mytchett Place so that the Duke could not find him? Did Malone know that he was being driven to insanity or suicide by a 'devilish scheme' that had begun a few days ago? He was being prevented from sleeping at night or even resting during the day. He ran through the list of disturbances: doors had been opened and shut loudly; people had run up and down uncarpeted stairs; the 'sentinel' stationed outside his room had deliberately clicked his heels. (Malone pointed out he wore rubber shoes.) He complained, as Malone wrote in his report, that 'Yesterday an enormous number of motorcycles had been stationed close by with their engines running to prey on his nerves. I assured him that there was no foundation for his suspicions, and said that the noise was perfectly regular as there was a large training establishment within a few hundred yards. This seemed to have no effect. He shook his head hopelessly and flapped his hands about on the arms of his chair listlessly. He then went back to bed.'

Yet no sooner had Hess retired for the night than he returned again, this time to ask to be excused for his behaviour as he was in a very nervous condition and, perhaps, did not mean all he had said. He rose several more times to go to the lavatory and did not sleep until, as Malone noted, 'I was relieved in more ways than one.' Once Malone had departed, Hess, in a bid to verify what Malone had told him, asked the new duty officer if there was indeed a training facility for motorcyclists nearby.

In Malone's private diary of 28 May 1941, he noted that Colonel Wallace and Captain Barnes were already 'very bored with "Death's Head"'. Wallace told Hess that his worth was now thirty-five shillings a week – 'no more'. A hardy Scot who had previously worked in a borstal, Malone was disappointed in the figure Hess now exhibited: 'I find it difficult to realise that this rather broken man who slouches into his chair careless as to his dress, whose expressions are unstudied, who is incapable of hiding his emotions, who swings in mood from cheerfulness to depression in a few hours, whose body reflects his mental pain and whose mind is cloudy with delusionary ideas (he sees Hitler's face in his soup, says Kendrick), who believes in second sight and dreams – that this man was the Deputy Führer of the Reich! He is such a second-rater, with none of the dignity, the bearing, of a great man.'

It was as if Hess had taken a vow of silence. During breakfast, a walk in the garden, lunch, and a long drawn-out afternoon, he spoke not a single word to his companions, who were treated instead to scowls or the blank face of a depressive. Dr Graham argued that he was now over the borderline between sanity and insanity. At three p.m. on 29 May Lieutenant Colonel Scott rang up Colonel Coates to brief him on the situation. At 5.45 p.m. Coates rang back to say that Graham would be relieved at the weekend and replaced by a trained psychiatrist. It was decided that that night Scott would dine with Hess, which he had not done before. Foley would join them and act as interpreter, and besides, the MI6 officer had news of his own for Hess.

Dinner was served at eight p.m. and Hess was amenable to a small glass of port. 'Jonathan was silent, although we tried to bring him into the conversation,' wrote Foley. After dinner Hess asked to speak with Scott then put forward a list of requests:

1. That the grille, if it was for his protection only, should be located on the inside and not outside as at present.
2. That he should not be kept to a regular timetable as to his getting up in the morning or going to bed at night. He admitted, however, that his only objection to the timetable was a feeling of restraint and that if the restriction was removed he would probably keep to the timetable as at present laid down.
3. That he should be allowed, at least, a summary of the news.
4. That he should be allowed to go into the garden at will.
5. That he would be prepared to give his parole at any time, subject to the restrictions on him being relaxed. Should his parole be accepted he would be willing that an officer should accompany him at all times for his protection.

All these requests were made in view of the fact that he had come here of his own free will and thrown himself upon the chivalry of His Majesty the King.'

The Commandant replied that he would have to refer the points raised to a higher authority for a final decision. After Hess had finished, Foley explained that a negotiator had been appointed by the Government to visit him. Hess immediately replied that he would not speak to him unless a German witness was present. Prior to his departure for England, Hess had searched through the list of the Auslands Organisation for civil prisoners of war and noted two names, Herr Kurt Mass and Herr Doctor Semmelbauer, whom he knew to be interned at Huyton Camp, near Liverpool. He retired to his room at 10.15 p.m. with a promise to deliver to Foley a written statement the following morning.

Hess's statement read:

His Majesty's Government has caused me to be informed, through Major Foley, that its representatives will probably visit me, perhaps in the near future. In this connection, I have to state that

> a conversation of a political nature with a representative of H.M. Government may take place only under the following conditions.
>
> 1. The name of the Government representative will be imparted to me in sufficient time to enable me, if considered necessary, to make a statement before his arrival.
> 2. Two German witnesses will take part in the conversation (I named the witnesses in question separately). They will be given time, with my co-operation, to write the conversation. The German text, signed by me, will be valid for the contents of the conversation in so far as my part in it is concerned.
> 3. For the purpose of recording the conversation, a German secretary, with typewriter, will be placed at my disposal.

For Foley the arrival of a German witness could be turned to his advantage. As Hess was unaware of the hidden microphones, he might drop his guard once in the company of a fellow countryman and disclose what he had so far refused to discuss, namely his knowledge of Germany's future military plans. Foley noted in a memo to C:

> It seems certain that it will be useless for a negotiator to come here unless the patient is allowed a German witness. This condition has a double aspect: one of general policy and, from our point of view, one of great practical and immediate importance. The success and progress in the methods we are using depends almost entirely on our being able to record unguarded and unsuspected conversation. At present the special methods are functioning solely as an aide memoire. We are hoping that the Gods would deliver into your hands a Nazi of importance such as the Admiral or Captain of the Bismarck, who would be sent down to this camp. The German civil witness would be an alternative, although of inferior quality.

On Friday 30 May, Colonel John Rawlings Rees and Major Henry Victor Dicks, both members of the Royal Army Medical Corps and, more specifically, the Directorate of Army Psychiatry, came to lunch. Colonel Rees was a small, stout, balding man who relaxed by puffing his pipe in the small bedsit above the Tavistock Institute, where he had been the medical director since 1934. The Tavistock Institute of Medical Psychology had been founded in 1920 by a group of British psychiatrists enamoured of the new 'dynamic psychologies' of Sigmund Freud. Among its early successes was to unravel, with compassion, the terrors of shell-shocked soldiers – men who previously would have been shot as cowards. Number 10 had been contacted just two days after Hess's arrival in Britain by a Professor Namier, who had a friend who had known the Deputy Führer and 'observed over a period of years that he frequently suffered from fits of intense depression during which his condition bordered on the abnormal. During such periods Herr Hess appeared to be a split personality.'

Professor Namier believed that Hess had brought over multiple pictures of himself to 'convince himself of his true identity'. The memo to Number 10 stated: 'If, as Professor Namier supposed, Herr Hess was now going through one of these periods only a really good psychoanalyst could get out of him what we wanted to know.' At the time the professor's suggestions were dismissed because he had said that '[Hess]'s reaction to ordinary cross-examination would probably be either anger or sullen silence,' and as a result Cadogan had pointed out at the bottom of the memo: 'He harangued Mr Kirkpatrick for 3 hours, I think!' while another person added, 'I think Professor Namier is being rather too clever.'

Time, and the peculiar behaviour of the prisoner, had prompted a change in tactics. The day before Rees and Dicks arrived, Anthony Eden was examining the glowing testimonials of Mrs Toni Sussman, a German psychoanalyst from Berlin now working in London's Portman Square, of whom Dr Carl Jung wrote: 'She is, both theoretically and practically, thoroughly versed in my psychology and has rendered invaluable services to the introduction of my psychology to Germany.' The memo Eden read stated: 'Mrs Sussman might be able to work successfully on Hess and be able to give you quite a lot of valuable information on his character, and the way in which he should be handled, if she was allowed to talk with him or, failing that, if she could be given some of his manuscripts so that she could study his handwriting.'

While Hess spent the morning at his desk developing the written notes he would require for his forthcoming meeting with the 'negotiator', Lieutenant Colonel Graham briefed the two visiting psychiatrists on his recent behaviour. Rees had already familiarised himself by reading the combined paperwork produced by Coates at the DDPW, Hopkinson at the Foreign Office, Scott at Camp Z, Graham's own reports, and selected extracts from Foley's briefings to C. They met in Hess's living room and Rees explained the visit on the grounds that Hess had been sleeping badly and had recently displayed signs of worry, an explanation that was accepted quite naturally. Hess was 'quite friendly and calm throughout'. The only problem was that the conversation was hampered by Hess's poor English and Rees's lack of any German. Nonetheless, Rees identified the outstanding symptoms as insomnia and depression. Hess told him that ever since the outbreak of war, the pressure of work and subsequent worry had triggered such sleeplessness, and that usually he slept quite soundly. In Germany he would normally have taken homeopathic drugs for the condition, or Phanodorm if it was particularly acute. Rees explained that such a preparation was available in Britain and that he would attempt to source supplies. Hess said he was currently sleeping just three or four hours a night.

The depression evident in Hess's countenance was, as Rees noted, adequately explained by his current predicament: 'My impression is that the depression can be adequately accounted for as the result of his sense of failure of his plans and that it does not give any indication of a seriously diseased state of mind.' Rees, though, added a strong caveat: '. . . at the same time it might easily get worse and give rise to an attempt at suicide. He has the face and slow manner of speaking of a man suffering from a depression.' The physical injuries sustained by his landing had healed.

Rees's report is worth considering at length: 'Our conversation inevitably led to his talking about his plans and their frustration. He said several times that he was, like everyone in Germany, completely convinced about the result of the war, and that Germany must win by the use of her submarines and aircraft. He said that he, and the Führer also, had disliked the idea of war with England and had thought it unnecessary.' Careful to sustain his image as a man of medicine, not interrogation, Rees added, in parenthesis, '(I was not, of course, pressing him to talk on these matters at all, nor did I comment on them.)'

> He told me how, since the beginning of the bombing of England, the idea of the needless slaughter had weighed on his mind, and also the destruction of the ports and factories. He said that for six months this plan had been in his mind to come to England and make contact with what he had believed was a very large group of people wanting peace. The Führer would not consider anything of the sort and would never have allowed it. He had made his plans and borrowed Willi Messerschmitt's plane on the plea that he wanted to come 'for the sport'. Only his adjutant knew of his plan of coming to England. He told me that he had left a letter for Hitler.
>
> I was not, of course, cross-questioning him in any way about this material, which did not seem new and which was not specifically my concern, but having a good deal of experience of dealing not merely with neurotics but with delinquents and criminals from the courts in peace time, I got the impression that the story was in general true. When he spoke of the slaughter etc there was emphasis and feeling in his voice that I felt sure was not simulated.

> There probably are many facts which I do not know about the circumstances of this visit, and further evidence may be collected which may point in a different direction. Hess spoke a good deal about his discontent; the absence of books for which he had asked; the lack of news, which he can't understand; and the presence of bars and locks, which he evidently feels are unseemly for a man who has 'come with a flag of truce' and who is 'of flag rank'.
>
> He showed traces of suspicion about the various noises of which he complains: the machine gun practice in a neighbouring camp; the motor cycles (The Military Police Training Camp); and the aeroplanes which fly over.
>
> He showed what was to me extraordinary lack of insight and failure to realise his position. He also seemed to have no obvious appreciation of the impossible nature of his self-imposed task. He said twice to me 'the King of Britain would never let these things happen', and he was clearly surprised that the Duke of Hamilton had not forthwith arranged for him to talk to the King and that he could not see the Duke of Hamilton and Mr Kirkpatrick whenever he wished. He did say that he was in the hands of the 'war mongers'.

Rees's conclusions were that Hess was 'not insane in the sense that the law would make one consider certification'; however, he felt that he was 'mentally sick', 'anxious and tense' and of a 'paranoid type'. He summed up by stating: 'He is obviously an intelligent man and the consequent impression is of a somewhat confused condition in which there are both hysterical and paranoid tendencies. Whilst his judgment on ordinary matters of fact might be sound, his appreciation of more intangible problems would be unsound because of the intrusion of his own personal emotional difficulties. This man gives me the impression of being lacking in balance, a psychopathic personality, to use the technical word, and also of being someone who, because of the added depression due to his circumstances, might take impulsive action such as an attempt at suicide despite his alleged promise to the Führer not to take his life.'

When told of Hess's energetic display of the goose step in the garden, Rees took particular interest in this colourful response: 'This seems to me important because it probably epitomises the situation. The man has excellent intelligence, but he is childish in his outlook and consequently unstable and with bad judgment. He has clearly been dominated by many people, quack practitioners of various kinds, and most markedly by Professor Haushofer, whose dreams or visions of his [Hess's] mission have been taken as prophetic.'

The policy had been set by Churchill, in collaboration with Cadogan, the Permanent Under-Secretary at the Foreign Office, and C that Hess should not be treated as a captured prisoner and interrogated, but as a defector who required careful debriefing so as to slowly peel back each layer of intelligence. Among the Government's concerns was that Hess could be a plant, with the intention of teasing Britain into a trap. It was Foley's job to ascertain if this was the case. The following extract is from Foley's conversation with Hess on 23 May 1941:

Foley: You believe that under certain circumstances you can starve England?

Hess: We can dangerously reduce your tonnage when the U-boat war begins in earnest and, apart from that, a great deal has already been sunk and because of that you can no longer withstand.

Foley: And our measures to fight back?

Hess: You have had enough time to establish defensive measures. We have calculated in a percentage of U-boat losses which, until now, have never proved true and our losses always remain far below that level. Despite taking into account these calculated losses, our production is so much higher that we can endure without a problem. Against your protective fleet we will be able one day to carry out mass attacks by U-boats.

Foley: Mass attacks by U-boats? Is something like that technically possible?

Hess: Yes, when we have the necessary numbers of U-boats.

Foley: That means you are thinking of hundreds?

Hess: I can't be firm about the number, but compared to the attacks today . . .

Foley: When you speak of mass attacks of U-boats – until now the talk has only been of mass attacks of airplanes . . .

Hess: You must not compare the two. You must not say there are 400 airplanes deployed to one town and so 400 U-boats would be sent to one protected convoy. Obviously not. But in comparison to what has been deployed until now for one convoy, it will be masses more one day. The comparison is maybe confusing. But anyway, an equivalent will be deployed against a convoy.

From time to time, of course, on your side something will be invented, either a new tactic or a new form of defence, but until now it has always been the case that we, in a very short time, mastered the situation and changed our own tactics.

My purely personal opinion is that from the first day until now and without interruption, not only have we been more proficient according to our conviction, but we have been so lucky that I am of the personal opinion that there are powers [assisting Germany].

A little later Hess said, 'As things stand I can guarantee you that within a certain time span – and I do not want to be specific about the time – the point will come when you will have the choice either to accept those conditions or to reject them and then England will starve.

'Taking into account the whole of the situation, I assume that that will be the outcome. The prestige of England will be most seriously affected; just now it would not be so seriously affected, because now there is an opportunity, because I am the catalyst . . . One day England will have to capitulate.'

The conversation continued:

Foley: You see we cannot see ourselves being beaten.

Hess: You may not believe it, but in this case history will decide. I know it for certain, otherwise I would not have come here if I did not know this so precisely.

In the year 1917 England was very close to giving in because of the U-boat war, but let us compare this to the situation today. In those days we had the whole narrow German bight, the Heligoland bight which was always mined, heavily mined, and from which hardly anybody could get out. We could not go through the Channel and we hardly could get to the other side of the German bight. You see, a whole long journey could hold us up, whereas now we have a base which stretches from the tip of Norway all the way to Spain with countless numbers of U-boats which are, of course, not possible to spot.

Secondly we have the Channel. Even if it were closed, we are sitting on the other side of it and we have our U-boats on the other side. Thirdly, don't forget the numbers of U-boats. If the Führer tackles such a problem, whether it be the Siegfried line or arming the air force or whatever, then he does it with no expense spared. You see there is no comparison, especially now in the coming time, the U-boat war has not started in the way that the Führer [has planned].

The U-boat war has not yet begun, not properly. That which the Führer has announced, the U-boat war that will come. And secondly, you have to add, the whole of the Luftwaffe has been launched against the shipping, which we didn't have at all in those days. Thirdly you have to add the battle against the shipyards by the Luftwaffe. Fourthly, the battle against the ports, the docks, etc by the Luftwaffe, the destruction of supplies of raw

> materials and food etc by the Luftwaffe. I went to the works. During the winter our factories only had one problem: where they would store the finished machines, because it simply wasn't possible to use them all. The losses were, in comparison to what we have, very little. In one to two days we have made up the losses of one month. Everything else that was made in the other 28 days had to be stored somewhere, because the personnel to fly had not yet been trained, because the Führer is exceptionally careful, that is why the personnel are forever training.
>
> You would not believe the letters I get from troops who insist that they have been trained but they were not allowed to go to the Front. 'Could I maybe do something?' They are concerned that the war would come to an end without them having a chance to serve at the Front. I want to stress that I am not talking of propaganda here, but that I am speaking out of conviction when I am talking about those questions. You have to be completely open without any exaggeration when talking with each other, so that each can make a clear picture of the real situation as it really is. And only then it may be possible, rationally, to look for a way to make an end.

Further in the conversation, Hess explained that he was not driven by selfish nationalism but concern for others. 'I am of the opinion that something like this is crazy, since the war is not even necessary, so that you have to try and stop it. That which is yet to come – through our planes and soldiers – that we will bring to the Front, these will be attacks compared to which the attacks until now were only a prelude. That is terrible.'

He then hinted at the tremendous power Germany would soon bring to bear on Britain:

'In addition there are also new bombs with stronger explosives.'

That was a chilling statement. Among the contacts Foley had developed while in Berlin was Paul Rosbaud, the editor in charge of Germany's principal scientific journal, across whose desk all the latest scientific papers passed. It had been Rosbaud who had informed Foley of Otto Hahn and Fritz Strassmann's experiment at the Kaiser Wilhelm Institute of Chemistry in December 1938, where they bombarded uranium atoms with slow-moving neutrons, so splitting the atom and opening the door on a dark new world.

> **Foley:** New bombs as well?
>
> **Hess:** Our inventors are of course not resting in their ambitions to find new weapons, even better than that of their dear colleagues. This competition is good for the whole war effort. But because of all this, the situation is that if we really believe that the war will carry on, we can be relaxed in the face of this coming war.

On 28 May the Admiralty was sent a transcript of the conversation with Hess which had taken place five days earlier. 'You will notice that we are particularly interested to know what is the German estimate of our shipping losses. We should also be interested if you could find out whether Hess has any information on the production of "Midget" U-Boats. In doing so care will be necessary to distinguish between alleged "Midget" and the 300-ton type of U-Boat which is of course known to be in service.'

The added difficulty Foley had was that of having each intelligence service scrutinising the efforts of his team. The secretly recorded interview transcriptions were circulated to the intelligence section of each force, with Naval Intelligence quick to spot a flaw:

> Will you mind very much if I draw your attention to something that has been happening during talks with your special prisoner? We have received here an interesting record of conversation which moved on to naval matters. Unfortunately, on each occasion that the prisoner mentioned something of outstanding interest e.g. underground submarine bases, the companion interrupted with

> a repetition of the crucial word, so either diverting the prisoner's train of thought or giving him a pretty good clue to what we are interested in. You will probably have a copy of the record and will be able to confirm that this happened. Would it be possible tactfully to point out to the companion that this method of handling is a bit dangerous? I happened to hear my chief suggesting that some complaint should be made and myself suggested that the matter could be best referenced to informally. I hope this won't give offence – but the underground submarine bases might be rather important.

The Admiralty conclusion was as follows: 'J [Jonathan] is uninformed, but probably not intentionally deceptive, about naval affairs. He has absorbed current views and propaganda about naval policy as part of his wider belief in the supernatural inspiration of German activity and the infallible guidance of war policy by the Führer. There is probably no detailed naval intelligence to be got from him. His naval ideas are evidently based on the propaganda in which he has been taught to believe.'

Nonetheless they proposed a number of further questions to be put to Hess:

- i) What rate of sinkings do you and the Führer think necessary to bring England to defeat? Is that the Naval Staff estimate?
- ii) What rate of sinkings does the Naval Staff claim in its information to the Führer?
- iii) How can the German fleet hope to achieve anything without an aircraft carrier? (This is to be leading, not a direct question)
- iv) Why does the Führer allow German lives to be sacrificed owing to the incompetence of the Italian fleet and its officers?
- v) What does Radar think of Dönitz's privilege of direct access to the Führer?

vi) Why is nothing being done in German naval construction to provide ships which could protect the operation of invading England?

Naval Intelligence also included a section on 'General Interpretations':

1. Proceeding from the naval remarks (we know something about) to the other remarks of J, the following seems clear:-

a) J sincerely believes in the certainty of German victory, the leadership of Hitler, the divine mission of the German people.

b) His views are instinctive rather than empirical. His particular opinions derive from his general faith in Hitler and the German people.

c) His arguments are mixed and full of non sequiturs. This could be due either to a tumbling out of ideas from an inspired disciple, or to a calculated, if rather naive, determination to bring in all the debating points. The former seems more probable.

Note: The genuineness of his protests of sincerity and desire for understanding to finish the war, become the crucial problem.

2. This would point to J's believing in the possibility of ending an unnecessary war and allowing the great work of Hitler's for the German people to proceed uninterrupted.

3. Another interpretation would be that he came with Hitler's knowledge to try to do in England what Germany succeeded in doing in France in the summer of 1940 i.e. although the German General Staff probably knew that France could quickly be overrun by arms, an attempt – largely successful – was made to split the Allies by humanitarian and seemingly sincere propaganda. Similarly J, though believing implicitly in the German victory by arms, may have been sent to make the same attempt.

4. Both (2) and (3) may conceivably be true. J was sent to effect (3), and was chosen to do it because he himself believed he was doing only (2).

   PROBLEM: If J is so dedicated to Hitler why did he deceive him by coming over secretly? (For J this may be no paradox: the morality of the converted is not our rational morality.)

   CONCLUSION: The only suggestion I can offer for elucidating the problem is to ask J:-

i) Will the Führer approve of your coming over here to end the war by mutual discussion in a spirit of fine supernational humanitarian feeling?

ii) If he says 'Of course' ask:

   Then why did you not tell him why you were coming?

   It seems that J is 'possessed' and genuinely and subconsciously 'guided'. He is most vulnerable to an approach from the starting point of accepting as facts his obsessive beliefs. The glorious destiny of his race, and the benevolent alliance with that race of all the powers which transcend mortality, should be acknowledged, and the threatening implications for Britain admitted. From this starting point he might be led on to give instances of the supernatural assistance or inspiration already afforded, and his faith undermined by reminders of instances when other 'hostile' powers prevailed and disasters such as the sinking of BISMARK [*sic*] were suffered. The effect should be, as always when a faith is assailed, to provoke unguarded and fervent arguments for the truth of the obsession, resulting in useful disclosures.

Both the Army and the Air Force contributed their own suggested questions. Those from the army were prepared on 7 June and handed over by Major General F.H.N. Davidson:

PART I. Future Operations

1. What was the forecast of operations for 1941 and in what

priority? The conversation might be led on to the following points:-

a) Continuation of offensive in the Middle East.
b) Intentions towards Turkey, particularly as to whether there was any idea of tackling military action.
c) Attack on Russia.
d) Occupation of Spain and Portugal, if necessary by force, with the intention of capturing Gibraltar or at least neutralising the Straits.
e) Any intentions for operations in North Africa with Dakar and/or the Takeradi air route as the ultimate objective.
f) Has an attack on Iceland or Greenland ever been seriously contemplated?
g) Is it true that invasion of the UK is off for the moment? Is it likely to be tried in 1941, or would that be the remaining final effort if a successful campaign were waged against Russia?
h) What is the axis plan for Japanese action in the Far East – if any?

2. What do the German General Staff really think about the outcome of the war? Do they think they can win it outright or produce a situation where we will be ready to compromise? In the former event in what stages and how long?

PART II. Germany's military effort

1. What is the man-power situation in Germany, with particular reference to the armed forces? How many divisions are there? Is there any intention to expand them or will the claims of industry and agriculture entail a reduction, always assuming that fresh sources of man-power cannot be tapped e.g. by occupation of the Ukraine.
2. How many armoured divisions are there and how many is it intended to form? Have the armoured divisions been reduced in strength in that they now contain only one tank regiment instead of two in order to create a large number?

Is it not planned to eliminate gradually light tanks from the armoured division in favour of medium and possibly heavy?

3. How many light armoured colonial divisions?
4. What is the policy about the motorisation of divisions? How many motorised divisions are there now, and is it intended to increase the number?
5. How many infantry divisions have been made into air-landing divisions etc.
6. How many SS divisions exist? Are they all motorised? Is there any intention to convert them into armoured divisions or have any of them been already so converted?
7. What is the priority of production, aeroplanes or AFV [armoured fighting vehicles]? Or is it all so well organised that the manufacturer of both proceeds at full blast?

PART III. The Army Higher Command and the Party

1. Are there any changes in prospect for the High Command and the Army? Which senior generals are likely to be retired and which to be promoted?
2. What are the relations between the Party and the Army? Does the Party attempt to interface with strategy, presumably by seeking to influence Hitler? If so, does the Army resent it, and if there is any rivalry for the Führer's ear who is he more likely to listen to when questions of the widest strategical implication are involved?
3. How does the Army react to the unpleasant task of 'holding down' conquered countries with Gestapo everywhere – and all the cruelties as carried out in Poland, etc. Surely Hitler and the Party are laying up a terrible score of bitterness and retribution.

PART IV. The Horrors of War

1. Is there any question of the Germans using gas or adopting some form of bacteriological warfare?

2. What about secret weapons, or new weapons, or new methods?
3. What about the effects of bombing in Germany, as regards actual damage both to the life and war effort of the nation, and the morale of the German people?
   NOTE: It is important to assess accurately the effect of bombing on the Germans, so that we can attune our bombing policy accordingly, it might be well to show Hess some of the effects of bombing in London, especially the destruction to Hospitals, churches, and other beautiful buildings.
   This should pave the way for discussion on the effects of bombing, and the futility of wanton destruction, and thus lead him to give away the real view and feelings of the leaders of Germany as to how the German nation is likely to react to increased bombing.

PART V. Propaganda

Though strictly speaking not a military question, propaganda may well have a very important bearing in the breaking down of the German national morale if efficiently carried out. Can we therefore induce Hess, by discussion on this interesting subject, to give away how and where our propaganda succeeds or fails, both in Germany and in German-occupied countries.

The least effort appeared to have been applied by the RAF whose questions filled a single sheet of A4:

QUESTIONS FOR HESS FROM THE AIR MINISTRY

1. What is the main policy for expansion of the GAF [German Air Force] and what is likely to prove the limiting factor – aircraft or crews?
2. Is there serious concern about the failure to win the war with existing types? What new types are being produced and when are they likely to become operational?

3. What are the chief 'bottlenecks' in the aircraft and aero-engine industry?
4. Very few war trained, as opposed to pre-war trained, pilots have been shot down. Are they being used as instructors and in the transport and glider organisations?
5. What is the present strength of the GAF and what further expansion is projected?
6. How is morale being affected by the heavy night losses?
7. What is the present and projected strength of the glider organisation?
8. What are the reactions to the growing strength of the RAF?
9. What is the general policy for the co-operation of the army and the air force during operations?

6

A Psychiatrist in the Rain

The room was dark when Hess awoke. In the distance an air raid siren had began its lugubrious drone, tugging him from sleep and setting his nerves on edge. He peered out of the window but could see nothing and so he began to pace, through the bedroom into the living room, a sharp about turn and then back again. The process, thirty steps in total, took about ten seconds, and was one he repeated again and again and again. Outside the grille, the guard on duty noted his movements and the fact that, by the time Hess eventually climbed back into bed, it was six o'clock and the dawn light was filtering through the curtains.

He slept late, rising at 10 a.m., and after breakfasting and dressing, he was escorted downstairs where Captain 'Barnes' took him for a walk in the garden. The psychiatrist came with the rain, and while Hess noted the latter and so returned to his room, he was unaware of the former, and the arrival, mid-afternoon, of Major Henry V. Dicks.

If the atmosphere at Mytchett Place had an unsettling effect on Hess, he was not alone. Major Dicks would later write of 'the detective novel atmosphere necessarily surrounding this place of mystery . . . even to the newcomer who was not to be closely confined here, the place bore a forbidding enough aspect.'

After displaying his green pass to security, Dicks was admitted into the house, which he noted 'had been refurbished in haste and furnished with heavy antique pieces from the Ministry of Works' store'. He perceived an attempt to create an atmosphere of 'dignified comfort'. The sofa in the officers' lounge was quite comfortable, but stubbing one's toe on the Tommy gun which poked out from under the bullion fabric fringe ruined the effect. Dicks was aware that in official paperwork Hess was referred to as Jonathan or 'J', but within a few minutes he learned that among a number of staff, the man who had recently been deputy Führer as just 'he' or 'that man'.

In the lounge Dicks was joined by Foley, his two senior officers, and the Camp Commandant, where the intense secrecy of their task was reiterated once again. As Dicks later wrote, 'The political officers managed to enhance the sense of mystery and "hush-hush" by impressing on all comers the necessity for the utmost secrecy and discretion in accordance with their instructions . . . The psychiatrist suddenly found himself a participant in the inner history of world events.'

Dicks had, however, been there before. At the age of nineteen, he had served as interpreter when Winston Churchill visited Murmansk in 1919 to assist the White Russians against the Bolsheviks. Born in the Baltic province of Estonia to an English father (an exporter and shipowner), and a German mother, he spoke both German and Russian fluently and was now considered one of the leading psychiatrists of his generation, having already published, in 1939, *Clinical Studies in Psychopathology* which had since become a popular textbook.

He was also Jewish.

At the conference that afternoon the political officers, Lieutenant Colonel Scott, the Commandant, and Major Dicks drew up a 'plan of campaign'. Foley was adamant that at such an early stage Hess must not know that he was being scrutinised by a psychiatrist. Since his status as a captive remained unclear, they need not reveal Dick's official capacity, as they would have been expected to do under the Geneva Convention if Hess were classified as a prisoner of war. Foley then made it clear there was hope that Hess 'might make important revelations of German plans and intentions' and that 'vital intelligence data' could be retrieved. Dicks' role was to assist in the 'management' of the subject. The task was defined as 'discreet supervision, and as far as possible, diagnosis; help to the camp officials in management' and assistance to the political officers in collecting 'useful information'.

The cover story was straightforward. Dicks was the new 'camp doctor' sent to replace the present medical attendant who, it would be said, had been recalled to Scotland.

Now that the ground rules had been firmly established Dicks was sent upstairs, escorted by Foley. The game was afoot.

Unaware that he was about to receive company, Hess was sitting at his desk, the evidence of drafts of his diplomacy plans strewn across the surface. He looked up as the door was unlocked and the two uniformed officers entered and, as Dicks noted, 'oozed hostility and suspicion'. Once in the room, Dicks began to mentally dissect his subject's physical appearance:

'It is fair to say that the first glimpse of Hess produced an immediate reaction: typical schizophrenic. His skull-like face wearing a profoundly unhappy, grim expression, with his eyes staring into infinity. The contrast between photographs previously seen in the illustrated papers and the man as he now appeared was prodigious. He was gaunt, hollow-cheeked, pale and lined; whereas the full face produced an impression of baleful strength, the profile disclosed a receding forehead, exaggerated supra-orbital ridges covered with thick bushy eyebrows, deeply sunken eyes, irregular teeth which tended to be permanently bared over the lower lip in the manner of "buck teeth", a very weak chin and receding lower jaw. The ears were misshapen and placed too low in relation to the height of the eyes.'

Hess was 'barely civil', and when Foley excused himself there was 'an awkward tense feeling'.

The awkwardness began to diminish when Dicks offered medical assistance, always a point of interest to a man as obsessed about his health as the Deputy Führer. Over the next few hours Dicks began to revise his initial opinion, perceiving Hess as full of pathos rather than hostility. He was impressed by the contrast between Hess's 'official' attitude as an important representative of the strongest power in Europe, and his own private simplicity. 'His personal equipment was of the simplest: his watch was of steel, his linen and other personal accoutrements simple and modest.' During the conversation Hess produced pictures of Ilse and his son and said that his own personal interest was that of a mountaineer who had no greater wish than to return to a 'little chalet' where he could devote himself to the country pursuits and his son's education.

As Dicks wrote: 'His interests had been in philosophy and matters of health and welfare. He took a special interest in a rehabilitation centre for disabled industrial workers which he said was his own creation. There was a schoolboy-like pride in his attitude when he related details of his flight, which he said was made secretly without the Führer's knowledge. A mischievous smile came upon his face when he said that in fact the Führer had extracted from all his immediate entourage a promise not to fly, because of the risk of losing his best men through accident. This promise had been given in the first instance for a year, and Hess said that the year had just ended and, as the Führer had forgotten to renew the promise, he had felt absolved from this obligation.' Dick also noted his vanity. Had, wondered Hess, the BBC broadcast his arrival in all its details, and had they interviewed the crofter who found him?

As a break, the psychiatrist suggested that they walk in the garden. The rain had stopped and he was interested in how daylight and the outdoors might further illuminate his new patient's mental outlook. 'Outside of interest he showed a curious lack of contact with ordinary things. He had never played tennis and did not even know how to score in the game, and it transpired during a brief walk we took in the grounds that he did not know the names of extremely common flowers.'

Instead Hess turned repeatedly to his wound, his dignity, and to the fixed idea that his confinement as a prisoner was due to the plans of a small clique of warmongers led by Churchill. Surely, he explained, it was they who were keeping him from establishing contact with the large movement for peace and friendship. Hess's view was simple: British life was divided between the good and the wicked. The Duke of Hamilton represented the chivalrous court of the king, which was currently being thwarted by the wicked circle of politicians.

The two men sat on the grass, under the shade of the beech tree. Conversation was difficult – stilted – with any attempt to draw Hess into a political discussion breaking on the craggy rock of his stern countenance. The sound of a distant bugle provided a brief insight. Upon hearing the noise Dicks began to point out 'the childishness of some military practices' and to observe that the British on the whole had very little use for military life. He ended his little soliloquy with the comment, 'Somebody or other has said that you can do everything with bayonets except sit on them.'

Hess immediately replied, 'Yes, yes, that was Napoleon, but he did try it just the same,' then added in a melancholy tone, 'Of, course in the end he came a cropper.'

The duality in which Hess experienced his new environment was demonstrated at dinner where – to the consternation of the cook in the kitchen towards the back of the house – two distinctly separate messes were in operation. While the Commandant and the regimental officers of the Brigade of Guards detachment dined in one mess, situated in the old billiard room, Hess, his three 'companions' and his new doctor dined in their own mess next door.

Dicks noted the admiration with which Hess looked upon the 'Guardsmen'. He was flattered by the fact that he was guarded by

'His Majesty's own Bodyguard' and admired those young officers with an aristocratic appearance who escorted him to and from his room. However, when he reached his own mess, his attitude hardened and his suspicions increased.

On the first night Dicks witnessed at first hand Hess's fear of being poisoned: 'The first meal in the mess provided evidence, which was to be repeated on many subsequent occasions, of the strength of Hess's poisoning fears, which were sufficiently great to obtrude themselves into his behaviour. An orderly served soup in plates. It was practice to serve first the senior officer acting as president of the mess, then the prisoner and then the rest of us. When all had been so served, Hess quickly interchanged his own plate with that of the president. During the meat course (on this occasion slices of beef on a dish) he took some bits as far removed as possible from the top piece, to which in the normal course of events he should have helped himself.'

In the summer of 1941 the Brigade of Guards was still in the fortunate possession of a rather fine wine cellar and so, as a matter of course, a 'quite decent' table wine was served with dinner. Hess refused, and also passed on the subsequent offer of coffee and tea. Over the next six weeks Dicks noted the manner in which Hess ate:

'Another notable feature was his capriciousness in the matter of food. He would refuse a course or take only a little potato and greens. When sufficiently urged by other people in the manner in which a child might be cajoled, he would then heap an enormous portion on his plate and eat ravenously. He would sometimes save, for example, pieces of bread and cheese which would have to be taken up to his room . . . this capriciousness was accounted for on his own evidence by constant conflict between greed and the fear that his inside would retaliate by giving him cramps or other forms of indigestion.'

Hess, it was later revealed, had for years meticulously followed the prescriptions of Rudolf Steiner that vegetables grown under artificial conditions should be avoided. At home in Munich he ordered his supplies from a specialist greengrocer who cultivated his vegetables in natural manure.

After dinner on Dicks' first day he accompanied Hess back to his room and gave him a physical examination. He noted his round shoulders and narrow chest, and that his ankle was healing nicely. Hess said it was giving him practically no trouble at all. He was also grateful for the attention and the assurance of a doctor that he was well. After the examination he told Dicks that he had not been sleeping and asked for sleeping pills. 'He asked for a number of herbal and nature-cure remedies with which orthodox medical practice in this country was not acquainted.'

Dicks' immediate recommendation was that an officer of the guard should spend the night in the room next to Hess and mount round-the-clock inspections. He ordered a new supply of drugs: barbiturates, morphine, chloralamide and potassium bromide. While the full array of natural barbiturates that Hess requested was unavailable in London, the psychiatrist secured what he could, including tincture of belladonna, gentian and rhubarb and a few cans of camomile tea. In conversation with the Commandant, Dicks explained that all possible steps should be taken to minimise those events that were feeding the prisoner's paranoia.

The next few days went smoothly, as recorded in the diary of Lieutenant Colonel Scott:

Sunday 1 June

Z had a rather restless night. There was an air raid warning for about an hour and a half. Several shots were fired during the night by the French Canadians in the neighbourhood. Both these incidents seemed to worry Z. However he came down to breakfast at 0900, spent more of the morning in his room, but after lunch walked in the garden and also sat out for a considerable time – in fact till about 1800 only coming indoors for a short time for tea.

Col Graham left in the afternoon. Major Dicks now has charge of his case – he is still treated by Z with a certain amount of suspicion.

Monday 2 June

Z had a restless night so did not get up for breakfast, in fact he stayed in bed till 1200 and came down to lunch. He complained of his lunch again being over seasoned and now says that it is a deliberate attempt to starve him. He went straight to his room after lunch and wrote hard all the afternoon and didn't come down till 1730 when Major Dicks went up and brought him down to walk in the garden. He went to bed soon after dinner.

Tuesday 3 June

Z came down to breakfast this morning after having had a very good night. The doctor gave him a drug which Z himself had asked for which seemed to have the desired effect. He went for a short walk after breakfast which was not announced, with the result that he was seen by three civilian workmen who were building an incinerator in the camp lines. They were removed by the Provost Sergeant but too late.

It rained hard for the rest of the day, so that Z was unable to do anything but sit in his room and write his long journal. It cleared a bit after dinner and he had a short walk with Major Foley. A corporal from Pirbright came over to cut his hair which seemed to make him happier.

Roughly fifty yards from the main house, just before where the lawn merged into mature woodland, stood an old oak tree whose trunk was so wide it required the arms of the two tallest sergeant majors to reach all the way around. The canopy of branches hung low and obscured the view of half the house, acting like a green eyepatch on those who sat under its shade. Here, on the afternoon of 4 June, Hess 'sat under a tree in the garden in the most uncomfortable position, refused to speak to anyone, was morose and in a fit of deepest depression'.

The night before he had arisen constantly and frequently visited the lavatory, where he stayed for half an hour at a time. After an afternoon contorted under the tree, he returned to the house for dinner and then went back outside and 'walked up and down in an agitated way – again refusing company'.

The despair evident from his countenance was, however, absent from his pen when, at some point during the day, he wrote his first letter to his wife and son:

> R. Hess
> England
> 3.6.41
>
> Dear Little Mother,
>
> Dear Buz,
>
> Since after the first visit to the Duke of Hamilton on the morning of my arrival in Scotland, I appealed to the chivalry of the King of England and laid myself under his protection, you need not worry about me. I have been allotted a house in a beautiful part as residence; it is well guarded by Scots Guards.
>
> Do not expect me to write often – I do not like writing, since I know that every line will be read by the censor.
>
> Many will not understand my step, but all who really know me know that I could not do otherwise after seeing the possibility of even trying in this way to bring about an understanding between England and Germany, and to save much suffering on both sides.
>
> [He then introduced a quote from Goethe: *By the eternal Iron grade laws, all of us must complete the circle of our being.*]
>
> Heartiest greetings to you and to all at home. Hail the Führer.

There was a brief postscript:

> 'Write to the General – of whose dreams I often think –'

At 2200 hours, Hess asked if he might be permitted to retire to bed earlier than usual. This was granted and he was escorted to his room by Foley and Wallace, and surprised them both by saying 'Goodnight', a small courtesy perhaps, but a word which, up until then, he had never uttered and therefore now triggered an immediate alarm.

Thirty minutes later Foley, Wallace and Major Dicks asked for an emergency meeting with Lieutenant Colonel Scott, who recorded that they had

> communicated to me their anxiety that Z might attempt suicide in the night. They had based their anxiety on the following:-
>
> 1) He had written for the first time to his wife – the letter containing a somewhat significant quotation from Goethe.
>
> 2) He had asked the doctor to go up earlier than usual.
>
> 3) On going to bed he had turned to wish his companions 'goodnight'. A thing he had never done before.
>
> 4) He had been overheard muttering to himself 'I just can't stand this anymore.'

Dicks agreed with Foley and Wallace's concerns, stating that such was Hess's state of depression that it 'might produce a tendency to suicide'.

Scott then replaced Lieutenant Hubbard as Hess's guard for the night with Second Lieutenant Malone, who had 'considerable experience of mental cases', and instructed him to go inside the grille in order to keep a closer eye on their charge.

The suicide attempt feared by Foley did not take place. Malone later reported that despite a restless night, Hess did get 'some sleep' and emerged for breakfast at nine a.m. in a 'highly excitable' state. Afterwards, citing his lack of sleep, he retired to his room to rest. At one p.m. on Thursday 5 June, Foley informed him, as he lay on his bed, that a high representative of the Foreign Office would visit Camp Z the following Monday to listen to his proposals for peace. The reaction was not what Foley expected. Instead of displaying any sign of relief, he 'seemed somewhat dazed and not fully to understand the importance of my communication'. He then complained of severe pains in his head and Foley thought he might faint.

At 4.30 p.m., Hess left his room to walk for 'some time' in the garden, where the flora and fauna appeared to have a rejuvenating effect on him: during dinner he was 'most talkative' and even went so far as to explain that his fear of poisoning did not extend to his present company, or to 'any officer or other rank in this house'. However, he did know that 'refugees from Germany' would stop at nothing to destroy him, even bribing the staff in the house to administer some deadly potion. The reason was simple: it was in their interest to prevent a settlement between England and Germany. In a gesture of concern to his companions, Hess pointed out that it would be a matter of indifference to these German refugees, trained in the dark arts of the assassin, if, while killing their intended target, they should also murder his fellow diners. Attempts to reassure him, both of his safety and that his concerns were but phantoms, proved unsuccessful. 'His mind was no doubt influenced by his early youth in Alexandria where such customs prevailed,' recorded Foley.

Once the plates were cleared, Foley suggested an evening stroll and, despite the light summer rain, Hess readily agreed. When they were alone he asked if news of the imminent arrival of a negotiator was serious and 'not merely a method of soothing him'. Foley assured him of the seriousness of the Government's intentions and, thus reassured, Hess's mood further lightened and he began to talk 'cheerfully and vividly of general matters', including his flight to Scotland. Hess agreed to the delegates and the presence of a single German witness, and said that he had an agreeable recollection of Lord Simon. He informed Foley that he would not read or speak from a prepared text but would use *sdeithwerter*, a series of very short notes or minutes, instead. 'He appeared to be a changed man,' wrote Foley. So much so, in fact, that after an hour's exercise he joined the officers in the drawing room and even accepted a glass of port before retiring just before midnight.

The following morning, Friday 6 June, Hess set to work on refining his *sdeithwerter*, which he jotted down in pencil on plain white paper. Inspecting it today, the writing is fluid, with little evidence of revision, though there are some paragraphs that were scored out.

In the evening, Colonel Wallace succeeded in segueing from a discussion about Hess's health (the pains in his back and head were no doubt stress-induced and his nerves would soon settle after Monday's appointment had passed, assured Wallace) into his views on peace. Was he, wondered Wallace, alone in his beliefs or were there others in high places in Germany who felt as he did? '*Ja, ich glaube schön*,' he replied. 'Yes, I believe there are.' Wallace wrote, 'He appeared reluctant to answer this question. This reply might be of some interest, as it appears to indicate that there is some kind of internal dissension.'

An update of events at Camp Z was sent that evening to Winston Churchill in Downing Street:

> When he found himself in his new quarters behind barbed wire and bars he began to profess great anxiety: he complained that he had fallen into the hands of a clique of the Secret Service and began to complain that his mission had failed and that there was nothing for it but to put him into a prisoner of war camp like an ordinary prisoner of war.
>
> He went through several days of increasingly severe depression, so much so that the medical officer became anxious for his

> reason and feared that he might attempt suicide. He was, accordingly, told that it might be possible in the course of a few days to arrange some responsible person who might give him a sympathetic hearing, and he has since shown a rather more hopeful disposition.
>
> From his conversation it seems doubtful whether Hess possesses any detailed technical knowledge of military affairs, but it seems quite possible that a certain amount of information on political matters might be obtained, or inferred, in the course of a number of conversations.

As the days and hours ticked down to the time of the conference Hess's agitation rose. On Saturday he did not appear for breakfast and ventured out only briefly for a short walk between showers of rain. On Sunday his mood swung severely. He apologised to Dicks for his behaviour and 'thanked us for stopping the noises at night; he said he had realised these had not been engineered maliciously'. Yet when asked about his health in the dining room at lunchtime, he said that he could not concentrate, that earlier he could not read Liddell Hart's *Dynamic Defence* as it was too difficult, and that he could not find the German equivalent for English words that he didn't understand.

> He took soup from the tureen, but did not eat it. He refused plain boiled fish. The meat dish was roast beef, sliced and not from the joint, Yorkshire pudding, cabbage and potatoes, all served from a common dish. Colonel Wallace, who sits at the head of the table, served himself first. Hess sits on his left and is served second. On this occasion, Hess asked Colonel Wallace whether he could have the food which he, Wallace, had already selected for himself. Of course, Colonel Wallace agreed. Theyexchanged plates. Hess remarked, 'You will probably think this an *idée fixe* and perhaps somewhat hysterical.' He helped himself to apple pie but refused pastry and custard. This is the

most demonstrative [*sic*] instance of his fear of poisoning which we have experienced.'

That evening Foley communicated to C:

'I have reported these facts because, in view of what appears to us to be a serious deterioration of his mental health, you may care to warn the gentlemen who are visiting us tomorrow that they may find it difficult to conduct reasoned and logically thought out conversations. He stated again today that he found it difficult to concentrate on the preparation of the work he has to do on Monday.'

Foley had suggested that on the day of the conference Hess should eat in his own room with an officer on guard, but now revised his suggestion and explained that 'it might perhaps be preferable for him to lunch with the visitors and us, otherwise he may imagine that his food has been specially selected and doped, with the object of dulling his mental powers.'

Dicks meanwhile was under pressure to deliver a preliminary report prior to Lord Simon's arrival, so that it could be used as an aid to discussions. In a paper submitted the day before the planned conference, the psychiatrist stated his initial conclusions, which are worthy of quoting at length:

i) An abnormal and neurotic preoccupation with his health, leading him to be a faddist and 'abstainer', and a frequenter of unorthodox practitioners from homeopaths to chiropractors.
ii) A suspicious attitude, amounting in Col. Graham's opinion to a definite delusion of persecution.
iii) An urge to be a saviour and bringer of peace.
iv) A fatalistic, in some ways superstitious, view of life: astrology, the phases of the moon, etc. interest him, as well as quasi-magical cures.

These traits of personality, viewed together, make it possible to venture on a diagnosis on psychological grounds. He shows to an abnormal degree certain typical characteristics of the paranoid personality: egocentricity based on a deep feeling of insecurity, a fear of injury or disease. The commonly accepted psychological interpretation of such an attitude is that the patient has a severe conflict about his own value and position. For whatever antecedent causes, such as people who are unable to feel confidence in the goodness of others, and while withdrawing in one sense into 'self', are always looking for an 'ideal' outside, which or whom they might love, in order to assuage their inner loneliness. Such an ideal is very apt to be a person of the same sex, regarded as a better edition of the patient himself – often an older man, of paternal authority, who embodies the qualities in which the patient feels deficient. In this way, by an identification, the patient's own sense of inferiority and lack of relatedness to life is at least temporarily ameliorated. He becomes the fanatical adherent of 'causes' and 'movements'.

A reasonable deduction from the above would be that in Hitler Herr Hess had seen the perfect father authority who would make the bad world right. The moment he felt that Hitler was ruthless and destructive, he must have experienced great anxiety. If Hitler was capable of so much murder, he might turn on Hess also. England, as the victim, becomes somehow an object in a state of extreme danger analogous to his own. At the same time he begins instinctively to look for another 'pure' object of veneration: the gallant Duke of Hamilton, or the chivalrous King of England.

He cannot, of course, admit or even allow himself to know that he feels this. The Führer is still perfect, and one must be loyal. To lose the 'ideal' by which one was buoyed up and 'inflated' would mean a breakdown of one's personality. Yet he is tremulously hoping that the Führer will 'understand' – implying that he HAS doubts of the validity of his former sheet anchor. In order to preserve intact the façade of this unswerving loyalty for reasons of his own mental stability, he had to delude himself that he is doing the will of the Führer, as he imagines him to be – a peace bringer.

He must therefore, at least consciously, reject the bad and aggressive qualities of his idol. I believe, however, that his flight was impelled by a deep doubt of Hitler, a feeling which he could never voice. The conflict became too great. His feeling of guilt at the aggression of the Führer is reinforced by guilt at being disloyal to him. He could save his mental integration only by some dramatic act of 'redemption', which at the same time had the effect of removing him from the fateful spell his idol had cast over him.

From the psychological point of view this attempt has failed. The 'bad impulses' have not been eliminated. He has had to dispose of them by a typical abnormal mental twist i.e. in attributing them partly to an obscure 'hidden poisoner' by whom he feels himself persecuted, and partly to his bad feelings inside – his complaints, fears of illness. The presence of this abnormal system of thought, of which there is ample daily evidence, is a manifestation of incipient insanity.

In addition, we clearly see his mental anguish and oppression increasing daily as the conference he has asked for approaches. So long as it was shadowy, he could blame us for keeping his message from the powers that be. Now, by our repeated demonstrations of good faith, he is faced with his own feelings of complete inadequacy for his task. He therefore has now to imagine himself ill: his head is so bad – he cannot concentrate – his mind is a blank etc.

This ill-feeling of a man who dreads being caught at a disadvantage is a familiar excuse, on hysterical lines. His resistance to any suggested form of remedy: greater rest, tonics, light treatment, massage, relaxation and suggestion etc, is complete and childishly obstinate. His inner realisation of his own inferiority in the face of really cultured and competent men makes it imperative for him to feel 'ill' in order to save his self-esteem which had been falsely bolstered up by Hitler's favour.

He has reasoned nothing out; he was driven by inner necessity. He admits he is no negotiator and feels at a disadvantage. His hope of becoming something other than Hitler's shadow – an important, even heroic, figure in his own right – is vanishing.

Clinically, he is deteriorating into a rather pitiful *malade imaginaire*, suspicious, self-centred and uncooperative. It is even possible that he will experience a complete breakdown just before or during the forthcoming negotiations, when he will be put to the test.

Yet his implicit faith in the chivalry of the English shows that quite a slice of his 'love' is detached from Hitler and, at least potentially, belongs to us, from the considerations stated above, and his mental torment is, at least in part, a 'kicking against the pricks'.

Dicks then went on to note a Practical Conclusion:

It seems to me that we have instinctively handled this man wisely, and that the orders to be extremely considerate may bear some fruit. He must be humoured in such things as will increase his confidence in the English as providers of 'good', 'non-poisonous' sustenance for body and soul if he is to serve ultimately some useful political purpose.

Anything which suggests Third Degree would extinguish his last desperate hope of goodness in this world and probably drive him clean over the border. He is at present in the state where he can still come out of his morose hostility for a little while, even if only to recoil seemingly as far back into the old attitude; and he responds to encouragement and demonstrations of good faith.

As to whether he is worth encouraging from the point of view of politics or of military intelligence, I am not competent to say. He has quite a good intellect. He was too distraught to complete a certain brief test of his intellectual capacity, but the result of that part which he carried out suggests a high level of cunning.

> Yet he is a very limited person, afraid of initiative, docile and very anxious, a creature of impulse rather than reason, and at present his emotional state, described in detail above, is highly unstable and critically near paranoid insanity.

Hess comprehended clearly that his thoughts were beginning to slip. He was exhausted from lack of sleep and cursed the guards who woke him each night by shining torch light directly into his face. He listened to their explanation, that it was to 'make sure that I was still alive', but doubted its sincerity. He had detected a pattern, an interrogatory jigsaw of which this was just one piece. Air raid sirens were a logical part of war and, gauging by the ambulance drive, he calculated that he was no more than a few hours from London. If so, the disturbances that broke his sleep three or four times a night could be excused. However, the sirens and horns mounted on the house surely served no purpose other than to torment him. He strained to hear the noise of motors or anti-aircraft fire, but heard nothing. When waves of exhaustion rolled up during the day and he retired to bed, they were beaten back by the 'constant slamming of doors; people running up and down stairs on a stairway' which, judging by the direction of the noise, ran directly above his room.

If the persistent noise was designed to set his nerves on edge, the drugs he believed to be carefully concealed in his food served to unbalance his mind and so reduce his peace plan to piece meal. He noted carefully the effects of each concoction and its method of delivery, milk being the preferred vehicle. After refusing a glass on a number of occasions for fear of what its cloudy contents might conceal, he relented with almost immediate regret. A short time later he became dizzy, was gripped with a 'terrific headache' and could no longer see straight. The partial blindness soon passed, but gave way to a rising inner hilarity that swooped him up so as only to increase the height from which he then tumbled down into the 'deepest depression and weakness'. If these were the weapons trained against him, he decided that he would resort to his natural cunning: 'From then on I had milk and cheese brought into my room every day, but merely to deceive people that I was eating that stuff.'

As the conference approached it became clear to Hess that serious impediments were being put in his path. He could feel his memory beginning to slip; events once viewed with crystal clarity began to blur while straight, clear ideas were soon knotted.

'I suspected that I was to be prevented in this manner from making any proposals for an understanding and that, moreover, Lord Simon was to receive the impression that I was mentally not normal because I was not capable of answering the simplest questions that were put to me.'

Thus Hess later claimed that he began to fast for the three days prior to the conference, sustaining himself with water. He wrote about the day of the conference, 'I had some wine brought up to my room, but instead of drinking it I poured it away. Major F [Foley] was informed by me that the wine had caused a miracle, my memory had returned completely. I shall never forget his horrified and confused face.'

7

A Lord Comes Calling

On the morning of the conference Hess dressed, with great care, in his German uniform. The fastening of each polished button served to pull him together, leading Lieutenant Colonel Scott to comment that he 'seemed to regain a portion of his former self.' At one o'clock prompt Lord Simon and Ivone Kirkpatrick arrived at the gate and used the pseudonyms of Doctors 'Guthrie' and 'Mackenzie' to collect the camp passes, after which they progressed up to the main house where they were served lunch in 'A' mess. These were the two names to be used on transcripts and all official paperwork to prevent news of the meeting from leaking. Over lunch the pair rehearsed the questions. Kirkpatrick had advised Simon to stir Hess up by demanding to know why Germany should make peace with Britain if she 'was going to sign up with Russia and bring Russian bolshevism into Europe'. Perhaps then Hess would clarify whether Germany's intent against Russia was indeed war. Hess meanwhile was to be served lunch in his room in the company of Captain 'Barnes', but he again refused to eat and at one point retired to his bed. Eventually Dicks persuaded him to fortify himself with a glass of port and a couple of glucose tablets.

At two o'clock the stenographer arrived, followed a few minutes later by four officers from MI5, who accompanied the German witness. Afterwards the officers retired to the officers' lounge where Foley extended the members of MI6's sister agency the courtesy of an informal briefing.

At 2.30 p.m. the conference began. In the sitting room were Lord Simon, Ivone Kirkpatrick, the shorthand stenographer Lieutenant Reade, and Captain Barnes (who was acting as interpreter). The following is a full transcription of the meeting, with only the necessary repetition of German removed:

Lord Simon: Herr Reichsminister, I was informed that you had come here feeling charged with a mission and that you wished to speak of it to someone who would be able to receive it with Government authority. You know I am Lord Simon and therefore I come with the authority of the Government, and I shall be very willing to listen and discuss with you as far as seems good anything you would wish to state for the information of the Government.

Interpreter: He is very grateful indeed that you have come. He realises that his arrival here – his journey – has not been understood by anyone here. Because it is such a very extraordinary step to take that he can't expect us to. He would like to commence by explaining how he arrived at his decision. He came to the decision when he was with the Führer during the French campaign.

Simon: I would like to know if he would prefer to say 'I came to this decision' repeating his words again. It is better in the end because you sometimes get confusion.

Int: Yes, I see.

Simon: Would you mind repeating the last sentence, I have not quite got it. Mr Shorthand writer, would you repeat?

Secretary: I arrived at the decision to come here after seeing the Führer during the French campaign in June.

Int: He was definitely of the opinion – he and they all were of the opinion – that they would conquer England. And he was of the opinion that we must demand from England those details, material such as the merchant fleet, which had been taken from us by the Versailles Treaty.

(Hess speaks)

Int: The Führer promised him . . . The Führer was of the opinion that the war would be a reason for a closer rapprochement between the countries, one which he had always attempted to bring about.

(Hess speaks)

Int: The Führer's aim ever since 1921 had always been to further this rapprochement between the countries and (that was) the aim which he had always had in view ever since he came to power. And he told the Reichsminister that even if the country was conquered, they could not impose any severe conditions if any spirit of negotiation was to remain.

(Hess speaks)

Int: Apparently the Reichsminister had the thought that if anyone in England knew this fact at that time, it might be possible to arrive at an understanding. Then came the Führer's offer at the conclusion of the French campaign. This offer was, as is known, refused.

Int: And this confirmed my resolution that I must go through with my plan.

[There then followed a long pause].

Hess: Following that came the air battles between Germany and England, which definitely caused heavier loss to England than Germany. I had then the impression that England would not give way without losing considerable prestige.

Int: It was then that he decided that he really must realise his plan, so that by his own presence in England, England would be enabled to consider an approach.

Kirkpatrick: What he really said was *anlass nehmen* – his arrival here would be a peg, a ground for starting negotiations without a loss of prestige.

Int: Yes, Sir.

Hess: I was of the opinion that there was a general atmosphere of distrust to counter apart from the actual conditions which might be attached to the final settlement. I must confess I had to face the most critical decision in my life. I believe my resolution was strengthened – not only on the German side, but also on the English side – by a picture of rows of children's coffins. And also the coffins of mothers followed by children. I now want to approach the problem and to talk about the psychological aspects, which, I believe, is the case here.

After the defeat in the Great War the Versailles Treaty was imposed on Germany. And no serious historian now supposes that Germany had any war guilt. Lloyd George said the peoples stumbled into the war. I read an English historian – Farrar – who at that time wrote about England and Edward VII. This historian lays at the door of Edward VII – the politics of Edward VII – the guilt of the war. Germany had this treaty imposed on her after the war, which was not only a tragedy for Germany but also for the whole world.

All attempts of politicians who were in power in Germany before the Führer came into power were unavailing. The Führer's first thought was to attempt negotiation and to attempt amelioration of the terms. He demanded a 200,000 army for Germany, a few aeroplanes, a few tanks, a few heavy guns, that was all. Not permitted!

He suggested that gas warfare should be abolished through international convention, and the bombardment of civilians also. He suggested that bombers should be abolished internationally. After this experience the Führer had to decide to go forward on his own initiative. His first aim was to cleanse the relations with the neighbouring powers. The relations to Italy were already laid down – fixed. He even made a pact with Poland. He allowed France to keep Alsace-Lorraine for ever. He continued to make offers to England in some form or other. The only offer that was accepted by England was the Naval Treaty.

The reason for the cancellation of this agreement was that England always attempted and continued to work on the side of Germany's opponents.

Simon: The cancellation of what agreement?

Int: The naval agreement.

Hess: For this reason the Führer was unable to let Germany be handicapped. Then came the union with Austria. A democratic principle was realised on this occasion, for 95 per cent of the population afterwards voted for Germany. Then came the Czech crisis. The French minister Pierre Cot had announced that Czechoslovakia would serve as an air base in a future war of France and England against Germany. In addition the maltreatment of German subjects over there gave them the excuse to . . . Then came Munich.

Simon: Will you forgive me for one moment, there is just a point I did not quite follow. Herr Reichminister was saying: 'the ill-treatment of Germans' meaning, I suppose, inside Czechoslovakia – Sudeten Germans – which gave somebody the excuse . . .

[The stenographer interrupted: 'It was not really the excuse – *handhabung* is the German word. He means the reason, the sound reason, for intervening'.]

Simon: The grounds.

Hess: I would like to emphasise that this maltreatment was not invented. The Führer said how happy he was that a possible means of understanding had been arrived at after the Munich agreement. Unfortunately messages then arrived from England stating that Chamberlain had stated that he was only trying to gain time for further rearmament. *The Times* confirmed this at the death of Chamberlain.

In addition to this, the historical fact is that England always seeks to build up a coalition against the strongest continental power. It is also known that General Wood stated under oath at the Foreign Relations Committee – made the following statement that Churchill had stated to him in 1936: Germany was getting too strong and had to be destroyed.

Simon: What is the Foreign Relations Committee . . .

Int: The United States Foreign Relations . . .

Hess: In addition came the fact that the rest of Czechoslovakia was, as before, being financed by England and France for purposes of further rearmament. The Führer was forced, as the responsible statesman, to get rid of this possible danger in the middle of Germany. The corridor was created by the Versailles Treaty. England must imagine what it would be like to have a corridor going right through the middle of the country – say for Ireland.

But the Führer was also ready to deal with this question by negotiations and on the fifth and sixth January, 1939, he made the necessary approaches to Beck, the Polish Foreign Minister. The suggestion was to return the entirely German town of Danzig to Germany. The idea was that Poland should retain the Corridor but Germany required two extraterritorial lines: a road and a railway.

And the Führer wanted to guarantee Poland's frontier. The German people were horrified . . . The German people were horrified at this suggestion. Only the Führer with his authority was able to make this suggestion. In the middle of 1939 the German suggestion was again made to Lipski, the Polish Ambassador. Poland was, of course, ready to accede to this suggestion. It was only prevented from doing so by British influence. Poland was even prepared to accede to the German request even eight days before the war. Then the mutual assistance pact was signed with Great Britain. Poles, that is to say members of the Polish Foreign Office, have made these statements since that time. The reasons again were the maltreatment of German subjects.

Simon: The grounds for intervention?

Hess: Yes. Neutral journalists have confirmed these atrocity stories. I could show you photographs of German children who died with their tongues nailed on to a table. Then came the war. After the Polish campaign the Führer made his first offer of peace to England and France. In the times to follow that, the Führer had received authentic information that England had plans against Norway. This was confirmed, that England intended to occupy certain parts of Norway to serve as bases for further operations against Germany. Our troops, when the Führer gave the signal and moved into Norway, the German troops were received as if they were Englishmen who had been expected. A nephew of Mr Churchill's who was a journalist in Narvik confirmed . . . Told the people up in Norway that English troops would be arriving. The Cossack-Altmark affair and the laying of mines in Norwegian territorial waters preceded this action. These were the two first contraventions of international law in this war. Apart from flights over neutral territory and so on.

In the autumn and winter news was also received of similar plans in Denmark. Air bases and a naval base were going to be established there with the probable intention of closing the Skagerrak. The plans of the Entente in Belgium and Holland then became known. An attack through Belgium and Holland was intended, aiming at the *Ruhrgebiet* as soon as sufficient war material had been accumulated behind the Maginot Line. And it also became known that maps had been printed for this purpose, which indeed were found later. England and French quartermaster staff had already been in these countries. Proofs were obtained that the motorised section of the army would be refuelled in these countries. This was all proved by the finding of various documents in La Charité. I have specially brought up these points because I know that they are held against us and play a considerable psychological role.

With regard to the breaking of international law and of various treaties – I believe, although I am not entirely familiar with English history, that England would have acted in the same way given the same circumstances. I only remind you of Copenhagen; the expression 'to Copenhage' does not come from Germany. I could lay out a whole list of broken treaties and broken international laws. I would like to remind you of Lawrence of Arabia.

It is well known that he resigned from his rank of colonel because England did not keep his word to the Arabs. The reproach of the suppression of small nations comes ill from England's mouth. We do not repress any of the smaller nations. Apart from the disarmament, the Czechs feel themselves in very good heart. It is certain that Germany has not handled any nation as the Boers, the Indians and the Irish. There's no Amritsar episode in German history. We have not created any concentration camps for women and children, as was the case in the Boer War.

And the German people have not forgotten that the Armistice was concluded on the basis of Wilson's fourteen points and that these were not adhered to. The armistice terms were broken in one particular respect, that of the interning of the German fleet. It is well known that the Versailles Treaty was also broken in one of the most important points, that of the disarmament. The Versailles Treaty laid it down that other countries should also disarm after a certain time to the same extent as Germany herself.

It has often been suggested to me that England did in fact demobilise her army and perhaps her air force. But England's most important weapon is her navy. If the thirteen modern capital ships which were the basis of the British fleet had been taken as the basis or the equivalent for the German army, then Germany would have had a very large, a gigantic army with all modern weapons. With Germany's geographical position, the army is for Germany what the navy is for England. And I believe that we must avoid . . .

Kirkpatrick: The reason is, we're talking as man to man, we should make up our minds to eliminate from the conversation these mutual recriminations.

Hess: And I'm certain that leading Englishmen who do know the situation will not make these reproaches. These reproaches do play a considerable role in the minds of our people. And the mistrust, the suspicion, which the German people has for the British is certainly not less than that which the British has for the German. German people ask themselves constantly: what guarantee is there that England will keep to her treaties, her pacts, in any better way than she had done previously. In addition there is considerable bitterness in Germany because they know, the German people know, that the Führer did not want the war on the civilian population by means of bombing raids.

The Führer made the suggestion at the beginning of the war that such bombing attacks should not occur.

[There was then a long pause before Hess resumed.]

Despite this, ever increasing attacks made by the British Air Force on the German civil population resulted. England makes the suggestion of Rotterdam. I'd like to point out that Rotterdam lies within the so-called 'fortress Holland'. Because of that Holland decided to capitulate. The English attacks on the other hand have not this advantage that they prevent further shedding of blood. Despite these attacks on the civilian population, the Führer hesitated, and hesitated again, to order any counter measures . . . But eventually the mothers of children and relations came to the Führer and pleaded with him and asked him why he did not order an attack to be made.

The victims were practically always in towns which had absolutely no military importance. When the Führer had come to the conclusion that common sense did not prevail in England despite his warning and other offers.

Kirkpatrick: When the Führer saw that, despite all his delays, reason did not prevail, then he decided to counter-attack?

Hess: Then he decided to counter-attack, and according to the precepts of Lord Fisher: 'Moderation in war is no use; if you strike, strike hard and wherever you can.' And I can confirm that it was always – several times – very difficult for the Führer to give the orders for these attacks to be made. He was very upset. I am a personal witness of this. The entire time he felt for the English people who had become the victim to this method of waging war. I now want to examine the situation as we see it in Germany.

Simon: May I just interrupt here to say, with the permission of Herr Reichsminister, because I listened closely to his account of the German view of the war since it began and, naturally, I will read all he has said again, I have not interrupted. I wish to be a good listener . . .

Hess: Yes.

Simon: Which is the compliment which I wish to pay him and that is why I have come. He will, of course, understand that I could not accept this account of the war and I hope he will plainly understand that if I do not contradict or challenge what he says about it, it is not because I agree, but because we must in this matter agree to differ; and because the real purpose why I have come is to hear from him about his mission.

Int: Herr Reichsminister wanted to emphasise, and perhaps he had not done so sufficiently, that when you did not contradict him he did not read that as a sign of acceptance.

Simon: But I want to make it quite clear to him, you see. I think I have made my words clear. I do that partly because I wish to be courteous, but I do it also because I wish to come to what is the real point that is coming now. That's all right as long as we understand each other.

Int: I assumed that, anyway, many differences in opinion could arise from the various points.

Simon: Yes, of course. That is really a matter that will ultimately be decided perhaps by history, perhaps not in a very few years.

Int: He has only put forward his views so that you get a true picture of what German people thought.

Simon: Yes. I quite understand that. And, no doubt, Herr Reichsminister will understand also that in developing his mission he must remember that the British people are a proud people – *Herrenvolk* – and will not easily accept such reproaches, were it not that we are talking here together in a friendly way, and I wish to hear what are the proposals he has come to make here. I think that is why he has come.

Hess: The reasons for my flight was that among the leading personalities, the leaders of Germany, we were absolutely convinced that England's position was hopeless. It goes so far that we ask ourselves on what basis England can possibly hope to continue the war. All our aircraft factories are still standing. A very large number of factories have been added since the beginning of the war and others are being completed now. Our production is such that last winter we had difficulties in storing the production. The fighting front did not require them because their needs were covered by the production of one day.

We built up these dumps because we wished to train the flying personnel right up to the last detail. We must be believed when we say that we have trained a sufficiency of personnel to use a tremendous force of material against England. The flying personnel which is now coming along is approximately the same number as the entire British Expeditionary Force to France.

Simon: I don't understand that; he is speaking of a comparison of two totals; he said that his flying personnel that is now coming along—

Int: He means the flying personnel that is at present fully trained.

Simon: The total, he means?

Int: Yes.

Simon: I mean, whatever the proposition is, it's so simple, I mean creating two totals; I don't understand what the two totals are.

Int: The two totals are that he has the completely trained forces at present at their disposal.

Simon: Air forces?

Int: Air forces.

Simon: Equal to?

Int: Equal to the BEF in France.

Simon: Does he mean the tanks and the—

Int: The total number of men.

Simon: And what is the total number?

[Hess then speaks . . .]

Simon: Probably Herr Reichsminister knows what is the total number he is assessing?

Int: The total numbers are, he imagines, in hundreds of thousands.

Simon: That isn't clear to me. Herr Hess is stating that the number of air personnel now ready to serve in Germany are equal to something; well, he must have a figure in his head then. It is much simpler to state the figure than to go half way round the world divided by six. What is the figure?

Hess: The training plan is arranged so that hundreds of thousands are turned out, not tens of thousands. It is well known that Goering works on a very large scale.

Simon: He is a very large man! (laughter)

Hess: It's well known that the level of training is a very high one. I continuously get letters from flying personnel who complain that they're being kept behind the lines, when they have already long ago completed their course of instruction. I am aware that England is also receiving reinforcements of men and machines. But we are quite certain we shall maintain our lead with regard to material, personnel, especially when one considers the geographical and strategical position of Germany. It's perfectly obvious that when one considers the distance between here and France and Holland, and the distances we have to fly to get to Germany – the difference in the bomb-weight carried – a big difference in being able to make use of the weather. Especially in autumn and winter, when it is much more difficult to make these long flights in bad weather than short ones just over from France.

By reason of my personal interests – I am acquainted with Messerschmitt and all the leading personalities in the flying world – I have an extremely good idea of what is being prepared to attack England. Without being guilty of exaggeration I can state quite definitely it will be terrible. What has happened so far in England is only a foretaste of what is still to come. And I want to emphasise that that is the reason why I have come. Because this is something quite inconceivable, the forms which such aerial warfare will take. I consider it my duty as a human being to warn you and to make my appearance here.

England's possible effort in this direction cannot be compared to ours. It is quite obvious that we have done everything we can ever since the outbreak of war to safeguard the civilian population, above all by making pill-boxes and shelters, by propping up cellars, and what we can do in such a small space of time we have shown in the construction of the Siegfried Line.

Simon: Would you mind repeating the last sentence again?

Int: And we have shown what we can do in this respect – the Siegfried Line.

Hess: The evacuation of civilian personnel in towns which may be heavily attacked has been organised with true German thoroughness. Such things function in Germany. You press on a button and it happens. Up till now it has been entirely unnecessary; we have not even thought of doing so. Our losses, in comparison to those which England must have suffered, are very small.

Simon: May I just interrupt you there? Herr Hess, I find a certain difficulty in following this. You told me earlier, you know, that Herr Hitler was most averse to making any attack on towns in this country, but you said that, though that was his policy and he is the undisputed ruler and leader of Germany, that great bitterness had been expressed in Germany by the civilian population. I do not understand how the civilian population can with great bitterness complain of being heavily attacked from the air unless the truth be that they have suffered terribly; and it appears to me to be quite inconsistent to say at one moment that there has been great bitterness in Germany on the part of the civilian population because of the attacks from the air of British bombers, and then you say a little later on that nothing at all has happened which has upset Germany in the least and that all the plans are quite perfect and that all that happens is that everybody takes shelter.

To me these two things are not the same.

Hess: I did not say nothing occurred, but that the losses which Germany had incurred in this form of warfare must have been very considerably less than those which England suffered.

Simon: The right view then is apparently that there has been heavy loss in Germany from British bombing attacks. That must be then the result.

Hess: They were very much smaller than those England must have suffered.

Simon: Forgive me interrupting, but I did not see how the things agreed.

Kirkpatrick: Even so, we have only lost 30,000 civilians and if they're very much lighter, they must be negligible, and if they're negligible, how about the bitterness?

Simon: But your information is – and therefore you stated here, and I, of course, listened with respect to what you say; one can measure other things by your statements – and your information is that the German population has not seriously suffered to any great extent by British bombing.

Hess: They have suffered.

Simon: It wasn't intended to interrupt you, but if two things don't seem to me to agree I like to know how it stands. Another question, do you mind? You see, you have been describing to me how everything in Germany is ready: vast quantities of aeroplanes and pilots and, no doubt, of other material too, which if it was used, would finish off the war by attacking England. I am rather inclined therefore to ask you, well then, why do you go on losing men in Crete and in Iraq, and in other fields of war, when you have in your hand something which is going to defeat us straight away? Why does the great German strategy prefer that?

Kirkpatrick: If Germany, as you say, has such a fighting force in its hand which can finish off England with one blow, why, with such a weapon in its hand, does Germany need to run around in the Balkans, in Crete, if it has such a wonderful, powerful weapon in its hand, to strike us dead.

Hess: Firstly, I didn't say that she had it in the hand, but that this will come.

Kirkpatrick: You said that there are already people who have been trained, flight personnel, en masse, already existing – and aeroplanes – in the numbers of our expedition corps – that is to say hundreds and thousands. And Lord Simon says if this monstrous weapon exists already, in Germany's hand, why the running around in the Balkans, with certain bloodshed, which is completely unnecessary, if England could be struck dead this summer.

Simon: Which is what you intended to do last autumn.

Kirkpatrick: Which was tried, in vain, last autumn.

Simon: Your view is, you see, in the last autumn we suffered much more than you.

Hess: Yes.

Simon: Surely, what a curious thing then that the invasion stopped!

Hess: I don't say that we possess these things already, I saw that they were coming out; one day sooner or later this weapon will be in our hand and I don't say it will be decisive, that it will win the war, I only say that it will be more terrible than anything that has gone before.

Simon: If I may say so, Herr Hess, I can quite understand the argument if you put it like that; I think I do understand what it is which you are placing before me for the information of the British Government. Your view is – your message, if you like – is that you believe there will be in the future a far more violent and terrible, overwhelming attack on this country—

Hess: Yes—

Simon: —than there has yet been, and you say that the thought of this is one which makes you unhappy because it involves terrible loss of life of innocent people, women and children, in both countries. And, as I understand you, you say that the mission with which you charged yourself is largely inspired by that fact. I understand that. We won't argue about what will happen if we did all this today, but you really are making a statement for the British Government to consider in view of what you believe will be future developments, isn't that so?

Hess: Yes.

Simon: That, I think, is the sore point. Well, if I might suggest it, because it necessarily occupies some time, would you feel it convenient, would it suit you, to tell me for the British Government what is the proposal you suggest should be forwarded or considered?

Please continue as you planned. I am quite content and very willing to listen. That is, after all, what I have come for.

Hess: I would like to tell you about U-boat warfare.

Simon: Yes, I would be grateful if you would.

Hess: The mere fact that they have sufficient flying personnel and aircraft does not mean that we have made clear their formations ready for actual combat.

Simon: Hm, I know.

Hess: Aerodromes must be built. Formation flying must be practised. The question of weather, which is not very suitable in winter.

Simon: I quite understand. What you are putting to me is the formidable evidence which, in your view, will hereafter, in the future, constitute an overwhelming force. It is the elements. Now, about the U-boat . . .

Hess: Our losses of the civilian population are considerably less than those which we normally have from road accidents.

Simon: Yes. In Germany do the soldiers drive the motorcars very fast? [Laughter]

They do in this country. They make a lot of accidents.

Hess: The Führer has a few locked up occasionally and he gets furious.

Simon: I dare say that's a very good way.

Hess: In Germany as in England the civilian morale is highest where the bombing attacks have been made and the people are in some way hardened. In the last World War it was demonstrated that the toughness of the Germans is no less than that of the English. And the collapse in the last war did not come from the front but from the home front. And this enemy behind the lines has been liquidated. The Führer is loved as never before.

If England – as I hope it will not – gets into the same position as we were in 1918, and later England would be equally attached to a man who came at her hour of trial and boosted her up, as happened in the case of Germany.

And the German people know what would happen to them if they had to capitulate. England and French politicians in their speeches have made this quite clear in speeches since the beginning of war. I do not know who said it, but someone went so far as to say that the time would come when the German people would have to beg at the field kitchens of the Allied troops.

And we can be believed if we say that we have used these facts for propaganda amongst the German people. The blockade was also responsible for the collapse. There is no question of this at this moment. Rationing was introduced from the very beginning. And our performances in these matters have been recognised everywhere. In some respects we have been able to increase our rations because we were so careful in earlier times. Raw materials are assured.

Int: Do you agree to that, Sir, that their raw materials are—

Simon: I didn't mean to—

Int: Would you like to ask him to expand the point, if you agree that—

Simon: Well, I don't think we can conduct the conversation on the basis that I agree to everything that Herr Hess says unless we expand it or argue about it. I am waiting – I say, it with great respect – I am waiting to be informed of the matter for which I was invited to come down here.

Hess: Yes.

Simon: And now I am waiting, I suppose, for two hours – I don't know how the time goes – I came down here in order that Herr Hess might have the opportunity for which he asked of explaining to a representative of the British Government his mission, and I haven't heard a word about it yet, so that, while there are many things we can talk about, I should be sorry to have any controversy on anything except the object of his mission. I understand in order that I may see what you have to say about your mission in its proper framework, it is necessary to have a sketch of what lies behind. I quite understand and I am making no complaint but I am being silent – patient. [Hess laughs at 'patient'.]

Simon: Yes, that is what I recollect we were going to have after the air—

Hess: The leaders of Germany have decided that that is the critic point.

Simon: The decisive point.

Hess: The numbers of U-boats are very considerable, especially with regard to those which are at present under construction and being finished. The strength of the Führer lies in the fact that he is able to make his plans long-sighted – taking the long view. And with regard to the decisive weapons against England, he has worked on a very large scale – decisive work has been done, especially aeroplanes and submarines. And he has decided to safeguard the construction of U-boats against bombing attacks because he had already foreseen that England would attack these factories or these wharves or these shipyards. The same applies, of course, to U-boat bases. The great decentralisation of manufacture is the best protection. Three-quarters of Europe is engaged in building U-boats, some factories even building parts and not knowing that they are intended for U-boats.

And we have the possibility of using our big rivers in this respect for the construction of U-boats—

Simon: Does he mean for the construction of U-boats or does he mean the bringing of the U-boats down from the places where they are?

Int: He hasn't finished his sentence, Sir.

Hess: —because for that reason we are able to put our assembly plants very far inland. And then as you said, bring them down the river.

Simon: Bring them down the rivers.

Hess: Down the rivers, yes. A river that can take a thousand-ton barge can take a 750-ton submarine.

Simon: Might I just ask, Herr Minister, if it is convenient, a question about that? We in this country are under the impression that we have bombed very heavily and successfully the U-boat yards, say at Kiel, and U-boat construction is going on there?

Int: He believes you are not quite right in the picture about the truth of these attacks. It is not possible to produce that from aerial photography. And as for reports by agents, we have our own experiences to judge from.

Simon: Yes, I merely told Herr Hess, I am not an expert on that, but I read the papers carefully, the confidential papers, you see, and I would have said that we had delivered very heavy attacks and very successful attacks on the shipyards where U-boats were being built in Kiel, and, I think, in Bremen and, I think, in Hanover; I don't feel sure about Wilhelmshaven, I don't know whether you do build U-boats as near as Wilhelmshaven.

Hess: But these are not all our wharves for building U-boats. I have just suggested that we use our rivers for the purposes of . . . and we are using . . . and we are in the process of expanding these methods.

Simon: I may tell you that U-boat crews – sailors, German U-boat sailors who have been made prisoner – have, as I am informed, complained bitterly that the U-boat production which they were assured would take place, the additional U-boats – had not been forthcoming. They may be wrong, of course, they may be telling a prisoner's [laughing] tale, but that is what I am told they say. Is that not right?

Kirkpatrick: I think that is quite right.

Simon: I am very much interested in what you say and, of course, I quite appreciate it when you say that Germany has vast production, as well as great powers of organisation, because the Germans are wonderful people about those things. I quite understand that. But what I have great difficulty in understanding is the suggestion that we have not done a great deal of damage to your U-boat shipyards. But we undoubtedly think we have.

Hess: And as regards newspaper reports. Yes, I can give you an instance. I was in Munich on the ninth of November, 1940, when a British air attack was made on the city. English papers reported that very heavy destruction had been caused, above all, on the railway tracks. I witnessed that no bomb hit any railway tracks.

Simon: Well, Mr Hess, in the last war, in the latter part of it, I was a ground officer in the British Air Force, and I was especially concerned with night bombing and I had the reports every morning early at dawn. And constantly we received reports that our bombers had smashed up the little triangle and we sent machines over to photograph the next day and the railway lines were never broken at all.

Hess: *Jawohl.*

Simon: And I should have supposed that the German plan of building U-boats, in parts, at various places away back in the interior and bringing it together . . . I should have thought that was due to the fact that it was not safe to continue to construct along with borders of the sea.

Kirkpatrick: He said that the Führer planned this long before any attack took place; in other words, the Führer foresaw that we were going to make attacks.

Simon: It's my fault, I have interrupted you. It is my fault entirely. You were just saying that, in the view of the authorities in Germany, this U-boat warfare will get more intense and was really the decisive point.

Hess: Yes. A little time ago the Führer announced the beginning of the real U-boat war. I can assure you that the U-boat warfare as announced by the Führer has not yet commenced. I would like to say a few words about the strategical . . . In 1917 we have a very small base of operations, the so called Heligoland Bight. And to the west of it. We also had a few small bases on the Belgian coast. That was so closed by mines that we had tremendous losses. We now have bases which extend from Norway to Spain. At that time it was impossible to get through the Channel with U-boats. We are now on the other side of the Channel.

The convoy system has failed in comparison to 1917–1918. In addition, our U-boat warfare is supplemented by the air arm. We can be believed when we say that our new constructions are coming along also on these lines. In addition, it was not possible before, we are able to destroy ships in their harbours and in their shipyards. We destroy the shipyards themselves. We destroy the dumps inland. We also destroy the factories for the home production. Many, and Lloyd George amongst them, have admitted that England was very nearly on the brink of a catastrophe in 1917 by reason of U-boat warfare. Despite the fact that the position was then for Germany a worse one, considerably more unfavourable.

Fresh inventions which have been announced in this field have so far not had any success. Although inventions of this kind have been announced since the outbreak of war. We are convinced that we shall arrive at the decision on the basis of tonnage. And we are convinced that our figures regarding the loss of tonnage are correct and these figures are confirmed by American experts.

Simon: When Herr Hess says 'our figures' does he mean the figures which have been published from time to time in the German broadcasts?

Hess: Our monthly official—

Kirkpatrick: The official returns. Does Herr Hess say that they have sunk practically the whole of our merchant fleet?

Simon: At that rate, you see, what has happened is that you have sunk the whole of the British Merchant Navy, you've sunk it all.

You see, it wouldn't be worthwhile having a discussion. I said it merely as a matter of interest, that's all, I mean in a friendly way. Nothing amuses the British people so much as the German figures about sinking British tonnage.

Hess: Yes?

Simon: It makes them laugh . . .

Hess: Be that as it may, but I'm afraid that the day will come on which the English people will no longer laugh about that.

Simon: I don't attach very much importance to that really.

Hess: I'm afraid that day will come. I'm convinced that day will come.

Simon: The day may come! The day may come! But the statement was that the German official figures show that they were correct. If they were correct, you know, it's a pity we are not all dead.

Kirkpatrick: Otherwise the country would have starved already.

Hess: No, here Lord Simon is not completely correctly informed, I believe. The figure which has been stated in its totality by Germany is not by a long way the equivalent of that which was the total English tonnage at the beginning of the war.

Kirkpatrick: The total tonnage was 15 million.

Hess: 15 million?

Kirkpatrick: Yes. And the Germans claim to have sunk 12 million tons.

Hess: Yes.

Kirkpatrick: Also, seven million tons which have been so badly damaged that they can no longer be used; they are not included. So we have practically no ships left.

Hess: Yes.

Kirkpatrick: Which would mean for us, with our Middle-East expedition corps and for other war operations, which for our island would mean no more shipping at all.

Hess: But here I still have . . .

Simon: I beg your pardon. There is only one thing I can suggest, don't let us dispute it, it was merely an interjection. I quite understand the thing that matters in your argument. You are telling me that the authorities in Germany are convinced that they will be able to have greatly increased U-boat attacks to put our own tonnage in greater difficulties. That's quite a statement one can understand. I won't discuss it.

Hess: Yes.

Simon: But believe me, we are not quite so hard up just yet – not just yet . . . I don't want us to quarrel about it. I want to get to your mission.

Hess: They are also entirely convinced that America can produce no revolution in this case. American ship production cannot be sufficient to cover these losses. They know exactly how many aircraft America can produce in a given time.

Int: He says that is quite a false conception to imagine we can carry on the war from the Empire and abandon the Mother Country.

Hess: Germany would not consider on that account, merely with the pretext of the island, excluding the heart of the British Empire from the struggle. If on account of lack of tonnage England were to capitulate.

England created concentration camps in the Boer War and, according to the monument, some 26,000 women and children perished in them. And we would not hesitate to—

Kirkpatrick: The meaning is, exactly: starving out the British Isles in that event.

Hess: We would not consider occupying these countries because we would have to feed the people. Assuming it has not already been occupied. In the event of capitulation we should only occupy a number of important air bases. And we would shut them off from the hungry population so that our own soldiers could never see that population. That is a very hard point of view.

England has the possibility of making a finish under the most favourable conditions. I don't know whether you are already aware of the conditions of making peace.

Simon: I will reply. I think we are now coming to the real reason for our interview. I quite understand what you have already been saying, but we now come to the point. If I might suggest it, Herr Reichsminister, I would ask you briefly to tell me what is the mission which you have undertaken; you can say it, I have no doubt, quite clearly and briefly: I think that is the most important thing for me to know.

Hess: The conditions in which peace could be made, I have heard from the Führer in the course of a great number of consultations. I must emphasise that these conditions have always been the same ever since the outbreak of war. With regard to my self-chosen mission I have always asked the Führer whether these conditions – or about these conditions. When I was considering the question of this flight I always made enquiries of the Führer as to the conditions of peace. So that I could be absolutely certain that something had not been altered in the meantime. I should have added beforehand that I had the intention of making the flight more or less from January until the moment when I actually made it. I have not undertaken the flight then because England then had the successes.

Simon: May I just ask you through the Captain? One of the first things you said in our conversation this afternoon was – I think the very first thing you said – was that you arrived at your decision to come here after seeing the Führer at the time of the French campaign. That was what you said?

Hess: Yes.

Simon: Well, you see, that was long before the first of January last. That's what you said. You said – it was almost the first thing you said – 'I arrived at the decision to come here after seeing the Führer at the time of the French campaign.' And then you said you were confirmed by that campaign in your resolution that you must go through with your plan, and that means to come here. I had thought, therefore, you see, that the time – the date – when you first made the plan and intended to come was not in January last, it was before that.

Hess: Yes. I made various attempts to get here in the period between the summer and January, but that for one reason or another – the weather and difficulty in getting an aeroplane – I had been unable to get here.

Simon: But I gather it is right to say that you arrived at this decision to come here after seeing the Führer at the time of the French campaign.

Hess: Yes.

Simon: I think I had better, if you will allow me, ask you one or two questions. May I? Because, of course, it's bound to be asked. Could you tell me – would you tell me, do you come here with the Führer's knowledge or without his knowledge?

Hess: Without his knowledge. *Absolut.* [laughs]

Simon: Well, I mean, one wants to know. You made the plan, you see, to come again and again and you have on each occasion before entering on this mission, or planning to come on this mission, on each occasion you have always enquired from him of his view on the conditions of peace.

Hess: Yes.

Simon: But I have it from you quite clearly – and indeed I so understood – that in fact you came without any knowledge of his or any authority.

Hess: Yes, surely.

Simon: So that suggests two questions, perhaps. One question is: why come now? You thought of it again and again, why come now? That is one question.

Hess: Yes.

Simon: You see, it's a little difficult to understand and I think that the Government will naturally want to know because they would say 'why has he come now?' Well, what is the reason?

Kirkpatrick: I'll translate the whole story to you.

Simon: Yes. Well, may I ask him a question? Why does he come now?

[Hess began a conversation with Kirkpatrick who then spoke]

Kirkpatrick: Really the delay took place owing to a whole series of difficulties. First of all he tried to get a machine from General Udet; he wouldn't give it him because he knew the Führer wouldn't permit him to fly. Then he got in touch with—

Simon: That is true, is it? He had forbidden you to fly?

[Hess laughs]

Kirkpatrick: When he had been turned down by Udet, he got in touch with Messerschmitt, a friend of his, and various things had to be done; he could not fly the machine at once, several things had to be prepared, extra tanks put on, then he had to do a bit of training and he did not have much time, you see. That took some time and then by December it was the first time everything was ready. After December there were all sorts of weather difficulties, he had to have really ideal weather conditions to start his flight to Scotland: he was alone with his two-seater machine, and so on. So, what with the postponement because of the weather and the postponement because of Wavell's victories, May really was . . . On the tenth of May he made one attempt and so on.

Simon: It wasn't then really world events, external events; he just missed his opportunity.

Kirkpatrick: But he did abandon the project for the moment in view of Wavell's victory.

Simon: I know. Well, that was one of the questions, you see. Now you must not mind if I put the other, because you will see it's a sensible question. You have said, Herr Hess, that you do not come with the Führer's authority or sanction or knowledge. Well then, you are going to tell me about these conditions of peace, you have not done so yet, but is the view that you are going to put before me held by other people?

Simon: Are there other important people in Germany who share the view you want me to listen to?

Hess: May I ask for this to be translated for me, please?

Int: Are there other people in Germany who hold such an opinion – other leading people?

Kirkpatrick: That's not the whole matter. Here is an important question, you must forgive me for asking it, for you will see that it is important. It is difficult to think that you came here without the Führer's permission, isn't it? Is what you will tell Lord Simon your own private idea, or do other leading persons in Germany share that idea?

Hess: The ideas are those of the Führer – and they are what determines things – simply and solely.

Kirkpatrick: And you know nothing of the ideas of the other personages?

Hess: They self-evidently agree with the Führer from the first, that's an absolute matter of course. When the Führer says to you, 'These and those are my ideas', then you say, 'Yes Sir'.

Kirkpatrick: Yes, but are the other personages in the picture?

Hess: I don't even know that, whether each one of them is in the picture, to what extent the Führer has spoken to them as well, I don't know.

Kirkpatrick: So you can't really determine whether those ideas are in accordance with the ideas of the leading personages. All you can say is that, if those ideas are those of the Führer, then they would be approved by the others. But whether they are in accordance with the ideas of the leading personages, that you don't know?

Hess: That I don't know, but that doesn't really matter.

Kirkpatrick: These ideas are the ideas of the Führer he has been able to establish in long conversations with him. The ideas that would be accepted by the leading personalities in Germany, because it is their habit to accept everything that the Führer says or does. Whether these personalities know what's in the Führer's mind about peace conditions he does not know. Whether these ideas are shared by the leading personalities he does not know. All he knows is that they are the ideas of the Führer and that is good enough to be accepted by leading personalities.

Simon: I see.

Hess: But I can, you see – I already spoke to you recently – and I stressed it before the Duke of Hamilton – only very rarely in my life have I given my word of honour, because I consider that to be too sacred a matter. In this case I give my word of honour that what I have written down here is what the Führer has told me in the course of several conversations.

Simon: Do you think that the Führer also told others about this matter?

Hess: I consider it probable that he spoke about it to Goering, for example. I don't know, but I even consider it certain.

Kirkpatrick: It's probable, but he cannot affirm it. He thinks that he probably has discussed it with Goering, but he can't say for certain.

Hess: But that is totally without consequence. The only one who matters is the Führer.

Simon: We have reached the moment to know what are these conditions.

Kirkpatrick: He usually does not give his word of honour because it is an important matter, but in this case he is prepared to give his word of honour that everything that is written down on that paper represents the view as expressed to him by the Führer on several occasions.

Simon: So, those are the conditions. Well, now, I am greatly obliged to you. Would it be convenient to you if we were to hand them to Mr Kirkpatrick.

Hess: Yes.

Simon: Today is the tenth.

Kirkpatrick: The tenth of June.

Simon: I think you may just read them out. They are not very long and I am sure Herr Reichsminister has taken a lot of care to write them down carefully.

Kirkpatrick: *'Basis for an understanding'*:

1. In order to hinder, to prevent future wars between England and Germany there should be a definition of spheres of interest. Germany's sphere of interest is Europe, England's sphere of interest is her Empire.

Simon: Europe then, of course, means continental Europe?

Hess: Continental Europe, yes.

Simon: Does it include any portion of Russia?

Hess: Of course, the European Russia interests them and if Germany would conclude a treaty with Russia, England is expected not to intervene.

Simon: I only wanted to know what was the meaning of 'European sphere of interest'. You see? If Germany's sphere of interest is in Europe, one naturally wants to know whether Russia, European Russia, Russia which is not in Asia, Russia which is on the west of the Urals . . . Moscow and all that part . . . one wants to know, is that part of the European zone?

Hess: No, not at all.

Simon: Italy?

Hess: In any case that is my conviction and I'm sure the Führer does not have another view. I have to stress that the Führer didn't say anything with reference to whether the rest of Russia is included, but I assume that it is excluded. We are not at all interested in 'over there'.

Int: Does Italy belong to that?

Hess: Italy, of course, yes of course. Italy is part of Europe and if we make a contract with Italy then in this case also England should not get involved.

Simon: We had better go on.

Kirkpatrick:

2. Return of German Colonies

3. Indemnification of German nationals who, as a result of the war, or during the war, have suffered damage in the British Empire or through measures of the Government of the Empire or through any such circumstance such as pure tumults, entire, robbery, loot or so on, have suffered damage to their life or property. Reciprocal indemnification by Germany of British citizens.

4. Armistice and peace to be concluded with Italy at the same time.

The above four points have been repeatedly expounded to me by the Führer in conversations as the basis for an understanding with England. Beyond these no points were specified. With regard to Iraq, which came into the picture shortly after my flight to Scotland, the Führer only remarked that this country should not be left in the lurch. More definite observations were not made to me in this regard.

Simon: I don't quite know what 'left in the lurch' means, but it is rather interesting to know it's a remark made by the Führer apparently: do I get the idea right, that since Germany has urged Rashid Ali to revolt and had promised him German help, that Germany under these terms should not leave Iraq without support? May I just repeat, I didn't quite understand the sentence about the Führer and Iraq. You say there, before you left Germany, the Führer, I don't know your expression in German – said that Iraq must not be left in the lurch, and I was asking what that meant, did it mean, I am asking, did it mean that since Germany had promised her help to Rashid Ali and had encouraged him to revolt against British influence that in the peace settlement Germany must see that Iraq had German support?

Hess: The Führer had just stated shortly before I left Germany that Iraq must not be left in the lurch.

Simon: I wanted to know what is that supposed to mean?

Int: He can't explain that, he says.

Simon: I think I had better ask you, please, Herr Hess, if you will explain these conditions a little more. You have had constant conversations with Herr Hitler about them, and I am sure the conversations couldn't be written down on two and a half sheets of paper, it must have been much longer than that.

There are one or two other details that I want to know. I don't know quite what is meant by Germany having Europe as a sphere of interest, and I am sure you must have discussed it with the Führer, as you know so well his mind. What, for example, would happen to Holland?

Int: The Führer told him when they were talking about the occupied countries, that some people say perhaps he would keep everything he had occupied; the Führer answered to that: 'I am not crazy.'

Simon: You will forgive me for asking, because, after all, that's why we have met, isn't it? The first thing the Government will ask would be that. If the Führer feels that he mustn't leave Iraq in the lurch, it may be that England feels that it mustn't leave Holland in the lurch. I am quite sure that you, when you conversed with the Führer whom you know so well, in such intimacy, I am sure that the discussion must have included some discussion as to what was to happen to Holland, and it would be no use my reporting to the British Government, if there was to be a sphere of interest in Europe, if I couldn't answer that question.

Hess: I have tried once to get some answer to the question from the Führer. [He said]: 'I have not racked my brains over this question yet, that will all have to come later.

Simon: I think, I must ask a similar question about some other great countries. Norway, you see, according to your view, Norway which used to be quite an independent state has got into trouble because of the action of Britain. Well, I do not agree, but that is the German view. Well then, as Norway has never done anything wrong to Germany, what is to happen to Norway when the war is over? Is she to be made subject to Germany?

Hess: I firmly believe no. The Führer has made no specific statement on this subject. He said, 'I have now got something else to think about.'

Simon: No doubt, but you will forgive me, I am sure, for seeming rather pressing. It isn't that I want to make you uncomfortable at all but, after all, this is what I have come here for and it is not much use making reports to the British Government if I don't understand what the reports mean, you see. Let us take Greece. Did Greece do any wrong in defending her own territory? Surely not. I mean, Germany has got no quarrel with Greece. But before Greece was invaded, Greece was informed publicly that Germany had no quarrel with Greece.

Hess: An entirely nonsensical idea that at any point we thought of retaining Greece.

Simon: If Germany is to have the sphere of interest over the Continent, she is to have the sphere of interest over Greece.

Hess: When I say 'sphere of interest', what I wish to imply is, in the future England is not to concern herself with what goes on in Europe if it comes contrary to German policy. Or form coalitions against her on the Continent. In the same way as we do not mix ourselves up in the domestic affairs of the British Empire, in the same way it is required that Britain should not mix herself up in the domestic affairs of Europe.

Simon: But there seems to be a difference. The domestic affairs of the British Empire are British. Are all the domestic affairs of the Continent of Europe German?

Hess: No. That's not what we're asserting, and neither do we have the intention to trouble ourselves with the details in those countries, such as England does with the Empire.

Simon: I made the observation that it might be that the affairs of the British Empire were domestic affairs, but I wanted to ask whether all the domestic affairs of the Continent of Europe are German?

Hess: No, not at all.

Simon: You see, I can't help feeling a little that this phrase about the sphere of interests on the Continent is rather a little vague.

Hess: The German people wish to be assured that England will not mix herself up in the affairs, in a general sense, of any European country.

Simon: I see. Do you know, Herr Hess, whether the Führer has communicated to Italy these ideas and Italy has consented to be under the authority of Germany?

Kirkpatrick: He's changed it. In the first question he has changed 'Germany' to 'the Axis'.

Simon: Oh, I see. Would you mind reading it?

Kirkpatrick: *In order to prevent future wars between the Axis and England there should be a definition of interest spheres. The interest sphere of the Axis is Europe, and England's sphere of interest is the Empire.*

Simon: I beg your pardon. I saw you alter it but I didn't realise what it was. Then perhaps it is that Italy is to have her sphere of influence in the Balkans. Italy perhaps is to have her sphere of influence in Greece?

Hess: This is a matter which has to be resolved between Germany and Italy, but anyway England must not get involved. May I point out that there were times in English history when that was self evident. That was the time of Gladstone and Lord Salisbury, who kept themselves out of it – and those were very happy times. Will you please translate?

Int: In which connection?

Hess: That they did not interfere in European history.

Simon: You are making reference to the policy of Mr Gladstone?

Hess: Yes.

Simon: I would recommend to you a history of the year 1878 and there you will find out all about the Bulgarian question.

Hess: Well, those may have been questions of detail, but certainly not in the same way as England is now interfering. And the wars which came about between Germany and England came about only because England interfered in European matters in such ways that it would lead to war. That cannot be contested. The world war came about, or rather the war between England and Germany came about because England had alliances on the Continent, and now it is the same. I don't know if Lord Simon has understood this.

Simon: Yes, I know what you want to say about Lord Salisbury. Well, I will, of course, most faithfully report what you have said, Herr Hess, and I am very glad to have been available to receive from you the account which you have given, because you wished to speak to somebody who represented the British Government and it happened to have been me and I am very glad because we have met before. I will certainly report all this.

Hess: The day will come when England will be forced to accede to these conditions.

Simon: Yes. But I don't think, if I may say so, that that particular argument will be very good for the British Cabinet because, you know, there is a great deal of courage in this country and we are not very fond of threats.

It may be a difference between the German mentality and the British mentality.

Hess: You should not take it as a threat. It was not intended as a threat, it was intended as an expression of my own opinion. We should have to come to these terms only with the difference that it would be done after the expenditure of an enormous amount of treasure, the loss on both sides of irreplaceable lives, materials, tonnage, which was particularly valuable to us, and the industrial plant and buildings of all kinds. Not to mention prestige.

Simon: Yes, I see. Well, in any case I will report faithfully what Herr Hess has said to me and that, I think, is really what we met for.

Hess: I want to thank you very much for coming.

Simon: I was very willing to come. We both of us want to do, I feel sure, what is the best thing for our two countries, and for my part I am very, very sorry that this immense grave event should have brought efforts for peace to nothing. You must not ask me to agree whose fault that was, but I am very sorry that efforts for peace failed.

Hess: *Darf ich bitten das zu Übersetzen?* ['May I ask for the translation?']

Simon: I am very sorry that affairs are complicated, but you must not ask me to agree as to where the blame lies.

Hess: I didn't quite understand this.

Kirkpatrick: He is not quite able to share your opinion as to the responsibility for the war; this is a matter about which one has to have different opinions, but he is sorry that the war did break out between the two countries, and that the efforts at the time to preserve the peace were in vain.

Simon: May I just ask one or two things? Well, now, am I to understand that includes German South-West Africa?

Hess: Yes, all German colonies.

Simon: Because sometimes the statement has been made that the German claim did not include South-West Africa. I am authorised then, by you at least, to say to General Smuts [the South African prime minister] that it does include German South-West Africa?

Hess: Yes.

Simon: Very well then.

Kirkpatrick: And the Japanese islands as well?

Hess: Not the Japanese Islands.

Kirkpatrick: All the colonies except the Japanese Islands.

Hess: But now I still have several things to say which is for the Cabinet, but which I want to say to Lord Simon only. May I do that?

Kirkpatrick: He would like to add something alone to you.

Simon: But that will have to be done very slowly.

The conference broke up at 5.30 p.m. The officers from MI5 collected their witness, having been mindful not to permit Hess to speak to him. When Hess was left alone with Lord Simon, the self-control he had displayed over the past three hours dissolved. 'He repeated to me his fear that he was being poisoned. He asserted that noises were deliberately being made at night to prevent him sleeping. He thought he might be assassinated.' Simon was abrupt and insisted that he behave like a 'sensible brave man' and banish such 'nonsensical ideas'. Stung, Hess immediately pointed to the courage required to make such an arduous solo flight to Scotland. Simon changed tack and explained that he was in the care and protection of British officers and that such an accusation was an insult to their honour. However, as his tone changed so did that of Hess who 'hinted that it was an unseen hand in the kitchen' of which he was afraid.

The subject of honour was raised that evening when Hess asked Dicks to give his word that there were no attempts to poison him. Once Dicks agreed and the pair shook hands, Hess 'demolished a whole dish of cake' and, like Oliver, asked for more. Relieved the conference was now over, Hess was 'somewhat arrogant and truculent' and accompanied Foley on his evening stroll with a distinct strut in his step. Had he been aware of the manner in which his 'diplomacy' had been viewed, his feet would have frozen in mid-air. Kirkpatrick described it as 'a Mad Hatter's tea party'.

In his written report to the Prime Minister and the Foreign Secretary, Lord Simon wrote: 'At the request of the Prime Minister and of the Foreign Secretary, I saw this man on Monday afternoon. The interview lasted for 2 hours, Hess doing most of the talking.' (It was in fact three hours, from 2.30 p.m until 5.30 p.m.)

Simon had already studied the reports of earlier conversations between Hess and the officers guarding him, and this, along with his own interview, led him to certain conclusions:

> 1. Hess has come of his own initiative. He has not flown over on the orders or with the permission, or previous knowledge, of Hitler. It is a venture of his own. If he achieved his purpose and got us to negotiate with a view to the sort of peace Hitler wants, he would have justified himself and served the Führer well. When

he contemplates the failure of his 'Mission', he becomes emotionally dejected and fears he has made a fool of himself. I see no reason to infer that he fled from Germany in fear of his life.

2. Hess arrived under the impression that the prospects of success of his 'Mission' were much greater than he now realises they are. He imagined that there was a strong Peace Party in this country, and that he would have the opportunity of getting into touch with leading politicians who wanted the war to end now. At first he asked constantly to see Leaders of the Opposition, and even imagined himself as likely to negotiate with a new government.

He is profoundly ignorant of our constitutional system and of the unity of the country. He has constantly asked to have a further meeting with the Duke of Hamilton, under the delusion that *der Herzog* (German for Duke) – perhaps because of his rank – would be the means of getting him in contact with people of different views from the 'clique' who are holding Hess prisoner i.e. the Churchill Government.

He now realised that there is no Opposition to which he could display his wares, and hence made elaborate notes for the exposition of his 'Mission' with much detail and emphasis, to me.

Why has Hess taken on himself this extraordinary mandate? The main reason, I feel sure, is that his position and authority in Germany have declined and that if he could bring off the coup of early peace on Hitler's terms, he would confirm his position as Hitler's chief lieutenant and render an immense service to his adored Master and to Germany.

Hess is quite outside the inner circle which directs the war: he does not, apparently, know anything of strategic plans: his sphere of authority is that of party management . . . It is clear to me that Hess's 'plan' is his genuine effort to reproduce Hitler's own mind, as expressed to him in many conversations. He would never dream of making proposals of his own. Hess said emphatically that this was so. He has had in mind the carrying out of his 'self chosen mission' ever since the downfall of France, and he has 'always enquired of Hitler what were his conditions of peace, as to be sure that nothing was changed.'

After the loss of the Battle of Britain at any rate, it is easy to believe that Hitler might be content, at this stage, with the Continent of Europe. One proof that Hess is merely trying to reproduce what he has heard from Hitler is that Hess breaks down as soon as he is asked for more details.

To my mind he is not at all in the condition when he could keep up a 'bluff' of acting independently when really acting on instructions. There is nothing whatever in his bearing or manner to suggest a cool cold mentality of a clever agent. His value is that he is trying to reproduce things that Hitler has said to him about conditions of peace that would satisfy Germany. And it may be that Hess's sudden appearance with this cudgel of an olive-branch discloses that Germany is more uneasy than he pretends.

Churchill, meanwhile, wrote:

I have read the Guthrie-Jonathan transcripts which seem to me to consist of the outpourings of a disordered mind. They are like a conversation with a mentally defective child who has been guilty of murder or arson. Nevertheless, I think it might be well to send them by Air in a sure hand to President Roosevelt. Pray consider this. They are not worth cabling, but people have to go from time to time from here to Washington.

I see no sufficient foundation for Mr Guthrie's assumption that Jonathan is in fact reflecting Hitler's inner mind, although no doubt he gives us some of the atmosphere of Berchtesgaden, which is at once artificial and fetid.

I do not see any need for a public statement at the present time, and meanwhile Jonathan should be kept strictly isolated where he is.

8

Whistling in the Dark

At five o'clock in the morning on 12 June, with sunlight filtering through the apple trees and the camp at rest, the curtains of Hess's room were thrown back and the window heaved open, and so began a better few days. 'He is still in a better frame of mind, talkative and truculent. He stayed up again till 23.00 and had a long walk in the garden after dinner,' recorded Camp Commandant Scott.

The following day was glorious, with the temperature hitting the high seventies and the morning dew glistening in the grass. After breakfast Hess moved into the garden where, after first removing his jacket lest it be spattered with mud, he embarked on a little light digging in the flower beds. So contorted and ham-fisted were his attempts that it led Scott to conclude 'it was very obvious that he had never held a spade before'. After lunch, exhausted by his labours, he retired to his room for a lie-down, but rose around four p.m. to sit on the terrace. The next evening he requested, and was provided with, a bottle of whisky – with the seal intact -- and was in so cheerful a mood that his 'companions' noted his laughter on two separate occasions.

It was laughter in the dark. A touch of hilarity and emotional high before the fall. As soon as he downed the first small glass, Hess 'knew' the whisky had been tampered with and the seal cunningly replaced. He could feel his mood collapse. The next day, Saturday, 14 June, saw the laughter subside. It was a 'morose and silent' man who now sought solace with an enema. Hess's bowels had long been a source of fascination to him. He had read the pioneering work of Dr Kellogg, the American nutritionist who bestowed upon the world the cornflake, and appreciated that the classic, healthy stool should be brown, firm, and possess no more odour than a warm biscuit. The drugs on which he believed he was force fed had left him constipated and, while usually he preferred to loosen them by aid of a laxative, on this occasion he favoured the anal sluice. For three-quarters of an hour he fumbled in the bathroom, with what Commandant Scott described as 'his new toy' and on emerging 'he professed not to be relieved'.

His bowels still clogged and his mind now cloudy, Hess retired to bed with a sedative and a small amount of whisky and hot water, having first asked Dicks if the two substances were not incompatible. At a quarter to one in the morning, he began to shout for the guard. Smith was the senior officer on duty that night and found Hess sitting in his dressing gown and pyjamas in the sitting room. He 'looked drawn and pale, eyes sunk deep into his head'. In a state of extreme nervousness, Hess was incomprehensible, his English garbled and confused. Smith explained that he spoke German. Hess said that he had come to know and trust Malone, that he feared he might not live through the night, and so wished to give certain last letters to him. Smith told him that Malone was a soldier like the rest of the guard and, as such, was on duty and could not leave his post. He offered to do anything that Malone could do. Hess could trust him.

When Dicks arrived and confirmed Malone's alternative duties that night, Hess said he knew he would break down within the next 24 hours.

'You, Doctor, know it – You know it!'

Then he shouted, 'Your instructions are from somewhere not to help me!' He pleaded to be taken to hospital. Dicks, unable to make any progress, left him with Smith. Hess said he trusted all the members of the guard, but that he was 'in the hands of the secret service'. He was being poisoned, and there was nothing Smith or any of the others could do to stop them. From experience, Smith was aware that a 'pompous' tone went down well with Germans, and so he replied sternly that Hess's life and security were in the hands of the Brigade of Guards and '*ipso facto* secure'.

Hess replied that he, Smith, was unaware of what was going on, which angered Smith who insisted that, as the adjutant, he knew exactly what was going on; that 'Germans are not the only efficient soldiers', and that the Guards had the 'fullest control over all that went down here'.

Hess then changed tack and said he would like to drink some whisky, but that what had been brought to him the night before was poisoned. Smith tried once again to explain that no poisoning had taken place, but dispatched the duty officer to wake the house staff and fetch a new bottle of whisky. While waiting for the fresh bottle to arrive, Smith decided to pour himself a glass. Horrified, Hess clung to his arm and begged him not to risk his life.

When the new bottle arrived Hess opened it, poured himself a large glass and drank it down. He then went back to his bedroom and returned with a medicine bottle on which he had drawn a skull and crossbones in pencil, containing whisky. He presented the bottle to Smith and asked that it be analysed in secret, but that it was imperative that Dicks know nothing of what they were up to. Smith agreed, but as soon as he was handed the bottle he took off the cap and swigged it down, deaf to Hess's 'loud protests'.

'After which we had a long and muddled argument centring round this certainty on his part that he was being got at in every way. As the hour was growing late I got more and more tense. I told him that with the exception of the three officers and the doctor who attended on him, there was no person in the house other than selected soldiers from the Coldstream and Scots Guards Regiments. He contradicted that, whereupon I told him in German parade ground terms that I would not be called a liar by him. I do not permit this. Is it understood? Smith shouted.

Hess jumped to his feet and apologised, shaking Smith's hand, at which point the guard ordered him to go to bed and 'sleep peacefully'. He duly went, and within half an hour was, according to the Provost Sergeant, asleep and snoring.

In the morning Hess refused to speak to Dicks and instead demanded to speak to the Commandant on the grounds that he required an immediate transfer to a hospital. So concerned was Dicks by Hess's behaviour that he wrote a memo asking that Colonel Rees return to assist in his diagnosis and treatment:

'In my opinion, the patient's mental condition is now very serious. It may be that this crisis, in which he is undoubtedly suffering from persecutory delusions and is of unsound mind in the legal sense will go over, only to recur more seriously still. I consider that he is in need of skilled mental nursing and is not fit to continue living under present conditions if his recovery, and even safety from impulsive acts of self-injury is to be hoped for.'

When Second Lieutenant Malone returned to duty later that day, Hess shook him by the hand. Malone listened while 'Z', as he referred to him, stated that he was being poisoned on the instructions of a 'small clique' anxious to prevent his peace mission. Churchill knew about his torture, but the remainder of the Cabinet were unaware. Lord Simon had convinced him that the Cabinet were willing to negotiate for peace. The guard officers were being hoodwinked. No steps that they could take for his safety would defeat the machinations of the anti-peace clique. Malone protested that such a thing might be possible in Germany but not in England; and spent some time exploring the endless ramifications of such suspicions.

'He had an astute answer to every objection and argument, and indignantly repudiated my suggestions that he based his surmises on his experiences of methods used in Germany, but, as an afterthought, instructed me to go to Germany on his behalf at the end of the war to tell Himmler from him that, if such methods were in fact being used, they were to cease immediately.'

Hess explained that the drug used was of Indian origin and was administered through his food or medicine. One of the cooks was involved in the plot. He expressed great sympathy for 'poor Mr Smith' who had foolishly consumed his whisky.

What would you make of it if Mr Smith survived, asked Malone. Hess replied that he could only ascribe his own condition to the pills which the doctor had been giving him to make him sleep, but which had had the contrary effect. He then fetched a one-ounce bottle filled with whisky and an envelope filled with pills and asked if Malone would have them secretly analysed. So that the world might know how he had been done to death, he explained.

He then produced two letters in unsealed envelopes and addressed in pencil to 'Heil Hitler' and to his wife, Ilse. Would Malone dispatch them through official channels as soon as he was dead? He knew the letters would not go through, and also needed Malone to take charge of duplicates so that he might deliver them personally at the end of the war. Hess also handed him his wallet containing all his photographs of his son.

Malone said he would have to report to his superiors that he had been handed the duplicates as well as the originals. He couldn't conspire with an enemy prisoner regardless of how sympathetic he was to his plight. Hess begged that he keep them secret 'in the interests of humanity', but Malone pointed out that as an officer he could not honourably do so. However, he would ask permission to retain them and, if this was not granted, for the letters to be returned. In a fit of exasperation Hess flopped back in his chair, stamped the floor with one foot and 'flapped his arms about on the chair arm'. He then resigned himself to Malone's compromise.

In an effort to ease Hess's feelings, Malone said he was quite sure that he would be well soon enough and look back upon this episode and realise how mistaken he had been. However, 'Nothing I could say appeared to make the slightest impression.'

Hess then had another idea. Might one of the guard officers be allowed to buy a dose of luminal at the local chemist shop, then keep it in his possession and administer it as and when he required it? This way he would be able to circumvent the doctor and obtain some much needed sleep. Malone said that the problem with this 'solution' was that if Hess took the drug from the guard officer and still did not sleep, he would simply conclude that the guard was now in league against him. Nonsense, said Hess, the correct interpretation would be that the underlying drug he was being force-fed was so powerful as to neutralise the effects of the additional luminal.

And so the pair danced deeper into the maze.

During their conversation, Malone noted that a part of Hess was well aware that his mental balance was disturbed, and that he could describe in detail the symptoms which led him to believe that his nerves were being systematically 'destroyed'. He begged to be taken to a hospital for treatment and said how well he had felt back at the barracks in Scotland.

When it came time for Malone to leave with the letters, Hess had a sudden change of heart. No sooner had the door closed on him than he rushed to it, pressed his face up against the grille and shouted after Malone. Could he please have the letters back, it was useless for Malone to hang on to them if he had to report the matter. Malone duly handed them back.

Later that morning Malone returned again to see Hess, who now asked him to go to Germany after the war and inform his people that he 'died the death of a brave man'. Malone promised that, in the unlikely event that anything should happen, he would, of course, carry out Hess's wish. Then, in an effort to move off such a morbid subject, he steered the conversation to aeroplanes and was rewarded with immediate engagement. Hess's mood lifted and he became quite cheerful, even suggesting that Malone fetch a chess set – though he said, diffidently, that it was a good many years since he had played. (Malone noted in his report, '. . . and apparently forgetting that by his own reckoning there wasn't much time in which to improve his knowledge of the game, so imminent was his "death"').

Malone asked if there was any other game Hess might wish to play. The German suggested *Mühle*, then sat down to draw a diagram of how it was played.

While Malone and Hess were positioning their chess pieces, Foley was downstairs composing an urgent communication to C. In it, he reported that Hess's mental state had deteriorated seriously over the past 48 hours, and he advised C to press for an immediate visit from Colonel Rees. He stated, 'Jonathan refuses to speak to the medical officer and has informed him that he will have nothing to do with anyone in the building.'

Foley was frustrated, teasing out actionable intelligence which was, for the moment, blocked by the subject's behaviour: 'It is obvious,' he wrote, 'even to us laymen, that he is very ill. Under these conditions, we are precluded from doing any useful work from our angle.'

Forty-five minutes later, he sent a second report:

> 'At 10.15 this morning, Jonathan put on his uniform and asked to speak to the Camp Commandant, to whom he had three requests:
>
> 1. That he be allowed to speak to Lieutenant Malone.
> 2. That Dr Guthrie (he mentioned him in his official capacity) be asked to remove him without delay to hospital.
> 3. That the Camp Commandant procure luminal and phanodurm for him, but without the knowledge of the medical officer.

C briefed Cadogan at the Foreign Office, who wrote in his diary: 'C came in about Hess, who's going off his head. I don't much care what happens to him. We can use him. There is a meeting tomorrow between Winston and Simon about him at which I hope to be present and to get decisions on how to treat him and how to exploit him – alive, mad or dead.'

As the sun set, Hess could no longer fight off the darkness which now consumed him. He wrote two notes – to judge by the dates, one before and one after midnight – and left them on the night table:

Please give my uniform to the Duke of Hamilton, who may be good enough to send it to my family in peace time.

RH 15.6.41

I shall win the pure war of nerves (special sirens etc); I cannot win the chemical war against my nerves, especially as its end is not been foreseen. This means of defence are lacking to me.

RH 16.6.41

9

Into the Darkness

The atmosphere in Mytchett House on the evening of 15 June was 'very tense and charged with misgiving', according to Dr Dicks. Before midnight he made a late visit to Hess, who was in bed, and urged him to take sleeping tablets in order to secure a good night's rest. Sleep did not come. To his interrogators his mental disorder was a locked box, one that must be picked to access any fruitful intelligence. To Hess the view was reversed: a man unable to control his mind was liable to say anything, even treasonous truths. He was now resolute in his decision. He would not succumb to their poison, but would instead slip away into the darkness. He would escape, the only way he could, and in the uniform of an officer, a gentleman, a Luftwaffe pilot.

Sitting on his desk table were two cream-white envelopes from W.H. Smith. Folded inside them were two letters, written in pencil on stationery marked 'British Royal' and addressed to the two great loves of his life:

> My Führer,
>
> My last salute concerns you, for in the last two decades you have fulfilled my life. After the 1918 collapse you made it worth living again. For you and also for Germany, I have been reborn and allowed to start once more. It has scarcely ever been granted to men to serve such a man and his ideas with such success as

those subordinate to you. My heartfelt gratitude for all that you have given me and meant to me.

I am writing these lines in the clear knowledge that there is no other way out, however difficult this end may be. I commend my relatives, including my aged parents, to your care. Through you, my Führer, I salute our Greater Germany, which has progressed to an unexpected size. I am dying in the conviction that my last mission, even if it ends in my death, will somehow bear fruit. Maybe my flight will bring, in spite of my death or even through my death, peace and understanding with England.

Heil mein Führer!
Your loyal
Rudolf Hess

He then added five lines from Goethe's poem *Das Goettliche* to the letter:

According to eternal, iron, great
Laws
Must we all
Complete the cycles
Of our being.

The second letter was addressed to Ilse:

My dear All,

Since I am forced to put an end to my life, all my last greetings and thanks for what you have meant to me. The final step is nearing, my thoughts are with you, but there remains no other way out.

I have fully committed myself to a great idea – fate has willed this end. I am convinced that in any event my mission will bear fruit. Maybe, in spite of my death or because of it, peace will be the result of my flight.

These pages will also be a last salute to my friends, to the General and to Gerl and son. For you and Buz and my parents, the Führer will provide.

With all my heart, your remembering,

Rudolf

He then appended a final line:

> *Sooner or later we all have to die. Honour to the one who dies for a great idea!*

Among his papers he had also completed his note to his son 'Buz', written over the past four days and detailing his flight to Scotland. It now ended with the words:

> Buz! Take notice. There are higher, more fateful powers which I must point out to you – let us call them higher powers – who intervene, at least when it is time for great events. I had to come to England to talk about an agreement and peace. Often we do not understand these hard decisions immediately; in time to come their meaning will be clearly understood.

Hess decided to act in the pre-dawn darkness.

At 3.55 a.m. Hess, still dressed in his pyjamas, went to visit the duty officer. He told him that he was not sleeping well, and had him fix him a small whisky, with which he returned to his room. Five minutes later the guard heard him once again shout for attention. As Hess was standing well within the darkness of his bedroom, the guard did not see him, but heard him call for the immediate attention of the doctor. The guard passed on the message to the warder, who walked along the narrow corridor to Dicks' bedroom door. Bleary from sleep, and in no mood for another round of Hess's childish behaviour, Dicks marched along the 30 feet in dressing gown and slippers.

While he was still a few feet away the guard unlocked the wire mesh door that separated Hess's bedroom from the short hallway. With the door now open the guard stepped aside to allow space for Dicks to pass. It was then Hess launched his escape bid for oblivion. Bursting out of the shadows, meticulously dressed in his full air force uniform and polished black leather flying boots, he dashed through the open door, across the hall and towards the oaken banister. 'The expression on his face was one of extreme despair, his eyes staring, his hair dishevelled,' noted Dicks, who thought that, given the antagonism between doctor and patient, Hess had violence against him in mind. Dicks prepared to tackle him when, at the last second, Hess swerved and hurdled over the banister.

As Dicks watched Hess's left leg strike the oak rail and his body begin to hurtle to the floor 25 feet below, he also spotted a greater danger: a sergeant coming up the stairs, holding a hot cup of tea for his colleague on the watch. He dropped the cup, which clattered to the ground, and drew his revolver. Dicks only just managed to shout, 'Don't fire!'

There then followed a scuffle of heavy boots on the carpeted wooden stairs as both guards and doctor thudded down in pursuit. Hess's fall had been broken by the handrail of the lower flight of stairs and he now lay in a crumpled heap. He tried to sit up, pointed to his thigh and shouted, 'Morphia, give me morphia'.

The thud of a heavy body on a hard, tiled floor had awoken the house, and from every door poured members of the household: officers, orderlies, and members of the inside guard. In seconds, Hess was surrounded by uniformed men with guns drawn, yet the domestic help soon pushed through this barrier, anxious to bring him pillows, blankets, and the English antidote to any trauma – the inevitable cup of hot sweet tea.

Meanwhile, Dicks took his pulse and blood pressure every few minutes, monitoring Hess in case he had sustained any internal injuries. It was apparent that he had fractured the femur of his left leg and, between grimaces of pain, he chastised himself for foolishly failing to realise that the lower handrail would break his fall and save his life. 'His reactions were a curious mixture of schoolboy interest, with annoyance at having failed in his attempt and a certain desire to manage other people,' recorded Dicks.

Foley telephoned C to explain that the doctor was anxious that Hess be treated by a specialist surgeon, but before any treatment could be administered, Foley had first to secure permission from C to bring in another outsider. Brigadier Menzies signed off on the request, so Lieutenant Colonel Scott immediately ordered the adjutant to drive to Cambridge Hospital and collect Major J.B. Murray. A call had already been placed to ensure that the Major was on standby. Under his calm reserve and military training, Scott was calculating the cost to his career had his prisoner's plan succeeded.

During the wait Hess, now propped up with pillows and a woollen blanket draped over his body, continued to demand morphine in a manner that grew increasingly shrill. Foley told Dicks that he was now permitted to administer the drug, but the doctor was cautious, fearful that such a powerful painkiller might mask crucial symptoms or signs of internal injury. Instead, he planned to wait until the specialist arrived and carried out a thorough examination. For half an hour Dick tried to humour Hess, but as the shock wore off the pain increased. Foley and Scott, who recorded the injection in their later reports, thought Dicks did eventually administer a dose of morphine. In fact, it was merely distilled water that he had used as a placebo – an ineffective one at that – for minutes after the 'injection', when no effect was evident, Hess began to complain even more loudly about being swindled out of his chemical solace. Then, when it was apparent no drugs would be forthcoming, he gritted his teeth and calmed down. Dicks noted, 'This period of waiting for the surgeon revealed the fact that his mental state had become one of resigned calm and a quiet friendly co-operation with his helpers.'

Major Murray, a fellow of the Royal College of Surgeons, arrived at five a.m. and, after a careful examination of Hess, administered the first genuine dose of morphine. By now, drugged and exhausted, Hess succumbed to a 'childlike' trust in and co-operation with Major Murray, although he was briefly roused and displayed vocal chagrin when the surgeon cut off his prized breeches in order to access his broken leg. In any normal circumstance the patient would have been dispatched to hospital, but Murray agreed to perform the surgery in Hess's bedroom. While waiting for the arrival of a mobile x-ray unit and the necessary medical apparatus, Murray splinted the leg temporarily, after which six Guards officers heaved Hess back upstairs on an army camp bed used as a stretcher.

After a few hours' sleep, Hess awoke to see Bill Malone on duty and sitting by his bed. He asked for water, but when Malone reached for the bottle of water on the night table, he insisted it be drawn from the tap. He inquired about the health of Mr Smith, who had sampled his poisoned whisky, and Malone remarked that he was fine. Hess then raised the subject of the suicide note to his family.

'I was certain that I was on the verge of a complete and lasting nervous breakdown. I had seen the onset of this nervous trouble and I knew what it would end in. It all began with the glass of milk ten days ago. The second attempt was two days ago, by means of the whisky – either that or the pills were much more successful – and the reaction was so severe that for a time I knew I was completely out of my mind.'

He explained that a third attempt on his sanity would take place soon, rendering him completely insane. When Malone asked if he had genuinely tried to kill himself, he replied, 'I certainly did and I still will. I cannot face madness. It would be too terrible for me to bear, and for others to witness. By killing myself I would be acting like a man – I know that of late I have been behaving like a woman.' He said that ever since his arrival at Camp Z he had got up every morning at eight, 'but then came the period of no sleep, no sleep, no sleep. I began to go to pieces under the influence of drugs.'

Malone asked him about the promise he made to Hitler not to kill himself, but Hess replied that, on his word of honour, he had made no such promise and that he had merely written that in the knowledge that it would be seen by the British authorities and so stay the hand of those who wished to kill him by means of a staged suicide. He added that, should he succeed in killing himself, the German authorities would assume he had been murdered and take swift and violent reprisals against British prisoners of war. When Malone left the room, he reported the conversation to Scott.

At dawn, C called Sir Alexander Cadogan and briefed him on the suicide attempt. In the Cabinet meeting, Lord Simon reported on his interview with Hess. Afterwards, Cadogan successfully managed to persuade Churchill not to make the incident public:

'(I) rode prime minister off his idea of announcing the broken thigh – which wd. be simply silly. He agreed that in regard to H mum's the word.' Cadogan ended his diary entry, 'That's what I wanted . . . and I will now get on with my propaganda.'

Colonel Scott's report stated that 'Z's case has now definitely become one that can only be dealt with by trained mental specialists from an asylum. As I have previously reported to you, I cannot subject the young officers to the strain and responsibility of sitting with a patient who is insane. Apart from his two medical orderlies, now arrived here, no one in this camp is used to the diabolical cunning shown by a patient of this sort, or who are trained in the various methods whereby one can defeat the objects of a madman determined to commit suicide.'

Colonel Rees was at a conference in Ireland when he was contacted with the news of Hess's suicide attempt, and immediately flew back to London.

At five p.m. the x-ray van arrived and by seven p.m. Major

Rigby, the radiographer, had traced the fracture to the left femur and also discovered a crack in the thoracic vertebra. Surgery, however, was delayed until after Rees had arrived and had had a chance to speak with Hess. He arrived at eight o'clock, but the patient refused to speak to him until he had received relief from his swollen bladder.

Hess was unable to urinate and demanded a catheter be passed through the tip of his penis so as to drain his bladder. He would not speak to Rees until the procedure had taken place. While Rees agreed to his request, Dicks was of the opinion that such a procedure was unnecessary. Water retention was common after an accident and in time the bladder would void itself naturally. Hess, however, was adamant that the cause lay not with his crashing fall, but with the Veganin tablet Dicks had fed him earlier. Rees, frustrated by the bickering, told the surgeon to begin the operation.

At 9.45 p.m. Hess was anaesthetised with an injection of sodium pentothal, then Major Murray fitted a large steel Steinmann pin through the shin bone. The leg was elevated in a frame and 35 pounds of weights attached to the pin to maintain steady traction on the thigh and gradually straighten the fragments of bone. The operation ended at midnight, when a second x-ray revealed that the severed portions of bone were now correctly aligned.

Once roused from the anaesthetic, Hess again demanded that he be fitted with a catheter. Dicks refused. Hess then demanded to speak to Colonel Rees and Colonel Scott, believing that they would order Dicks to perform the procedure. When Dicks relented, a scene out of a risqué Charlie Chaplin comedy ensued. The doctor chose a soft, gum-elastic catheter but, as he prepared to force it into the urethra, Hess insisted that first the tip of his penis be rubbed with cocaine so as to anaesthetise it. Exhausted after being up for 21 hours, Dicks lost patience. There was no cocaine available in the house and, besides, the catheter tube was soft, pliable, and unlikely to hurt. Hess then felt Lance-Corporal Everatt, the male nurse providing assistance, grip his arms tightly so as to hold him in place, and Dicks began to force the catheter into Hess's penis. It was then that Hess began to scream, 'Help! Help!'

As Dicks wrote: 'Once again, scenting further drama, the denizens of our house of mystery poured from all the doors, with myself torn between my duties to the patient and my wish to reassure a group of officers who had been already considerably upset by the day's incidents, and their narrowly averted prospects of unpleasant courts of enquiry and displeasure in high places.'

Dicks managed to calm them down with a joke. (Sadly, the joke by a doctor called Dicks about the penis of the world's second most famous Nazi has not been recorded for posterity!) After the guards departed, Dicks turned on Hess in a rage, shouting, 'Aren't you ashamed of yourself? You, the second man in the German Reich, causing us all this trouble and bellowing like a baby; I shall do nothing further to relieve your bladder.'

Hess claimed he heard Lieutenant Atkinson-Clark, an officer of the guard who had come to assist Dicks shout, 'We are treating you the way the Gestapo treats people in Germany.' Atkinson-Clark insisted he merely said that they were 'not the Gestapo'. Whatever was said, Hess fell silent, the doctor, corporal and lieutenant left the room and, in time, he passed water naturally.

Lieutenant Colonel Scott's diary for the next day, 17 June, reads:

'He remained quiet during the day. Capt. Barnes had lunch with him. At 20.00 Z sent a message down to say that he refused to eat any meals unless an officer had his meal with him. No notice was taken of this request and Sgt. Waterhouse later reported that after several refusals to eat anything he eventually relented, asked for dinner and made a hearty meal of soup, fish and a sweet. Major Foley reported that he had had instructions from London to let him read *The Times* daily. This is the first occasion on which he has been allowed any news.'

*

England was enjoying a hot, sultry summer, but Rudolf Hess was not. The heat, combined with the extreme discomfort of his leg, elevated on a rack of weights, made sleep even more difficult than before. In the small hours of Wednesday 18 June, he awoke after just two hours sleep and asked the orderly (who now sat in his bedroom round the clock) if he might have a whisky. When the orderly turned around to fetch a little water to dilute the drink, Hess snatched up the bottle and tried to glug it down neat. Deep, sonorous groans were now the soundtrack of the bedroom.

Lieutenant Colonel Scott met with Hess, who lectured him on the various reasons why Dicks was intent on his murder. Scott told him that he was talking nonsense and had insulted the British Army, but Hess was persistent. He asked the Commandant to fetch him atropine, but without the doctor's knowledge, saying that it was his duty to thus protect him. When Scott asked him who in the camp he actually trusted, and suggested Major Murray, the surgeon, Hess was dismissive: 'He's only a surgeon. He knows nothing of my . . . interior economy.' He was then asked if he trusted Colonel Rees, and when, surprisingly, Hess said he did, Scott said that this was fortunate as he was visiting at three p.m.

Rees had a kindly bedside manner. He would listen and smile and nod his head while scratching notes on a pad. Hess felt safer talking to him than anyone else, but Rees was aware that it would not be long before the crooked finger of suspicion would fall on him, too. During their conversation, Hess pointed out that if his food continued to be poisoned he would have no option but to go on a hunger strike. Rees replied that this would be unfortunate as no one there had any desire to force feed him using a nasal drip – but do so they would.

'As is usually the case, his delusional ideas centre on different people at different times. I gather that on Sunday last it was the officers of the guard whom he suspected, whereas on Monday when I talked to him the Intelligence Officers and Major Dicks constituted the gang who were driving him to insanity. I was regarded as his one hope, but probably now I shall be regarded as in the plot also since I was, of course, unable to accede to all his requests for precautionary measures in connection with drugs.'

Rees concluded: 'There is no doubt, therefore, that Hess's mental condition, which was somewhat masked before, has now declared itself as a true psychosis (insanity).' Rees suggested at first trying sleep treatment or, later, when his leg had mended, 'electric convulsion therapy'. During the past month both Rees and Dicks had attempted to pin down Hess's emotional and mental history, searching for signs of an earlier disturbance, but he had been successful in shutting them down:

'Although Hess is secretive about most of his history it seems clear that there must have been similar attacks of this mental trouble previously, though probably they have been more marked this time owing to his circumstances. Hess may therefore be a mental patient on our hands permanently.'

Rees praised the decision to permit Hess access to news, which he thought 'very wise' on the grounds that it could make him more co-operative and even biddable – though to judge by his reaction to that day's edition of *The Times*, it was by no means a certainty because now, the battle between Hess and those who wished to engineer his destruction was far more engaging than the wider war. As Rees prepared to leave, Hess noted that his eyes flashed red and the smile fell from his face. The time it took the Colonel to cross the room and exit was all it took for Hess to realise that he too had been turned. He was alone in a house full of enemies.

Downstairs, Rees briefed Dicks on his immediate impression and suggested that he stay in place for at least the next two weeks in a hope that the addition of news would bring about some kind of breakthrough. Like a baton passed between two exhausted runners in an endless relay, it was now Dicks' turn to trudge back up the stairs, where he was surprised to discover Hess in a more communicative mood than usual. Hess had figured out the cause of his dilemma: a secret drug of Mexican origin had been used to influence key figures in the house, including, he confided, Colonel Rees. It was this drug that was compelling them to 'subject him to slow torture'. Dicks marshalled all his patience and understanding and, slowly and quietly, explained that the manner in which he was thinking was a well-known form of mental disturbance, which everyone who had so far examined him, agreed was the case. Could Hess not agree that his theories were 'fantastic?'

Lying back on his pillow, Hess said he only wished it were so, that it would be a relief to him to believe such a diagnosis as he would genuinely like to establish friendly and trusting relations with all the staff. Since he liked them personally, it was the collective desire to 'torture' him that he could not tolerate. So, sadly, he could not agree with Dick's view.

'We agreed that all methods of torture, mental or physical, were beastly, and he said that if he were spared, he would devote his energies to bringing about a universal renunciation of secret police methods. He repudiated the suggestion that such methods were practised by his friend Himmler, or subordinates whose honour he trusted.'

Feeling that he was making some progress Dicks offered, as a concession, that one of the guards would always take meals with him 'out of the common pot'. Further, that he would neither give, nor cause to be given, any medicine or injection in the hope that this might abolish his fears. Hess readily agreed, saying that he would even endure insomnia for the good of the experiment and that he liked the idea of companionship during meals. 'I had my evening meal with him and he ate well,' noted Dicks. 'He was friendly and contented.'

The new treaty lasted almost four hours. Hess, having stared at the ceiling as long as he could, finally cracked and called for one of his sleeping draughts. The next morning the new mood of détente continued: while Major Murray adjusted his splint, he said that he was 'taking a risk' and tucked into porridge, toast and a glass of milk.

There then followed two days of departures. On 19 June, Captain 'Barnes' (Baker) had a final lunch with Hess before returning to MI6 headquarters. The next day Colonel 'Wallace' (Kendrick) returned to the Military Interrogations Centre at Cockfosters, leaving Major Foley as the sole representative of Military Intelligence.

Scott noted in his diary, 'Z at his own request has been cut off all medicines and drugs and is very much better for it. It appears that his fear of poison in the drugs given outweighed any effect they should have had.'

The suicide attempt and its traumatic aftermath had left Hess spent. It was as if the madness had been burnt off in one fiery act, leaving him dozing in the embers. On 19 June, Foley found him to be having a 'good day', during which he spoke reasonably, read *The Times*, played chess, and ate without hesitation.

Outside of Camp Z both the British public and the rest of the world were anxious for news. With none forthcoming, rumour and speculation mounted with unhelpful results. In America, as the British Consul-General in New York, a Mr Campbell, was at pains to make clear, the Government's silence over Hess had triggered rumours that a peace deal between Britain and Germany was now in preparation:

> The cessation of all news of the whereabout of Hess, the decision of the Prime Minister to make no public statement, the secrecy of Winant's [the US Ambassador] visit to Washington, the temporary suspension of air-raiding by both sides and the private visit of Kirkpatrick to Ireland, have combined in the public mind to create out of the Hess case a series of steps towards a negotiated peace. Considerable use has been made by unfriendly people, including such an influential person as Herbert Hoover,

> of opportunities for speculation or rumoured inside information. At the same time there has been evidence of friends of the allied cause being adversely influenced and discouraged by this series of coincidences. The most serious result has been the introduction into the minds of some industrialists of doubts as to the advisability of vast plant expansion lest this rumoured peace negotiation should prove a reality.

While explaining that such rumour and speculation was only circulating by private conversation, Campbell explained that there was an 'undefinable' but widely held feeling of apprehension and uncertainty that was fertilising the 'soil of German propaganda'. He felt most strongly that such a miasma of doubt over Britain's fighting spirit should be removed immediately, and that 'all possible steps be taken to dispel any misconception that His Majesty's Government entertain the slightest intention of reaching a negotiated peace with Nazi Germany'. The point should be beaten like a drum 'on all suitable occasions regardless of repetition'.

'Hess is no more mad than Crippen, Judas Iscariot or Satan.' So declared Major Vyvyan Adams, the MP for Leeds West, to the House of Commons. The fact that his diagnosis, impassioned and eloquent though it proved to be, was based on nothing more than a perusal of the daily newspapers, combined with a default setting that meant if German propaganda declared it day he would instinctively retire for the night, was exactly the point of the debate. Why had the British Government refused to release any information about Hess's arrival?

The debate on 19 June had been instigated by the MP for Nelson and Colne, Mr Sydney Silverman, who had been frustrated by the Prime Minister's previous refusal to answer his question, 'whether he can now state the results of the investigation into the purpose of the arrival in this country of Rudolf Hess; whether Hess brought with him any proposals indicating how the problems of Europe might be solved?' Winston Churchill had replied that he had no statement to make 'at the present time' and had rebuffed each supplementary question with 'I have nothing to add to the answer I have given.'

In opening the debate, Silverman pointed out that conflicting statements had been issued by Cabinet members. The Minister Without Portfolio, Arthur Greenwood, had said, 'When a man occupying such an important official position in the Nazi hierarchy as Hess flees his country and puts himself in the hands of the enemy, it looks as though all is not well on the German home front. Disunity, doubt and disillusionment are growing, and will continue to grow within the German Reich.'

In contrast, Herbert Morrison, the Minister for Home Security told his constituents in Hackney, 'Hess, Hitler's right-hand man, is, like the rest of them, a brutal thug, whose hands, like his master's, are stained with some of the worst political crimes of modern times . . . This gangster is now in our hands. He is going to stay in our hands. It does not matter what kind of animal he is: whether he is Rat Number 1 or a Trojan horse, or just a baby panda sent over in the hope of finding innocents over here to play with, he is caged.'

If the Minister Without Portfolio viewed Hess's arrival as a crack in the edifice, the Minister of Labour, Ernest Bevin, disagreed, and asserted that he had been dispatched with his leader's blessing: 'I do not believe that this gentleman came here without Hitler's knowledge.'

The fact was, as Mr Silverman made clear, there were no facts, with the only statement of genuine interest being made by the Lord Provost of Glasgow, Sir Patrick Dollan, who in a newspaper interview headlined 'Hess – The Truth' explained that the Deputy Führer had arrived to meet with certain individuals or groups, whom he did not wish to name, and had planned to fly back two days later.

While Sir Patrick was shy on naming names, Major Adams,

when it was his turn to speak, narrowed the focus to the landed gentry. It was his belief that Hess had come to Britain to 'debauch our aristocracy' and with proposals designed to attract those who favoured peace at any price:

'There is such a mentality, and it is mainly to be found here and there in the corners among the well-born and well-to-do, those who have more money than sense, those who whisper the dangerous fallacy, "Better defeat with our possessions, than victory with Bolshevism," which is exactly what Hitler wants them to say.'

Adams insisted that 'appeasement is not dead among those whom I may call, for the purpose of rough convenience "the Cliveden Set"' – an expression, he conceded, which was as historically convenient and geographically inaccurate as the 'Holy Roman Empire'.

At the heart of the debate was a suspicion that Hess had brought plans to negotiate peace and, whatever they might be, the British people deserved to know. For, as Mr Silverman pointed out: 'This is not the Government's war. They are not bearing the brunt of it . . . The great burden, the tragedy, the misery, the suffering, and the cost are borne by the vast multitude of our countrymen. Do not despise them, do not distrust them. Do not think that you are entitled to mother them and coddle them and wrap them round in cotton wool.' He continued, 'There are many people in this country who believe, rightly or wrongly – the Government will not yet let us know – that Hess arrived here with a definite plan for peace. I would like to ask the Government a direct question: Is that the case or not? Can there be any reason for not telling us?'

The debate in the House of Commons raised the question of whether Hess, who had just been permitted a newspaper, should be allowed to read *The Times*' coverage of his own fate. Major Foley's view was clear: 'He will, I assume, argue that his peace offer is being withheld from the people by the clique. On the other hand, if *The Times* is withheld, he will suspect something more sinister. On balance, I am inclined to think we should allow him to read *The Times* and observe the reaction.' It was relayed to Foley that Sir Alexander Cadogan had agreed with his view and the newspaper was passed on to Hess.

As Foley reported a few hours later, Hess was 'Interested and amused at having a column of a parliamentary report to himself. Asked to be allowed to keep it. He regretted his broken leg had not been reported in the press.'

If *The Times* sometimes amused Hess and sometimes bored him, he also had a desire to read more widely, while also enjoying a broader view through pictures. So he put in a request for a weekly illustrated paper such as the *Sketch*, *Illustrated London News* or the *Tatler*. The request was supported by Dicks on the grounds that it would 'a) provide a pleasant distraction and b) because it would make less call on [Hess's] concentration.'

C wrote back in green ink: 'I have approved of his having the *Tatler* or *Sketch*.' A fortnight later, however, and after being mildly disturbed by his image of the Deputy Führer chortling at London's most recent debutantes, and how best to improve one's strawberry jam, Foley voiced his concern that, 'The *Tatler* is too silly, and is more liable to induce contempt than admiration for British life.' Instead, he recommended *Picture Post* or *Illustrated London News*, as publications heavy with pictures required less concentration. As he explained to C, 'My object is to make him more amenable to intellectual intercourse and subtly to foster opportunities for us to introduce various subjects in which you are interested.'

Six RAMC orderlies were now dispatched in pairs to monitor Hess in three eight-hour shifts that ran continuously around the clock, seven days a week. Each orderly kept a meticulous note of the patient, as evidenced by Lance-Corporal Everatt's report on 21 June: 'On taking over at 05.45 hrs Patient had had a fairly good night. Awake and talking until 06.45, he then slept until 07.15 hrs, passed urine 20 ozs and slept fitfully until 09.10 hrs. He then had toilet and treatment to pressure points. Did not want any breakfast. Spent the morning reading. Visited by MO [Medical officer, Dicks] at intervals and visited by Major Murray at 11.00 hrs. States he feels comfortable, but would like something to occupy his mind. Has been very cheerful this morning, passed further amount of urine.'

The next day, the rumble of tank engines began on a front that stretched two thousand miles as Hitler unleashed the German invasion of the Soviet Union. When Major Dicks told Hess, he uttered but a single enigmatic phrase: 'So they have started after all.'

10

Jagged Thoughts and Treacherous Suspicions

The book at bedtime for Rudolf Hess was the memoir of Sir Neville Henderson, the British Ambassador to Germany from 1937–1939. Henderson had believed more could be achieved with Hitler with a pat than a firm hand and, in February 1939, he cabled the Foreign Office that, 'If we handle him right, my belief is that he will become gradually more pacific. But if we treat him as a pariah or mad dog we shall turn him finally and irrevocably into one.' As Hess lay in bed, with his broken leg raised in a steel frame and the windows open to allow what little summer breeze there was to pass through the blackout curtains, he found his spirits raised with each page of *Failure of a Mission: Berlin 1937–1939.* So certain was he of Germany's success that he announced to the duty officer watching him read that he had now decided he would rather return to Germany than accept the governorship of any of the victorious Reich's new colonies.

The next evening, Saturday 13 July, Hess's ebullient mood ballooned further as he dined from a tray on his lap with Bill Malone, who was smartly dressed in his 'Blue Patrols' (for which he received a sartorial compliment). The subject of Unity Mitford began the conversation: Hess told the story of how she chased Hitler around Germany before shooting herself in the 'English Garden' at Munich upon the declaration of war. The doctor who operated on her was a personal friend of Hess and had assured him that she would be 'quite insane for the rest of her life'. From Mitford they moved to music.

Top (left to right): Goebbels, Hitler and Hess in SS uniform.
Bottom left: Rudolf Hess in 1933.
Bottom right: General Karl Haushofer, whose prophetic dreams inspired Hess's flight.

Hess indulging the passion for flying he had picked up during World War One.

David McLean, the ploughman who discovered Hess after he parachuted onto Bonnyton Moor, south of Glasgow.

The remains of Hess's Messerschmitt Bf110 on Bonnyton Moor, guarded by soldiers and police.

Dr Albrecht Haushofer, a brilliant scholar and poet and a talented diplomat who would write to the Duke of Hamilton at Hess's request.

Group Captain the Duke of Hamilton, who became the unwanted focus of Rudolf Hess's 'peace mission'.

Opposite, top: The House of Secrets; Mytchett Place, or 'Camp Z', as it was known, was Hess's home for one year.

Opposite, bottom: An aerial photograph of 'Camp Z', taken in 1941 during Hess's residence.

Sir Ivone Kirkpatrick, the Foreign Office's expert on Germany. He was the first to interview Hess after his arrival.

Anthony Eden, the Foreign Secretary, in conversation with Ivan Maisky, the Russian Ambassador to Britain.

Frank Foley, the brilliant intelligence officer who tried to unravel Hess's secrets.

The Lord who came to call: Lord Simon, who was viewed as an appeaser, was chosen to represent the government in talks with Hess.

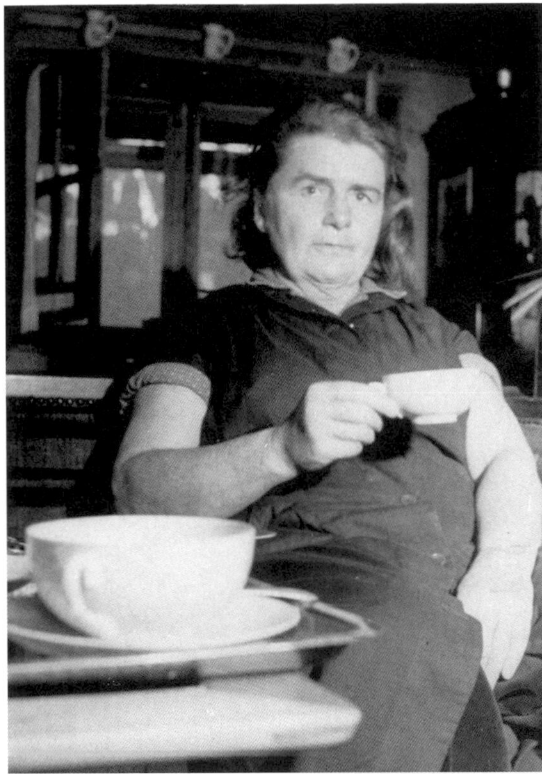

Isle, Hess's wife, in 1958.

Judgement at Nuremberg: Hess (*second from left, third row*) sits beside Hermann Goering.

Although Foley had previously reported Hess's lack of interest, Malone was keen to record that Hess was quite the aficionado who regularly attended concerts in Berlin, and was even aware of the bad echo that plagued the Albert Hall in London. (Before his suicide attempt he would press his ear up against the window to hear Beethoven played on a record player in the officers' anteroom.) Then from music, and with scarcely a missed beat, they moved to the Mass. Although the Roman Catholic faith was on the rise in Germany and Hess admitted to being more religious than most Nazis, he insisted that Germany would soon sweep away Christianity 'as being only a Jewish fable and replace it by a new German religion'. The pair spoke of Sir Oswald Mosley, leader of the British Union of Fascists, whom Hess had met, but admitted that he had not seen enough of him to form an opinion.

What had begun with Unity Mitford ended with *maquillage.* Was it because men like it, enquired Hess, that women in England used so much make-up? It was a feature he had always noted when meeting an English rose in Germany. The female ATS driver who drove him from hospital in Scotland had worn none. Was this, he asked, an army regulation?

Over a few hours the following afternoon, Malone struck up a revealing conversation with Hess, one recorded by the microphones for MI6 and by Malone's own pen that evening for the Camp diary. Hitler, explained Hess, was a great admirer of Britain, one who mourned the current conflict and who had stayed his hand as long as possible. He had capitulated to the persistent demands of the military to bomb England only after the British had bombed Germany. The Führer's affection for England was predicated on meetings with British friends, as well as with the Duke of Windsor, whom he considered to be 'the most intelligent prince he had ever met'. Germany was simply in the bull's eye of the British cross hairs on account of its rise to become the dominant power in Europe. Britain, insisted Hess, had throughout history always waged war on Europe's strongest power – as a close examination of its relations with Spain, the Netherlands and France revealed. Churchill, he said, 'worked unceasingly behind the scenes before this war to engineer the means for the destruction of Germany'. The Poles had been dragged into the war through the behaviour of the British. Polish diplomats had told the German Foreign Ministry that they had been willing to discuss the corridor to Danzig, but that the British had dissuaded them.

Propaganda, pronounced Hess, had been Britain's principal weapon during the First World War. It had done more to break down Germany's resistance than the blockade and was achieved by 'Socialists and Jews'; and it was specifically to prevent a repetition that the German Government had forbidden the public to listen to British broadcasts. According to Hess, German morale was incapable of withstanding defeat; it was, he said, 'A fatal flaw in the German character.' The British could accept defeat, which made them superior. He commented that now Germany had numerous victories under her belt, it might be possible to allow the public to listen to the BBC.

The current propaganda produced by Britain was poor by comparison to that achieved in the previous war, Hess said. He explained that when the British Ministry of Information was bombed, he had jokingly complained to Goering that this was a mistake, so important was it to the German war effort. However, he did admit there had been slight improvements and asked Malone if he knew the identity of the men who broadcast to Germany. Malone, in turn, asked Hess who was the real Lord Haw-Haw. The identity of William Joyce, the Irishman hanged for treason after the war, but who broadcast nightly from Berlin, was then a closely guarded secret. Hess said he didn't know, but then impersonated Lord Haw-Haw's distinctive delivery by declaring, 'Where is the *Ark Royal*?' This was a reference to one of Joyce's broadcasts when he – mistakenly – claimed that the aircraft carrier had been sunk.

There was one piece of propaganda to which Hess took exception: the idea that the Gestapo was behind the assassination attempt against Hitler at the Burgerbrau beerhall in November 1939. Had the hand behind the bomb belonged to the Gestapo, there would have been a more reliable timing device than two alarm clocks which, in turn, detonated the bomb seven minutes after Hitler had departed. Hess said he believed the would-be assassin, Georg Elser, was linked to two MI6 officers, Stevens and Best, who were ambushed on the Dutch border by Gestapo officers who had lured them into a trap by impersonating Generals unhappy with Hitler. 'Z inferred [*sic*] that they were not sufficiently important to be executed for their activities, which he seemed to think were puerile,' wrote Malone.

Like a verbal game of tennis, accusations of atrocities were batted back and forth. The average German soldier believed his British counterpart to be ten times as vicious. Red Cross planes were shot down on sight by the British, while lifeboats riddled with bullet holes and stacked with corpses stood as testament to Britain's disregard for the convention of rescuing sailors. The 'Rules' had been torn up when the British mined Norwegian waters. Malone pointed out that Germany had sunk hospital ships; Hess said he didn't believe it. He agreed that Polish priests had been shot, but they had been guilty of espionage. He conceded, however, that in 'political morality' Britain was fifty years ahead of Germany.

He said the Tommy guns cradled by his guards were disadvantaged because their high rate of fire made it difficult to maintain supply, but that their tremendous noise and its demoralising effect made up for this. 'The Führer is a great believer in the demoralising effect of noise,' and as a consequence demanded sirens be attached to bombs so as to maximise their terror.

The Communists Hess had battled against in his youth had been vanquished by the Nazi policy of constructing vast factories equipped with showers and recreation facilities: 'The workers realised what we had done for them.' He denied that Germany's pact with Russia had served to encourage Communism, 'because the German people understood Hitler's reasoning in making the pact. They knew he wanted to avoid encirclement, and they were perfectly aware of Britain's efforts over the previous six months to persuade Russia to come in with her.'

When the pair returned to talk of Christianity, he said Hitler had religious feelings but believed Christianity was alien to the German people. Hess believed in a hereafter, but not in a heaven including a God that resembled an old man with a beard. The new faith that would emerge in Germany would require 'externals and rituals' still to be devised. Stalin, he said, was mistaken to have eradicated religion without constructing a suitable replacement, and he believed it was the Nazi's hostility to Christianity that had prevented the Vatican from coming out in support of Germany's invasion of Russia.

The problem of the Jews for Hess, or plight for Malone, had a solution, Hess said. Hitler had 'decided to banish all Jews from Europe at the end of the war. Their probable destination is Madagascar.' The island off the coast of Africa was part of the French colonial empire, and in 1940 the German Foreign Office drew up plans for their eviction.

On the merits of leadership Hess praised Chiang Kai-shek as honest and dependable but dismissed the Japanese as untrustworthy, and with their eye fixed on Australia. Regarding Germany, he criticised Von Ribbentrop as too recent a Nazi, who would never succeed Hitler even if the Führer, Goering and himself all died. When asked whom he would like to meet in England (excepting, of course, the King and the Duke of Hamilton), Hess said General Sir Ian Hamilton, whom he had met before the war and whose memoirs he had not quite got around to reading. As the shadows of evening fell across the room and Malone's shift drew to a close, Hess, perhaps in tribute to his interlocutor's accent, announced plans to build a country house in Scotland and so asked for books on English country house design.

Hess's suicide attempt prompted a reassessment between Lieutenant Colonel Scott, Major Foley and Colonel Rees about the advisability of keeping Major Dicks in place. In the end they concluded that he should be replaced with a younger, 'rather less valuable' RAMC psychiatrist, though he should remain on standby should future crises warrant his presence.

His replacement was Captain Munro K. Johnston who, after 18 days, produced a medical report on Hess that diagnosed paranoia:

> He exhibits a marked persecutory delusional system. He distrusts those in attendance on him, and is convinced poison of a subtle kind is given in his food and medicine. He claims this poison affects his brain and nerves and is given with the intention of driving him insane. He explains his attempted suicide by saying better to kill himself than become mad. He regards this act as a noble one, and since the injury he sustained enforces a long period of inaction, without any further pressing necessity to justify his presence in this country, he is temporarily complacent and well behaved.
>
> On recovery from his injury, the danger of suicide will again become imminent, and the present superficial appearance of improvement is not indicative of any real progress. His moody introspection and the recent lengthy written statement he produced, with its bizarre ideas of persecution and torture and its quoting of witnesses and proofs are pathognomonic of Paranoia. In my opinion the prognosis is bad and he requires the care and supervision necessary for a person of unsound mind with suicidal tendencies.

In bed and trussed up with his leg in cast and sling, Hess was more conversational and, according to Foley, 'more disposed to examine the English point of view'.

MI5 had learned that a group of seventeen Polish soldiers, in collaboration with two British officers, were intent on tracking down Hess's location with a view to extracting revenge for the invasion of their native land. On Monday 7 July, Colonel Coates and Colonel Hinchley Cook of MI5 visited Camp Z to brief them on the details of the plot. 'Code words were agreed upon as warnings that the suspects had left their present location.' In response to the threat, patrols were withdrawn at night to inside the perimeter wire and 'steps were also taken to guard against the possibility of a heavy car being driven at the double gates, which would not have been strong enough to withstand such an attack.'

Hess meanwhile was hard at work on a long memo with the top note, 'I should be grateful if this memorandum would be given in translation to the Duke of Hamilton.'

The following day, he requested paper and envelopes so that he might write to his family. When he asked Major Foley what had become of the letters he had written before his attempted suicide (kept and scrutinised by MI6), Foley said that as suicide is a crime in Britain the letters had been sent to a 'higher authority' and would be kept as evidence, an explanation Hess was happy to accept. Later that day Hess wrote to 'MY dear all!' explaining that he had settled down to the idea that 'I am, in practice, a prisoner of war', yet one who enjoyed a more elevated standard of living: 'I must be pleased – with the prevailing heat – that I can live out in the country and have a garden with beautiful flowers at my disposal.' He said that his English had improved and praised the treatment by his dietary doctor in Munich, for he was now able to eat with impunity: 'This is particularly welcome . . . where one is given a lot of sweets, cakes etc.' As if to reiterate what he had so recently put down in print, the following evening Hess went so far as to send his congratulations to the Camp cook for his 'most suitable' diet.

Foley, meanwhile, had been working on persuading Hess to broadcast to Germany:

> He is ready to read his own script, provided the [British] authorities – the higher authorities – agreed . . . He told me he had been

> thinking things over and had slowly come to the conclusion that suspicion of those appointed to look after him was probably unjustified and that it came from his own psychosis. He then went on to say that someone had suggested to him that his fear of us was based on his experience of Gestapo methods. He denied strongly that there was any cruelty or torture in German concentration camps and prisons. He had visited them. He knew the Führer also was decidedly opposed to such barbaric practices. I happen to know a great deal about concentration camps and I have probably met as many victims as anyone. But I pretended to have only an academic and detached knowledge and let him speak.
>
> The strange thing is that one gained the impression that he honestly believes his own opinion to be the true one, and that he is genuinely opposed to the infliction of suffering and cruelty. We know from previous statements that he will not take part in blood sports of any description. His own anxiety has been so acute that he is interested in putting an end to any kind of cruelty, even in Germany if it is proved to exist.

During their discussion Hess asked Foley to produce evidence to support his claims of the abuse and murder of Jews.

'He went so far as to say that he would accept the evidence of a Jew of credibility. There must be many Aryans and Jews who could say much. I suggest that these two conversations are not without importance as they may be made to lead to the first serious stage in destroying his faith in his friends, provided we are able to convince him that he had been deceived and cheated by them, even in this matter.'

There were, said Foley, a number of reports or documents exposing the true nature of the camps: 'We could produce actual victims whose testimony would be even more effective. I am thinking it must be possible, progressively, to convert him into an active instrument of propaganda against Hitler if he is proceeded with quietly and gradually. I would thank you to be good enough to consider plans on these lines and to direct me if you agree.'

The only current documentation the British Government had to hand was the Atrocities White Paper, and although the authenticity of one section which had been passed on to Kirkpatrick was in doubt, it was nonetheless passed on to Hess.

Foley had seen the horrors of the German concentration camps. He had visited Sachsenhausen, the camp north of Berlin, to free Gunther Powitzer. This young man ran a car hire business, but was transferred to the camp after serving an eighteen-month prison sentence for 'race defilement' – a law Hess had helped draft – because of getting his non-Jewish girlfriend pregnant. Foley's cover as an MI6 officer in Berlin was in the passport control office of the British Embassy in the Tiergarten from where, each day, he bent the rules, issuing exit visas to as many Jews as he could. After *Kristalnacht* in 1938, he and his wife frequently hid Jews in their home overnight. Kay Foley said one man would leave a rose as a thank-you gift, and recalled that while some escaped, others were less fortunate: their wives would be called to the Gestapo headquarters to collect their belongings, only to be handed 'an envelope containing ashes'.

He had recently received a letter from Hans Friedenthal, the former President of the German Zionist Organisation, congratulating him on the CMG he had received for his service in Norway: 'You, my dear Captain Foley, have always stood for me as a representative of British freedom . . . We Jews have no order to award, but we have a good and long memory and you may be assured that the German Jews will not forget how often you have helped them.' In reply, Foley thanked Friedenthal and offered his solidarity: 'I am sorry to read of the immense amount of suffering your people are experiencing in Europe. The Teutonic beast is never satiated: the only solution is extermination. We in this country are working hard to that end and the time will come when they will plead for mercy. I hope that those who have suffered so much will be heard and revenged.'

*

Foley's hope that testimony to the suffering of the Jews might be the key to unlocking Hess from Hitler's hold was short-lived. After carefully studying the Atrocities White Paper, Hess wrote an appendix to his own 'Statement and Protest', which dealt with the 'alleged witnesses of alleged treatment' of prisoners in German concentration camps. He promised that, when he returned to Germany, he would launch an investigation to determine whether the facts described in the papers had been carried out by 'sub-leaders' against the 'will of leaders'. The evidence presented by Foley also included a book, 'written like a novel', by an inmate of an Austrian concentration camp. Hess then devoted the next five paragraphs to listing the abuses suffered by National Socialists interned in 'Arrest Camps' in Austria. He pointed out that 'with the exception of common criminals' the only people in concentration camps were Communists who had spread their vile political philosophy by 'word and deed', and that whenever Communism attains power it is followed by 'dreadful terror accompanied by the most bestial tortures'. He listed abuses in Hungary where priests had had their hats nailed to their heads, eyes gouged out, nails torn off, and stated, 'I am sorry to say Jews were nearly always responsible.' He explained that there was always an 'outcry . . . as soon as it became necessary to defend oneself against Jews'. Hess continued:

'I shall not undertake the investigation (I wish to emphasise the point) because of the curious treatment I have received in England, or because England desires it. As British subjects are not concerned, I refuse England the right to deal with the question of the treatment of prisoners in Germany. Otherwise I have to ask for the same right for Germany. Germany would then have to make it her business to investigate the English treatment of the Irish in Ireland, of Indians in India or Arabs in Palestine, etc.' The English concentration camps of the Boer War were once again referred to before his concluding sentence repeated that 'Germany has never sent women and children to concentration camps.'

A few days later, on 11 July, Churchill was briefed by C that Hess had shown signs of improvement, but was still stubborn with information:

> It has been found impossible to have free discussion with him on that Russian situation, and directly any military matter is touched upon, he either says that he knows nothing of such problems or complains that he is too tired to pursue the subject . . . He has also made a request to be provided with evidence of our contention that atrocities have been committed in Concentration Camps, as he denies hotly that anything of the sort has taken place. (The Foreign Office is producing the necessary documents.)
>
> Another request he has made is that he may see the pronouncement made in Germany after his arrival in the UK, and on this point I am awaiting the direction of the Foreign Office. In my opinion, it may definitely throw doubts in his mind regarding the complete confidence which he alleges Hitler has in his motives for coming here, and it will touch him on a sore point when he discovers that he was not to be regarded seriously in view of his physical condition.

What did Hess know? It was a question Foley asked himself daily and to which he still did not have an answer. In conversation, Hess was robustly confident about a German victory but, given recent newspaper reports, this should not have been so. The MI6 officer was concerned that Hess's confidence was pinned to his knowledge of what hidden armaments Germany now possessed but had not yet used. In his mannerisms and behaviour, Hess had the appearance of a man with secrets: 'He seems to have something on his mind which we have not fathomed.'

As Foley's report explained, 'We have been impressed by his absolute faith in a German victory in spite of the articles he has read in *The Times* about the British air offensive, the Russian situation, increased British production strength etc. We have been asking ourselves whether his faith is based in particular on knowledge that Germany was developing a new weapon which could be used with effect on some densely populated areas of England, or in some secret with regard to himself and his mission outside the statements he has made.'

For Foley it was Hess's silence that 'interests one more than his talk,' and Fortune now sent him a lever with which he hoped to prise open the strong box Hess so cautiously guarded. On 17 July, Second Lieutenant M. Loftus reported for duty. He was the son of a Member of Parliament and his mother had met Adolf Hitler before the war. Foley had suggested to Loftus that he use the family acquaintance as an easy introduction to 'gain his confidence and perhaps unseal his lips'. He suggested that Loftus offer Hess a bottle of Rhine wine as a tonic, and to indicate in a vague way that his family had been impressed by what they had seen in Germany. Conscious that each conversation would be recorded, Foley stated for the record, 'I wish to stress this request, as it would be unpleasant if the reader of these recordings should think that some of the sentiments and thoughts which were expressed were true and genuine . . . They were part of a scheme.'

The scheme began when Loftus joined Hess for lunch. The officer brought a copy of *Life* magazine with a picture of Hess standing alongside Hitler at the Reichstag. The caption, for which Loftus apologised, explained that the picture was taken six days before Hess 'deserted from Germany'. However, Hess seemed more upset at the pictures of the bomb damage to Westminster Abbey, which occurred during the heavy bomber raid on the night of his arrival in Britain. Looking at the historic rubble, he said that if the war continued neither Germany nor Britain would have any fine buildings left. When Loftus pointed back to the picture of Hitler and Hess at the Reichstag, and asked which of the two men he preferred, Hess laughed and replied, 'the Führer'. Loftus asked if Hess had already made up his mind at the time of the meeting to fly to Britain, and Hess replied it had been his intention as far back as Christmas. He said he had tried twice before but was forced back by bad weather. He spoke of Haushofer's dream in which he saw Hess alone in the sky, and added that the General had had a second dream prophesying his return.

When the conversation moved on to the paranormal, Hess admitted he believed in predestination, second sight and ghosts. Loftus asked why he had tried to kill himself, and he answered because he was afraid of going mad. He had flown to Britain to stop the war, and after he failed, he had begun to feel that he was deluding himself and that in Germany he was already considered mad. So – he then promised not to try again.

Loftus said that for anyone who believed in a 'personal star' it was a 'silly' thing to do. Hess agreed, adding that such a fate didn't fit with Haushofer's vision of his return flight. He then said, rather sadly, that if only he had been able to contact some influential people, together they could have stopped the war.

Loftus asked if he were sure Germany would accept Hess's proposals. Hess said that Germany is the Führer, before embarking on Hitler's passion for peace. On Russia, Hess said that invasion had long been Hitler's plan and was formulated during the writing of *Mein Kampf*. On Britain, he said the decision to invade rested with Hitler, and if he did decide to invade he would succeed.

Jokes were swapped about Goering, but Hess defended Ribbentrop (despite his personal feelings towards the Foreign Minister) and said that politicians depend on the press for their popularity, while he assured Loftus that Heinrich Himmler, the head of the SS, was 'nice behind his spectacles'. The pair's first lunch ended with Hess taking Loftus over to the wardrobe to show him his Luftwaffe uniform. Loftus couldn't help but notice Hess's eyes, which burned with an intensity he had seldom seen.

In his written report, Lieutenant Loftus concluded:

'I think he is one of the simplest people you could meet and I very much doubt whether he is at all intelligent, but he has what has lifted the whole mediocre bunch to power – that single-tracked blind and fanatical devotion to an ideal and to the man who is his leader. But he differs from the rest of Hitler's henchmen in that he is genuinely religious and sincerely humanitarian. He doesn't doubt for a moment that Germany will win the war and he sees himself building a house in Scotland. His chief interests seem to be skiing and architecture and, like so many Germans, he is a great admirer of our style of living.

'He has left a wife and small son behind him. The wife doesn't appear to concern him but he talks of his son, and told me how hard it was for him not to give the show away when, the night before his flight, the child asked him where he was going . . . I should say his mind is as virginal as Robespierre's.' Then Loftus stated that he could be as lethal an idealist as the French revolutionary had he been equipped with the personality and eloquence. Hess was quite capable of presenting two different faces to the world. To Loftus Hess was 'courteous in manners, has a disarming smile and laughs easily'.

A few hours later Captain Munro K. Johnston, the psychiatrist replacing Dicks, was introduced to his new patient and received a quite different greeting. Hess displayed an attitude of 'suspicion and correct formality' and appeared sick – 'gaunt, hollow-eyed and anxious'. When Johnston commented on how the British laugh at Goering's ostentatious display of medals, Hess said, 'So does Goering!' Hess added that Goering would have been too frightened to attempt his flight to Britain, but Johnston thought he detected Hess's jealousy of Goering's position.

Yet when the Commandant visited Hess on 18 July to drop off a book on English country houses, he noticed a steady improvement in his mental attitude. On 20 July, Scott wrote that, 'He seems to improve every day and one begins to wonder if Col. Rees & Major Dicks were right in their diagnosis that he is "permanently insane".'

As Bill Malone had received orders to report to divisional HQ and take up new duties as DAPM, he made one final visit to Hess who offered him, if not high-grade intelligence, then a thick slice of gossip. Hess explained that the German War Minister, Werner von Blomberg, who had married a young girl in a ceremony witnessed by Hitler and with Goering as his best man, had subsequently discovered that his bride had previously posed for pornographic pictures and had a criminal record. The marriage breached the moral code of conduct for officers, written by Blomberg himself, and when he refused Hitler's order to seek an annulment, he resigned in 1938. Hess compared him unfavourably with Werner von Fritsch, the Commander-in-Chief. Forced out of his position despite his attempts to defend his position against a false accusation of homosexuality made by Himmler, Von Fritsch deliberately walked into a field of fire when visiting the front line in Poland. Hess pointed out that Blomberg did not go to the front.

Malone asked Hess about Poland and Hess explained that he had never visited the country, but said the Polish Ambassador was so convinced there would be a revolution in Germany against the invasion of his country that upon his departure he said to those who saw him off from Germany *Auf Wiedersehen.*

Malone's departure pushed Hess closer to Loftus, with the German eager to take the young officer into his confidence. He explained that he had been visited by Lord Simon, with whom he had negotiated, and even offered Loftus a look at the typed transcription of their meeting.

As Foley reported, 'Jonathan began by revealing the identity of Dr Guthrie and by offering the minutes of the conference which, by the way, the DO [Duty Officer] did not read. It is interesting to read Jonathan telling the DO that the minutes were secret and that he could not divulge the fact that he had been offered them . . . He is sane enough to realise that he was committing a breach of faith . . .'

Loftus's role was two-fold: not only was he to try and draw Hess out, but also, where possible, to drive a wedge further into what

Foley perceived as Hess's faltering conviction about the reliability of German statistics. During discussions, Hess had admitted to Foley that his certainty of German victory was based on figures issued by his Government with regard to the sinking of British vessels by U-boats and aircraft – figures that Foley had tried to convince him were unreliable and artificially inflated by boastful German naval and air crews. While monitoring Hess's conversations with others, Foley believed that 'the reason why he referred to the subject so often was that our assertions have begun to have some effect and that he was beginning to doubt.' When Hess spoke on the subject with Loftus, the officer argued Foley's line.

Loftus had been briefed that Hess was likely to raise the subject of the Duke of Hamilton, which he promptly did, asking again that a meeting be arranged between them. One would have expected a tinkle of excitement to have rippled through Loftus when, on 27 July, Hess leaned over from his bed and whispered that he wished to make a 'secret statement', provided that Loftus did not repeat it to anyone else in the Camp. Instead, the Lieutenant felt 'perplexed' and, in order not to discourage Hess as well as to buy himself time to consult with his commanding officer, he suggested that he speak to his father during his next leave. Hess was delighted. A new route to circumvent his captors had now opened up, leading – so he thought – to a Member of Parliament sympathetic to Germany's position. After Loftus had left, Hess settled down at his desk and began to write.

'We do not know what this statement will be: it may be something quite trivial connected with his mission; the "clique" or his health. It should throw some light on Jonathan's saneness, and that too is important as his leg is healing rapidly and he would discard his splint in four to six weeks time,' reported Foley.

The question of Loftus's discretion was discussed by Anthony Eden and Sir Alexander Cadogan who were concerned in case Loftus might convey anything whatsoever that he 'may glean about Jonathan to his parents'. Foley was asked to confirm that there was no danger of this, and replied that 'Lt. Col Scott, his superior officer, at my request invited him to the orderly room and solemnly reminded him of his oath of secrecy and took from him a verbal assurance that he understood.'

Over the next four days, Hess remained hard at work on his report, stopping for visitors who included Colonel Coates, the Deputy Director for Prisoners of War. Hope, and a fixed task, had raised Hess's spirits, and sense of humour. When Lieutenant Hubbard, the duty officer, grew weary of his complaints at the quality of food and offered him a charcoal dog biscuit, Hess not only ate it, but asked for more. Then, when Major Murray arrived to x-ray his fractured leg, Hess (who was concerned that x-rays could cause sterilisation) made sure to cover his genitals with a metal lid.

While Hess toiled on his essay, Major Desmond Morton, the Prime Minister's intelligence liaison officer, was equally hard at work, reading through a vast pile of transcribed conversations between Hess, Foley and the other officers. He was unimpressed, and sent a note to Churchill on 28 July: 'I am reading all the conversations but have not troubled you with them. They are immensely long and equally uninteresting.'

On Friday 1 August, Hess delivered to Loftus a hand-written fifteen-page document, along with a couple of glucose tablets that Major Dicks had given to him just prior to his suicide attempt. Hess asked for the document to be passed on to the officer's father and the tablets sent for independent analysis. By the time Foley had translated the first page of what was an attempt by Hess to pin down the perpetrators of his abuse, he'd dismissed any hope he'd had of fresh intelligence revelations. The document had a legal feel, was well-ordered, and named 'witnesses' who would, Hess insisted, if forced under oath by the King, substantiate his allegations. Hess began thus: 'As I am conscious that my statements in parts sound fantastic, I have limited myself to cases for which I believe that I am able to submit proof or for which I am able to name witnesses.'

He described in detail the feeling that overwhelmed his body after Major Dicks had administered an unknown drug – 'a curious development of warmth' followed by a rush of euphoria, and a resultant collapse into depression and an 'extraordinary rapid fatigue of the brain'. The drugs had driven him to suicide as he had no wish to be 'displayed to journalists as an insane person'. Of the night in question he said, 'I wrote the relevant farewell letters in complete calm. When during the night it became abundantly clear that the same consequences as before were recurring, I jumped into the well of the house.' While he recovered physically, the same mental symptoms returned but had diminished in strength, which he put down to his growing ability to hide the tablets, that he now wished to have analysed: 'I suspect that the substance concerned is in them . . . But I cannot say for certain. I assume that the substance would be known of in a hospital for nervous diseases. Its presence in the tablets could be determined in a laboratory.'

Hess believed the narcotic abuse had begun immediately after his arrival at Camp Z. He then turned his attention to the Veganin tablets given to him as he lay sprawled in the hall after his leap. Not only had they failed to dull his pain, he said, but they deliberately prevented him from urinating, and when he told Lieutenant Malone of his concerns he was not believed. Only after Malone himself had taken the drug were Hess's fears confirmed, not by anything the officer said but by his reaction. 'He was completely distracted. His features seemed to show that he had suffered badly.' However, explained Hess, Malone had been silenced by Scott, who had ordered him to deny suffering any such ill effects. Since his discovery, the drugged Veganin was replaced with the genuine article, thus preventing him from securing a sample.

Torture by drugs then gave way to the physical variety. He described how his penis was abused by Dicks with the catheter, and how the doctor had deliberately arranged his splint so as to render him in agony for twenty-four hours. In the armoury against him, perhaps the most powerful weapon was neither narcotic nor physical abuse, but psychological. It was common practice for his fear to be magnified by his captors. On the same day, the same question had been put to him by Foley and Dr Gibson Graham: 'Has provision been made for your family in the event you do not return to Germany?' The news of the sinking of the *Bismarck* and the sadistic manner in which he was informed of the death of the captain and majority of the crew, was cruel, especially as they had made no mention that the *Bismarck* had sunk HMS *Hood*, Britain's biggest battleship. 'I cannot avoid the impression that my nerves had to be influenced in a negative sense.'

His sense of isolation had been compounded by the authorities' refusal to allow him mail. Foley had told him that perhaps Hitler had prevented delivery as punishment for his flight, but he refused to believe this and, instead, stated the prohibition on mail and news was 'imposed in order to affect my nerves'. The same reason lay behind their refusal for weeks to allow him to hear gramophone music or listen to the radio.

Towards the end of the document, Hess wrote:

My requests are:

1. That an enquiry be instituted on the basis of my statements. Those entrusted with the enquiry must be given full powers to release witnesses from the pledge of secrecy and to question them under oath; as they are nearly all officers, I presume that only HM the King can give such authority. Those entrusted with conducting the enquiry must on no account be placed under, or receive directions from, the War Office, under whose purview I apparently come, or from the prime minister.

2. That the Duke of Hamilton be given a translation of this statement. That gentleman promised me when I landed that he would do everything to ensure my safety. I know that in consequence the King of England himself has issued appropriate orders. It is for that reason that Guards officers are charged with my protection. May the Duke of Hamilton be good enough to ask

> HM the King of England to place me in every respect under his protection . . . I request that all those who have been charged with my care be removed.
>
> 3. That the representatives of the British People in the British Parliament be informed in proper manner that I appeal to them.

The principal hands behind his torment, he insisted, were Foley, 'Wallace', Colonel Scott and Dicks, while those who could act as witnesses were Rees and Graham, 'Barnes', Atkinson-Clark, Riddle and Malone, of whom he wrote, 'Mr Malone has always been very chivalrous towards me.'

What is interesting about the letter is Hess's perception of his perpetrators and how they had tried to use the idea that he is suffering a psychosis to silence his complaints:

> I have asked myself over and over again how it is possible to reconcile their thoroughly likeable natures with their treatment of me. I am, in fact, faced with a puzzle. I have no real proof, of course, for the suspicion that they are acting under duress, under a powerful suggestive influence or the like. But by their manner, whereby they win and inspire confidence in others, they have succeeded on both occasions when I have tried to complain to visitors, in suggesting to them that I am the victim of an *idée fixe.* In both cases they invited the visitors to take tea or lunch with them beforehand . . .
>
> This was the case with the visit of [Lord Simon] who was so convinced that I was a victim of a psychosis that he stopped my complaint the moment I started. It was the same with Col. Rees, who listened very attentively to my statement on the occasion of his first visit. When he visited me for the second time after, as far as I could observe, taking tea with the senior officers, he appeared completely changed and tried to persuade me that I was suffering from a psychosis.

He insisted Dicks, Foley and Wallace had made a habit of suggesting that all 'my sufferings' were attributable to a psychosis. What is interesting is that Hess said it was as a consequence of this repeated behaviour that he began to simulate the symptoms of psychosis. So had he embarked on an elaborate charade? 'If recently I have given the impression that I myself believed in this psychosis, it was only because it appeared to me that I should obtain more peace.'

He was the innocent victim of 'the most refined system of cruelty conceivable. To torture a man under the very eyes of those responsible for his protection; perhaps even to ruin his health for life, with almost no possibility of proving it.'

In conclusion of his statement, Hess wrote:

> 'Never would I have thought it possible that I should be subjected to mental and physical tortures in England, and that I should be exposed to the cruellest experiences of my life. I came to Britain trusting in the fairness of the British. As a veteran aviator I know that this has been displayed to an opponent time and time again. Since I did not come to Britain as an enemy, there was all the more reason to expect fairness. I came to Britain completely unarmed, at the risk of my life, with the intention of being useful to both countries. I still believe in the fairness of the British people. I am convinced that the treatment I have experienced was not according to their voice. I know too that the King of England himself gave orders for my safeguard and comfort. I have no doubt whatever that only a few persons are responsible for the kind of treatment I have received.
>
> Of course, I shall take care that the German public never hears of my treatment. This would contradict the very meaning of my flight to Britain, which was to improve, not embitter, the relations between our two peoples.

The response to Hess's statement was muted. While Dicks drafted a lengthy rebuttal of the allegation of torture by catheter, he dismissed the remainder of the text in a single line: 'For the rest of the document, this is so obvious that further comment is hardly called for.' Captain Johnston felt that Hess's quoting of witnesses in the text was 'pathognomonic of paranoia', that the prognosis was 'bad' and, as a consequence, Hess would require the care and supervision suitable for a person 'of unsound mind with suicidal tendencies'. Dicks agreed, stating on 3 August that the chance of recovery was 'less than one per cent'. Foley's disappointment was tempered by the news from Loftus that, having dispensed with the personal consequence of his mission, Hess had now embarked on a new document to deal with the politics behind his flight.

On Tuesday 5 August Scott records in the Camp diary: 'Z spent the whole day writing what is understood to be the political side of his mission as opposed to the personal which was the subject of his last effusion. He seemed in a very good mood and chatted with the duty officer at meals.' One of his guards noted that he 'wrote page after page until dinner time. His interest in writing was so deep that he failed to answer when spoken to at times.'

The next day he recorded: 'Z is still writing hard but promises to give Loftus the completed deposition tomorrow.' As good as his word, Hess dutifully delivered the manuscript, which consisted of 45 pages of foolscap paper, to Loftus at four p.m. on 7 August. While Foley immediately started the translation, the guards were alerted to a 'suspicious chap ... Observed taking too much interest in the defences and outer wire.' When the patrol examined the outer perimeter they discovered that a portion by the orchard had been tampered with, and Scott, therefore, instructed that Number 6 post by the gap be manned overnight by two men armed with a Bren Gun.

The second deposition was entitled 'Germany – England, From the angle of the German-Bolshevik War' and contained a note that 'I should be grateful if this memorandum could be given in translation to the Duke of Hamilton.' At one point in the document Hess stated that 'I am partly betraying military secrets by making these statements, but I think I can justify myself before my conscience and before my people. I believe complete frankness may help to stop a senseless war.' What 'secrets' he revealed focused on Germany's invincibility, her burnished breastplate and mighty sword rather than her Achilles' heel.

Hess began by stating that a second 'Versailles' was undesirable and even if Britain should emerge victorious – which she wouldn't – the ultimate benefactor would be the United States. The Reich, he explained, now had a massive stockpile of armaments and ammunition and had benefited from the raw materials sourced from France, and that Hitler was currently achieving victory over Russia so as to dispense with the long-feared 'war on two fronts'. Germany would then turn on Britain, and her U-boats had bases extending from Norway to Spain from which to launch an assault on British shipping. Should Churchill abandon Britain and fight on from Canada he would be leaving the population to be starved out, which would be an inhuman policy, but one which would reflect the nation that killed 26,000 women and children in concentration camps during the Boer War.

A key point of the document was to convince Britain not to underestimate the Russians' capability to become a mighty military power: 'only a strong Germany as a counter-weight, supported by the whole of Europe and by the confidence of England, can avert the danger.' Communism was at risk of growing in the British Empire as 'the dangers increased by the attraction which Bolshevism has for natives of lower standards of life, who have come in contact with European civilisation' [*sic*]. The document was also prophetic when it stated of Russia, 'Unless her power is broken at the last moment, Bolshevik Russia will be the world power of the future, which will inherit the world position of the British Empire.' Germany wished only the return of her former colonies and for Britain to refrain from 'meddling in the affairs of the European Continent', as she had done in the past under William Gladstone and Lord Salisbury.

Foley called in Colonel Wallace to read both depositions, the second of which he admitted 'contained some items of interest'. Foley's view was that 'a good deal of this gives the impression that he is whistling to keep his courage up'.

After producing two lengthy texts in two weeks, Hess rested over the next few days. When he again picked up the pencil it was to write to Ilse, whom he addressed as 'Dear Mutti' (mummy) and asked her to tell the general 'that I am curious to know when the second part of his dream will be fulfilled and when I shall stand smiling in front of him'. He greeted Major Dicks on his weekly visit with folded arms, a signal that he refused to shake hands. The next day, he argued with Loftus over lunch about the persecution of the Jews and the concentration camps in Germany, issuing his standard retort on the women and children who perished in Britain's camps during the Boer War. On 15 August he wrote again to his family, with his thoughts on the battle against Russia: 'My thoughts are not less with the Führer and with the whole nation, especially during this gigantic fight in the East. In great events I imagine the working of destiny. For that reason I am not quarrelling with the loss which destiny has imposed on me personally.'

He also wrote to his former adjutant whose arrest he had heard about:

> Dear Pintsch
>
> Among the rumours, I have heard that you were arrested in conjunction with my flight. I hope and I assume that it is not correct. But if it is the case – which would be very painful to me – I beg you to look upon it as a decision of destiny and as a part of the endeavour which I am convinced had to be made. Whatever the case, I thank you for your loyalty and your silence – otherwise I should not have been able to carry out my flight. I wish you all good, especially if, as I assume, you are at the front.

An insight into what Foley thought about Hess comes in his response to a long letter by Stephen Laird, who had written to the Government with his own thoughts on Hess whom he had known in Germany. Foley praised the letter as the 'most reasonable report' from Germany or a neutral source he had read. Laird wrote that Hess had been 'amazingly open with his friends about the stupidity of the present war' and while Foley said he could not confirm this, Hess's statements in England 'are in harmony with that trend of thought'. Foley said he and his team had asked themselves if Hess was putting on a pose for their benefit, but 'we are inclined to think that it was not and that he had been shocked by what he had seen in Poland and in the West.'

When *The Times* carried a report on the Anglo-American Declaration, Loftus was asked to seek Hess's view, which he wrote down:

> As I [Hess] have been asked to give my opinion on the eight-point declaration of the USA and the English Prime Minister, I make the following statement:
>
> The basis for an understanding between Germany and England, which I gave to the English government with the object of reaching a lasting peace was a very fair one.
>
> The declaration under reference is a kind of answer. It mentions Nazi tyranny. It contains a demand for the disarmament of aggressor nations which, according to Mr Rosevelt [*sic*] and Mr Churchill are Germany and Italy.
>
> As long as a declaration contains insults, I must refuse to make a statement even on a single point of such a declaration.
>
> I welcome it from the point of view of its effect on the peoples concerned. The German people have not forgotten the experiences which they made over a period of fifteen years when they faced, unarmed, their adversaries who retained their arms in breach of the Treaty of Versailles. Those experiences weigh all

> the heavier as Germany was in those days not an alleged tyranny, but a democracy.
>
> Signed: Rudolf Hess.

Camp Z was to undergo a security overhaul as a result of the attempted suicide of Rudolf Hess. The elegant country house was to be fitted with the accoutrements of an asylum. Where previous residents had shopped for antiques and *objets d'art* to decorate the rooms, Captain Johnston embarked on a tour of the latest mental hospitals and returned with a shopping list of requests – including lever plug-pulls to replace chains on the toilet. At a meeting at Hobart House attended by Foley, Rees and Scott, as well as representatives of the Foreign Office and the Department of Prisoners of War, it was agreed that Z should remain in his upstairs quarters (there had been suggestions of moving him to the ground floor) but that his bedroom, sitting room and the downstairs dining room, the only rooms to which he would gain access, should be equipped as in a mental facility with, among other changes, armoured glass, lest in a fit of madness he attempted to leap out the window.

In effect Hess was to be caged, as the report made clear:

> The dining room door at the foot of the front stairs will be permanently closed and the wire netting covering the well of the stairs will be extended to make a passage-way from the foot of the stairs to the drawing room; a door through this will be made, opening inwards. In the garden, wire fences will be erected from the north-west corner of the house to the double gates (leaving the carriage sweep and fire hydrant free). From the SW corner of the house, similarly, a fence will be erected running westwards to the perimeter wire. The area thus enclosed will be all that will be free to Z to exercise. Camouflage nets will be hung on the fences of the inner perimeter so that view is obscured from the outside.

As well as banishing the chain from the toilet, the WC was to be fitted with an observation swing door that would restrict Hess's privacy but keep him within sight of the guards. Yale locks were to be fitted to all doors on the landing and half landing.

Lieutenant Colonel Scott, as Camp commander, was anxious that a demarcation line be drawn on his responsibilities and those of his men. He argued that his role was to prevent Hess from being captured or escaping, not to prevent his suicide. As he had previously reported, 'It seems to me that a definite ruling should be laid down as to how far my responsibility is entailed and I suggest that it should only be so far as to guard against attack from outside and the escape of the patient. The doctor should be responsible to me for his safety against suicide not only within the grille, but also during exercise. I am quite willing that one of my officers should still lunch and dine with the patient who, I think, looks forward to his meals and a chat with the duty officer. But it should be clearly understood that this officer should not be responsible for him during these meals and a medical orderly should be present throughout.'

The meeting agreed to Scott's terms and the budget for the new security measures were estimated at £300.

On 22 August, Colonel Rees submitted a report to MI6, headed *The Future of Z*:

'The documents written recently, which I have seen, confirm the diagnosis that has been made previously of a paranoid state. In my judgment . . . this condition will continue without any real improvement, although there will be times of remission, some real and some apparent, because, as at present, the patient is masking his symptoms. Z will, therefore, be a constant suicidal risk and precautions must be taken. I understand that he will be out of his splint in about two months, and from that moment he becomes a greater risk even though he may not be down and out for another month.'

Yet Scott had another point to raise following Colonel Rees's report: 'There is just one further point which I should like cleared up; this is, if Z is to all intents and purposes certified as insane, what order should I issue in the event of his attempting to escape as regards warders or sentries firing on him?'

Hess, meanwhile, unaware of the upcoming changes to Mytchett Place, was more concerned with the progress made by Lieutenant Loftus in passing the depositions to his parents. When Loftus told him that he was meeting his mother on Friday 29 August, Hess made a point of checking his movements that day by asking the medical orderlies if he could speak to him. At this time, his days swung from good to bad and back again. The banging of a downstairs door, which he believed to be deliberate, appeared to dement him. He would bang his hands on his head, pull at his bedclothes and insist the medical orderly look out the window to discover the identity of the culprit. Yet when the last weights were taken down and the steel pin removed from his leg, he insisted that the event should be celebrated with champagne, which was duly served during dinner. When not concerned about his food being poisoned, he was fussy about its variety, dismissing dinner on one occasion as a 'hash-up' of lunch and refusing to eat it

As late summer turned into a golden autumn, Hess compensated for his confinement to bed by writing to Ilse about the countryside: 'You will, also, of course, be toiling away in the garden and with the cattle. The children will be helping with the haymaking. You can imagine how here the smell of hay reminds me of home. But on the whole the air in England is different from that at home, much softer than in particular with us in the southern districts and also in the Fichtelgebirge.' On 1 September he also wrote to his brother, admitting his concerns for the financial support of his men and how he could help: 'Is it possible that Freiburg [Hess's pet name for his former secretary, Hildegard Fath], to whom I send my best greetings, has not enough money for special expenses, such as monthly payments to his parents, Father Winkler's treatment, etc. If this is so my box can be found in the safe under yours. The key for this is in my cupboard at the top right-hand side of the bedroom. If the key cannot be found, you can force it open. The money is there for disposal. If necessary you can also have recourse to the packets which I have placed in there for my men, in view of the possibility that I might swallow too much North Sea water.'

On Thursday 4 September at two p.m. there was a knock on the door and a guard entered Hess's bedroom with a letter. It was from Lord Beaverbrook, the new Minister for Supply:

> Dear Herr Hess,
>
> You will recollect our last meeting in the Chancellery at Berlin. It has been my intention for some time to suggest that we should meet again and have some conversation. So perhaps, if this meets your convenience, you would tell me when I may come and see you.

Hess wrote an immediate reply:

> Dear Lord Beaverbrook,
>
> I thank you for your friendly lines of September 1 which I received today.
>
> I remember our meeting in Berlin and I am glad of the opportunity of seeing you again.
>
> I take it that the conversation is to be of an unofficial character and therefore is to be without witnesses. I think my English will in that case be adequate. If I am mistaken, I should have to ask you if possible for me to have a German witness present.

Foley was at first unsure about the meeting and pointed out to C that 'I think I should remind you that the Commandant's orders are not to admit anyone to this camp without a pass signed by Sr. A. Cadogan.' This note was copied and sent on to Beaverbrook.

On 4 September Beaverbrook wrote:

My dear Herr Hess,
I received your letter with pleasure.
It was my intention that nobody else should be present when we met, and that we should do the best we could with the English language. Whatever you say will be private. But if you think an interpreter necessary, I agree at once, and we will have a German.
Unhappily I have no understanding of the German language.
Yours sincerely,
Beaverbrook

Two days later Hess wrote back to Lord Beaverbrook, 'I see from your second letter that you consider the proposed conversation to be private and that you will make a trial with my imperfect English. Otherwise Major Foley, who is here, can function as interpreter should any great difficulty arise.'

Authority was granted for Hess to have access to a radio, which involved Foley driving into Aldershot to hire one that afternoon. By evening Hess's living room reverberated to the sound of dance tunes and broadcasts from Berlin, whose commentary on the Leningrad front he translated excitedly into English for the medical attendants. The prospect of meeting Lord Beaverbrook agitated Hess. Although able to concentrate on preparing a lengthy paper entitled *Germany-England from the Point of View of the War Against the Soviet Union*, he would, at times, lose his nerve, and inform staff that such a meeting was impossible in his 'current state'.

On Sunday he listened to the wireless, read *The Sunday Times* and wrote a short condolence note to Elsa Bruckmann over the death of 'the Führer's old comrade', her husband, Hugo: 'Over and over again my mind has recalled the deceased, that splendid man, who had such a noble character.' He also wrote to his secretary to ensure both his father and 'old Winkler' received regular funds.

The radio had earlier played *Schatzkastlein*, which had put Hess in mind of 'you and your poodle, Ami; Ami could have been Goliath in his mixture of rascal and soul'.

He awoke early on Monday morning with a stabbing pain in his gall bladder. Captain Johnston administered a morphine injection, allowing him to sleep most of the morning, but when he awoke at 11.45 a.m. he asked to speak to Foley and requested that he cancel his forthcoming meeting with Lord Beaverbrook – but then asked to be warned of his visit in case 'he was not feeling well enough to carry on an intelligent conversation'.

According to Captain Johnston, Hess's symptoms were psychosomatic, brought on by fear of the meeting. As Foley reported: 'The MO is convinced that Jonathan is exaggerating his pains as his pulse and temperature are normal; his appetite is even excellent. The MO would like to suggest that in order to avoid the possibility of Jonathan further developing these turns, it would be preferable if the visit of Lord B could take place without delay. He is of the opinion that any further visits would not be divulged to the patient until immediately before they are due to take place. The idea is that these visits prey on his mind and have a deleterious effect on his mental state.'

Previously Hess had asked Foley if he should raise with Lord Beaverbrook his complaints about his ill-treatment. Foley had replied that he had no objection and would translate them into English if he wished. Hess later decided it was best not to, but once again changed his mind and told Foley he might now put them in writing. 'I promised to translate into English for him. The MO is wondering what new complaints he will find, as he now has newspapers, wireless, the doors below his bedroom have been completely silenced and the bars on the cage have been replaced by an ordinary lock. These were the principal causes of complaint.'

11

The Man in the Homburg Hat

If there was a moment in which Rudolf Hess's fate swung in the balance, it probably took place on the evening of 8 September at 7.30 p.m. when the man in the Homburg swept into his bedroom, placed his hat on the bed, and began to talk as if a long friendship had been placed on pause by an unfriendly family dispute.

Lord Beaverbrook was the garrulous Canadian newspaper tycoon whose friendship with Winston Churchill (who had been a long and frequent contributor to his newspapers, often having his chauffeur drop off copy with instructions to wait for the cheque) had led to Beaverbrook's appointment as Minister for Aircraft Production and now Minister for Supply. A genius at logistics, who never took a written note, relying instead on his remarkable memory, Beaverbrook's new role was to work with the Americans in order to supply Russia with the necessary armaments to defeat Germany. Since the launch of Operation Barbarossa, the old maxim – my enemy's enemy is my friend – applied. Twenty-two days after this visit to Hess, Beaverbrook was to fly to the Arctic port of Archangel. From there, he would travel to Moscow for a meeting with Stalin about co-ordinating the first armament delivery. He wished to glean what he could from Hess, who had prepared a thirty-seven-page memo detailing his views on Russia.

The verbatim conversation between the Government minister and the German prisoner was, like that of the negotiation with Lord Simon, recorded by MI6's secret microphones:

Beaverbrook: How well your English has improved.

Hess: A little; not very much.

B: A lot. You remember the last time we talked, in the Chancellery in Berlin . . .?

H: Yes, surely.

B: And we talked in your office and you were understanding everything in English . . .

H: Understanding, yes. But I can't . . .

B: You weren't speaking, but you were understanding it all.

H: Understanding, yes.

B: Well, we've come to a bad pass.

H: Yes, surely.

B: Yes, Yes; I was very much against the war.

H: Me too; I know it.

B: You too, yes. Very sorry to see it come about, very sorry indeed; I regretted it greatly. I did my best for my part to escape, hoping greatly that we wouldn't be involved in this terrible world crisis. Now it's become terribly complicated. It's become such an extraordinary combination of complications that it's awfully difficult to see what can be done about it. It's awfully difficult to see how the whole thing is going to develop. The world is in terrible trouble. Little things begin big consequences and they roll on most majestically and there's no stopping them, no stopping them at all. It bothers me a great deal – continually – the whole tragedy of it, the terrible pity of it – frightful. Since I saw you I have become a member of the Government – in May 1940, with the formation of the new Government.

H: Nineteen hundred and . . . ?

B: May, 1940, with the formation of the new Government. I was not in the government after the war broke out, not until May, 1940. I began building airplanes, I'm now building guns and ammunition, filling factories and so on; after a world of peaceful pursuits, I suddenly find myself entirely concerned with the implements of war – nothing but the implements of war.

Now what do you think of all that? Extraordinary change in a man's life, who begins by being a newspaper man and ends up making bullets.

[H Laughs]

B: Extraordinary times. You're getting better?

H: Better.

B: You're improving.

H: Improving, yes. Twelve weeks now.

B: How many?

H: Twelve weeks.

B: Twelve weeks. That's a long time.

H: A long time. A long time for a man who above all doesn't get many visitors. [If] I was in Germany there would come my wife, my son and all my family and my friends, but here I have not, that is to say, I have, for example, the Duke of Hamilton, he would come.

B: Yes.

H: If he would get the permission.

B: Yes.

H: I asked for the permission.

B: You want to see him.

H: Four months ago I asked. He didn't get the permission.

B: Oh, so . . .

H: Yes, I would like to see him.

B: Yes.

H: If necessary, I would give the word not to talk about politics with him, if necessary.

B: Yes.

H: Could you mention . . . ?

B: I'll have a talk about it. I'll have a talk about it.

H: Yes.

B: I'll have a talk about it and I'll have a word with him.

H: Yes. The only man who is, so to say, so to speak, a friend of mine, even though I don't know him well.

B: Hm. I saw him on the airfield the other day up in the north. I flew out the other day to America.

H: Yes.

B: From one of the Scottish airfields. We had a conference out in Newfoundland and so I flew out from Prestwick in Scotland to Newfoundland in the night time in a bomber. It's a good way to travel.

H: Yes. Now in the night. I had once the intention to fly over the ocean in the time when all of the ocean flyers tried to get to America, at the time of Kohl, Fitzmaurice and so on.

B: Yes.

H: But at that time I didn't get the engine. It was very difficult at this time, but now today, it is much easier.

B: Oh yes, now you don't fly in comfort in a bomber, anything but comfort, but you do fly with extraordinary safety and great convenience. I think that the flights across the Atlantic have been extraordinarily favourable. I started the line after becoming Aircraft Minister. I think altogether we've flown a great many airplanes now and our losses are very small, and the losses are mostly in taking off and in getting down. Practically everything occurs in taking off or in coming in. Practically nothing else. Is that the radio you have over there?

H: The radio since two days – a long time – twelve weeks. No radio. I don't know why.

B: Oh, and it's just been moved upstairs now?

H: It has been bought for me since three days.

B: Oh. I don't see why they don't get you all those conveniences that you want, whatever . . .

H: I don't know it.

B: They don't give you the conveniences you want?

H: No, surely not. [Laughs] Five weeks I didn't get any newspapers, any news. The officers had been forbidden to tell me anything of the news in the world. I don't know why. Perhaps you can tell me why?

B: I haven't a notion.

H: It had been a terrible time for me, you know. Coming here from Germany as a German Minister and not to hear the news of the world.

B: Yes.

H: I don't know it.

B: Hm. You get newspapers now?

H: Now I have them. The day after my jumping down, I get them.

B: Day after what?

H: After I broke my leg.

B: You've had the newspapers since?

H: Since, yes.

B: You have them now, every day?

H: Yes, every day *The Times*, yes. But if I would not have done that perhaps I would not have the newspapers today. I am quite sure personally.

B: Quite sure you wouldn't have had them.

H: Yes, but I don't know why. I can't understand it. If an English like myself would come to Germany, you can be sure it would be done what we can for him.

B: How's the food. Is the food all right?

H: The food is all right, yes. The serving is good.

B: Well done.

H: Well done, yes.

B: You don't drink?

H: No. But you smoke perhaps, I think?

B: No, I don't smoke, no. You don't, do you?

H: No, strange. [Laughs]

B: I would have asthma. I don't smoke on that account. I haven't any excuse to offer – [both laugh] – except that my asthma keeps me from smoking. So you don't want any smoke and you don't want any drink.

H: Yes.

B: You don't even drink wine?

H: No.

B: Hm. I still drink German wine.

H: [Laughs] I hope you will drink it again in not too far time, but I don't know. Perhaps in two years, three years, it can be. [Hess appears to have thought Beaverbrook wished to drink wine in Germany.]

B: Yes, hmm. I don't know what is going to be the source of events at all. They are all so very obscure. It's not a situation that I can contemplate at all with any understanding or any grasp or any vision – about what's going to happen.

H: And it is very, very dangerous to play what England plays since those days with Bolshevism. Very dangerous.

B: Very dangerous? What's that?

H: Very dangerous to play with Bolshevism.

B: Yes.

H: The alliance.

B: Yes.

H: If you have in a short time complications between the Bolshevist women and the English women, Bolshevist work organisations and English work organisations, that must have results, you can be sure.

B: Yes. I can't myself tell why the Germans attacked Russia. I can't see why?

H: Because we knew that one day the Russians will attack us.

B: Will attack Germany?

H: Yes.

B: And it was really the intention to destroy the Russian machine. The Russian war machine.

H: Yes, Russian machine, and it will be good not only for Germany and the whole Europe. It will be good for England too if Russia will be defeated.

B: Yes.

H: It's a very, very great danger and they have armed, they have big armament – all silent.

B: In Russia, how much did they have? What sort of arms did they have?

H: Long before the war.

B: Yes. In Russia. What sort of war plant did they put up? Good?

H: Difficult for me to say: I can't tell it. Just that what I read by your newspapers, not more. Because before we attacked Russia we didn't know anything. It had been quite silent.

B: Hmm . . . Hmm. I would think they had very big munitions plants, you know; I would think they had very big plants in the Donau basin.

H: They must have. They must have. They must have. Otherwise it would not have been possible to own so many.

B: What were their tanks like? Were their tanks good in the days before the war?

H: I can't tell it.

B: Did you ever see them?

H: No. Never. I have never been there.

B: Were you never in Russia?

H: Never.

B: Hm. They appear to have a seven or eight-ton tank.

H: Oh, very much more.

B: Yes, I am sure; but the tank they fight with most of all appears to be a seven or eight-ton tank.

H: Yes. The medium, I think so.

B: They seem to have a very good tank in that seven or eight-ton tank. If appears to be very good indeed.

H: Fortunately we get now the party of Ukraine in the West of the Dnieper. The dam had been destroyed and there on the industry in the East does not get any power.

B: If the German intention was to destroy the munitions-producing plants of Russia, then they have gone some way – without a doubt. Some considerable way, without any doubt at all. But it's hard to see why Germany, for me to understand, why Germany – engaged in such a universal war elsewhere – should turn to fight

Russia without trying to complete first of all the war that she was engaged in. I can't understand it.

H: I didn't quite well understand that last.

B: Well, Germany is engaged in a great war with England, and England has proved to be a formidable foe, hard fighting.

H: Surely.

B: And a great air power – exercising that air power with great fortitude and endurance, standing very heavy bombing, and yet Germany, engaged in that war with England, turns aside to fight Russia. I would have thought Germany would have said, 'First of all, we must finish, get to the end of the war with England; until we get to the end of the war with England, we can't undertake to do battle with Russia.'

H: Yes. If Russia would have . . . but we had been sure that Russia would attack us before that. It is quite logical. In the time in which we are engaged with England, to attack us.

B: Now with what purpose would Russia attack Germany? What would be the object?

H: To make revolution – world revolution.

B: Yes, yes. The Bolshevik revolution.

H: Yes, the Bolshevik revolution. To come in Europe; Germany and then Europe.

B: They care enough about it for that?

H: I am sure. They have announced several years ago that they will not continue the world revolution, but it cannot be true.

B: I am going there now.

H: Yes, I know it. Congratulations. [Laughs]

B: [Laughs] Why do you look at it that way? [Laughs heartily] I don't look at it that way at all. I'd rather be going to some other part of the world. I used to love my journeys all over Europe and now you can't do those any more. I've got a magnificent house in the south of France that I want to go and live in – I'd like to go back to. But there's nothing else for it.

H: I wrote a special memorandum about Germany and England

and the Russian war. I'm sorry I wrote it in German, but you can translate it. I would give it to you to translate it.

B: Yes, I'd like to have it very, very much. Very much. I would like to have it very much indeed. I make no concealment of my views at all, you know. My political opinions are what they were. I fight for my country just as hard as any man can fight. There isn't any blasted thing that I won't do. There isn't anything that I wouldn't undertake. And fight like Jerry and teach my sons to do the same thing. But my political views are exactly what they were. I've no doubt at all that I stand where I was. My newspaper standards are . . .

[H laughs]

B: It's hardened them and we're all greatly strengthened. They don't lose their money and they don't lose many of their comforts and much of their liberties in life. But they're a better people. I am not sure that the war has been a curse to them altogether. The war has uplifted them; the war has strengthened them.

H: Yes, yes. But the same I can say by German people. And above all, in all parties and towns where big raids had been, the people is much stronger.

B: Yes.

H: Like here.

B: Yes. It strengthens them.

H: Yes.

B: Without any doubt. One thing we don't quite succeed in doing in England is to mobilise yet our manpower to the full. We've mobilised it all right, but we don't yet use it to the full. There will be, there must be, a great strengthening of the use of our manpower. You can't tell when this war will end, can you? You can't tell what permutations – you know the meaning of the word permutations? Too complicated?

H: Too complicated.

B: You can't tell what will be the outcome of it all.

H: Yes, the outcome, yes.

B: I mean what new situations will arise. There are so many. The combinations are so many. The whole world is in such a state of flux and reflux that you can't tell what sort of . . .

H: One I know, I am quite sure that Bolshevism will be stronger.

B: As a result of the war, stronger?

H: Stronger, yes.

B: Do you think so?

H: Oh yes. Firstly in Russia itself, and because they had been just at the beginning of their industrial and they will continue and one day they have, I don't know how many hundreds of millions of men, and they have raw materials more than they need today, but they will employ them and one day they will be, I am sure, a big concurrence in the world power.

B: Hmm. Of course they are going to get a great setback to industry over this present war.

H: For a short time. They have developed their industry of today is not a long time and they can continue that in the middle of Russia.

B: You'll tell me if you get tired, won't you?

H: On no. I don't.

B: If you get tired at all and feel you want to sleep. Just tell me and I'll . . .

H: Oh no.

B: I don't want to raise any issue with you or discuss anything that doesn't at all concern the mere wide issues of politics and so on. I would have you understand I'm not trying to discuss intimate things with you at all, not in the least.

H: I wrote that all about Russia in my memorandum, you will see it.

B: Yes. You think Russia will emerge from the war beaten, but in a short time recover and become stronger?

H: Stronger, I am quite sure.

B: And Japan. What about the Eastern world? What do you see there?

H: Difficult to say. I can't tell.

B: You don't know enough about it?

H: Not more than you.

B: No. Well, my view is that Japan is moving.

H: Yes, yes. It seems.

B: My view is that she's on the move, but she doesn't mean to be engaged anywhere if she can help it, that she doesn't mean to go to war if she can avoid it, but that she's on the move; I think she has great aspirations in the East. And America? What do you think about America?

H: I think one day America will get it, the war.

B: Yes, I think so too.

H: I am quite sure. It will not change very much, because they are today in the war, practically. But they will go in.

B: Yes. Why do you think the war broke out?

H: Why?

B: What do you think was the reason for the outbreak?

H: It is difficult to say it in English for me, but I told all that in a talk with (Lord Simon).

B: Lord Simon. I heard Lord Simon.

H: You didn't read the protocol on those?

B: I didn't read it, but I listened to Lord Simon on the subject.

H: Yes.

B: But I didn't want to get you to deal with it extensively at all, but just in a gossiping way. The war came so quickly, so swiftly. I think that Chamberlain here, who was Prime Minister and who is dead, you know, I think he would have honestly, as far as I could understand him, I think he would honestly like to have escaped it.

H: Yes. I had the protocol, just two or three pages, I think, about this point, if you want.

B: In English?

H: In English.

B: Tell me where it is and I'll just read it to refresh my memory.

It's rather beside the point what made war break out anyway. It's like asking a man who made you fall downstairs, isn't it.

[H laughs]

B: So many reasons. You've got any other friends here besides the Duke of Hamilton?

H: No, I have no . . .

B: Except me.

H: No. But you are here [laughs]. You will become one.

B: Hmm.

H: This is my record to you that I have something . . .

B: To occupy your . . .

H: Could I tell it you? Could I write to you?

B: Oh yes. And not only that, but when I come back from Russia – I'm going to Russia very soon – and when I come back from Russia, if you desire it, if you wish it, I'll come and see you again.

H: It would be very kind.

B: Yes. I will do.

H: It would be very kind.

B: Yes. I've been meaning to write to you for some time. I've been intending to write to you for some time. We necessarily, you and I, both being in politics, sit down and talk about politics, but I don't know that I want to talk politics with you exactly. It's not so great a desire on my part to talk politics.

H: It is here in the drawer, if you would be so kind in the second drawer at the right. Perhaps it would interest you too, the reason why I come here.

B: Yes. I remember that, more or less.

H: Even about the beginning. I went to the Führer one year ago and I told him.

B: England has proved to be remarkably strong in the air, you know.

H: Yes.

B: The air has been the great surprise of the war for me. The strength and resource of England in the air. The English airmen are very good.

H: Yes, surely. Oh, we knew it from the Great War.

B: They have an aptitude for the air. It surprises me. My son is among them. My son is very distinguished.

H: Yes.

B: I find them all air-minded, air conscious.

H: Yes, surely. But I think the German pilots too.

B: I would think so too.

H: That is the pity.

B: You know my views on the Germans.

H: You have the best men and we have the best men.

B: Certainly.

H: And one will kill other, and I think for nothing.

B: This is all your conversation with Lord Simon?

H: With Lord Simon, yes.

B: Did you find him an agreeable fellow?

H: Yes, surely . . . [pause]

B: Well, the people did stumble into the last war, of course.

H: Yes, of course.

B: The last war; and I'm afraid we've stumbled in again, haven't we?

H: Yes, surely.

B: It could have been.

H: I am quite sure.

B: I think so too. What page do you come to this . . .

H: There's the beginning.

B: Oh, yes. Chamberlain has stated that he was only trying to gain time for further re-armament – I don't think, I think Chamberlain wanted to –

H: *The Times*, itself – I wrote . . .

B: Yes, I see that you quote *The Times* – and his death. Well, I, I – Chamberlain genuinely desired peace; he genuinely desired . . . here you are: 'We have had misfortunes and we have had great disasters, and we have had terrible events following swiftly one another.' But I do think he desired it, you know.

H: Yes, I don't know him personally.

B: I'll say not.

H: Yes.

B: It is quite true, of course, that England always built up a coalition against the strongest power. That was the traditional English policy always.

H: And to-day, I am sure too [laughs] – in the last years . . .

B: Did you have all this taken down in shorthand at the time?

H: Yes, it had been taken down in shorthand.

B: All taken down in shorthand?

H: Yes.

B: Must have been a funny meeting. [Laughs]

H: [Laughs] Yes . . . And I get it now some corrections. These are mistakes in . . .

B: Beck; what was Beck's object in all this? I would have thought that Beck, the Polish foreign minister, would have fallen under the influence of Germany. Why was it that he did not fall under the influence of Germany?

H: Under the influence?

B: Yes.

H: I don't quite understand quite right.

B: You know Beck?

H: Personally, no not.

B: No. Well, Beck is the type of man who would have been likely to have fallen – who would have been likely to have come into the German sphere.

H: Oh yes; he did so, he did so.

B: He looked that type of man to me.

H: And he had the intention to come to an understanding, a real understanding, surely I know it.

B: He turned his back on Churchill. He turned away from Churchill.

H: Yes. I did not know that. [Laughs]

B: Oh yes, he did so.

H: When? When did he so?

B: Before the war, turned away from him. He would not deal with Churchill at all. I would have thought he was easily in the influence of Germany.

H: Yes, he had been.

B: The French were not any good, were they? No spirit left.

H: No.

B: The French.

H: No; they ran.

B: Did you know how bad they were?

H: How bad they were [chuckles] in the . . .

B: How weak in character they were?

H: Yes, yes.

B: The Germans knew that.

H: Yes.

B: We did not, you know.

H: Yes.

B: I always said it! I always said it before the war.

H: Had been communist influence, Marxist influence.

B: Breaking down the national spirits.

[. . . Silent pause while Beaverbrook reads]

B: Oh! Plans against Norway . . .

H: Yes.

B: . . . The nephew of Mr Churchill who was at Narvik, he was on my newspaper.

H: Yes. [Laughs]

B: Yes. He was there for me, you know. He had been in Finland. It was before I was in government.

H: Yes.

B: And I was still running my newspapers. I am still looking after my newspapers, and that boy; his name is Romilly . . .

H: Yes.

B: Giles Romilly – and he is not a conservative like Churchill.

H: Not!

B: No, he is socialist, left wing socialist, quite left wing, not acceptable to Churchill at all. Churchill never took a great view of his politics. Have you had dinner? What time do you dine?

H: Oh, much later.

B: Much later?

H: Yes.

B: I don't mind a bit if you want to go on with your dinner, you know.

H: Oh no.

B: I am rather interested in reading this for a few minutes.

(Silent pause while Beaverbrook reads)

B: When you came to England I went down to Churchill's room in Downing Street and he showed me the photograph—

H: Yes.

B: —And said, 'Who is that', and I said 'Hess!'

H: [Laughs] He did not believe it at first.

B: I did not either.

H: I can understand it.

B: Moderation in war is no use, you say.

[H laughs]

B: It is true that moderation is of no use?

H: I know it.

B: What?

H: War or not war, but if war no moderation . . . But I think war is not necessary, between Germany and England.

B: Did you expect England to fall before this time?

H: No, never. I have never been here.

B: You did not – you got to expect that she would fall before now.

H: Expect is a . . . ?

B: I read here, 'The reason for my flight was that among the leading personalities, the leaders of Germany, we were absolutely convinced that England's position is hopeless.' Well now, did you think that England would fall. You arrived, I think, about the first of May, did you?

H: Yes. It will fall, I thought. I think it will fall one day. I said nothing more. But it was not in those months. In one year, two years, three years.

B: You did not expect England to fall by the first of September when you came here?

H: No, no, not at all. Oh no, not at all. But I thought it would be better for England to come to an agreement than to fight three years.

B: I don't think England can be beaten, you know, she's got such enormous resources of resistance, such vitality.

H: Yes, but the tonnage is deciding.

B: The tonnage at sea?

H: Yes, the tonnage at sea.

B: Yes, of course. If we lose our tonnage we lose our lifeline.

H: Yes, and you will lose it.

B: Yes, we lose to the submarine.

H: Yes I am quite sure.

B: And the air.

H: The last war it had been on the point, you know it.

B: Yes.

H: It had been very near to the point.

B: Strange to say I was a minister in the last war. In every war I am a minister.

H: Yes, you have been with Lord Rothermere – Northcliff.

B: Yes. I was the minister for information – the Minister of Propaganda.

H: Yes, yes. I know it. [Laughs] We in Germany, we have learned very much of your propaganda of the last war. You must confess it.

B: Well, I hope you won't take anything from it this war.

[H laughs]

B: This war is not very good.

H: No, not good. And one day I had heard a bomb had fallen on your Ministry of Propaganda, of Information, and I told them, 'That is wrong – you have not to do so, you have to bomb our ally.'

B: [Hearty laughter] It is better now, there is a new man there, a man called Bracken.

H: Yes, Yes.

B: Tough fellow . . . I think England is very strong in the air.

H: She is! Yes?

B: Oh yes, much stronger than I ever expected.

H: Yes, but nevertheless Germany will always be stronger, I am quite sure, and I wrote it here in my memorandum why.

B: Yes. We have great air power – the nation is an air-minded people, just as they were sea-going people years ago, now, of course, they are an airborne people.

H: Yes, I know it. But nevertheless, I am quite sure, certain circumstances, we will be always stronger.

B: I look at the English with a very detached eye. I am, as you know, a Canadian.

H: Yes, you are Canadian.

B: Yes, I see them very clearly.

H: I think that the following will be in my memorandum as well.

B: Yes.

H: This point here.

B: Yes, 'In a year' – yes, I see, I see that – 'the total force devoted to the air.' It takes a lot of men to service one airplane, does it not?

H: Yes.

B: Yes, terrible.

[H laughs]

B: I forget what the B.E.F. in France was, the British Expeditionary Force, I expect it was about 500,000 men.

H: The British force had not been 500,000 men.

B: Not 500,000 men?

H: No, I think about 300,000.

B: 300,000 in France.

H: Yes, I think so, I am not quite sure, but I think so, yes.

B: I think it was more than that, you know

H: More than that?

B: Yes, I think so.

H: I thought less, but I had not been quite . . . know it now . . .

B: Were you a pilot in the last war? You were too young?

H: In the end of the last war. Oh yes, I have been in the last war from the first days, from 1914.

B: Were you? I thought you were too young.

H: Oh no. I had been 20 in 1914.

B: You were 20 in 1914, were you?

H: Yes, and I had been footman, I had been opposite to your English troops, Arras, Vimy and so on. Had been a bad fighting, not very nice. At Verdun I had been too. I had been wounded at Verdun. And then in the last days I get an airman, a fighting man.

B: You were at the University in Munich, were you not?

H: Yes.

B: I cannot understand entirely Hitler's tactics at the present time. I cannot understand the events.

H: In what – ?

B: I cannot understand the way in making war.

H: But I told it here.

B: No, I don't mean why he made the war. No, I can't understand quite now, I can't understand the campaign for 1941.

H: Of 41?

B: Yes, that is this year. I understand perfectly the campaign of 1940, that is clear to me. If he was going to Russia why did he go to Yugoslavia? I don't understand.

H: He had the danger that English troops and soldiers come in from Yugoslavia and so on.

B: He is too clever for that. He would have said, 'Bring them right along.'

H: In the last war he had been at Salonika too. It had been a danger at Salonika.

B: He would have said, 'Bring them right here'. He would have liked to have them at Salonika. Because if they had come in at Salonika he could have beaten them up.

H: Oh, not sure; if they are the English soldiers – are good soldiers, we know it. It is better to prevent it. [Laughs]

B: Yugoslavia would never have let them in either.

H: Oh, we had not the intention to fight against Yugoslavia, we had a treaty with Yugoslavia, and then it had been broken.

B: I cannot understand why he went to Yugoslavia. I cannot understand why he went to Greece. Since he went to Greece I cannot understand why he did not go on from Crete to Cyprus – to Syria.

H: Oh, it is not so easy. You have a fleet – [laughs] – and you have air – troops too.

B: Oh that airborne power was perfect there, that airborne power was very great; the battle for Crete is a tremendous story, tremendous story, the story of that battle is one of the big stories of history. The English fought – as terrible as useless – at Crete. They fought very, very hard.

H: Yes.

B: Hm

H: Yes. Oh you are good soldiers, I know it; it is because that we are . . .

B: The Germans fought at Crete with great, great theory and with tremendous shrewdness and cleverness. The campaign was well directed, you know, well thought out and the punches were good and well delivered, you know. The English fought very, very hard; very hard indeed. I would agree with your statement as to the numbers in the German Air Force compared with the B.E.F. if you take all the personnel into account.

H: All the personnel, yes, yes.

B: I would agree without any doubt.

H: Yes, that is a mistake, I didn't . . .

B: If I read it I would agree, I would not misunderstand it. Tremendous force of material against England means bombs and . . .

H: Yes.

B: And magnesium bombs. Yes, I think I understand. The Americans are making some very fine types of bombers, big bombers.

H: Yes.

B: Their big bombers are very fine – Fortresses. The Fortress is the greatest bomber in the world.

H: Scorned?

B: Rejected; nobody wanted it.

H: By whom?

B: By the Americans, by everybody.

H: And who did take them?

B: Well, it came over here and it was suddenly put to use over here and was discovered what a great airplane it was. It turned out to be tremendously useful. It's the greatest airplane of the world without any doubt. The very greatest. Wc have three new types – the Stirling, Manchester and Halifax. All built in my time; all built while I was at the Ministry. All brought out during that time – very big types; very heavy, carry big loads you know. But the Fortress has universal advantages. Then there's something called the B.24 – that's a very fine machine too. The Consolidated B.24, made by the Consolidated Company.

H: I don't know it.

B: It's a fine airplane. What I shall go to Russia in. But I shall go without guns, and take my chance on getting through. [Both laugh] Yes, Germany has a big advantage in bomb weight, you know; very big. I don't think any war can be ended by bombs.

H: No, I told the same here; Germany will not be beaten by bombs and England will not be beaten by bombs. But we will surely, if the war continues some years, we will destroy one another, our factories, our harbours and our towns.

B: My house in town has been blown up; a place called Stornoway House; a bomb fell on my kitchen; a beautiful house in the Park – the kitchen was attached to the house – the bomb fell on the kitchen and the blast went into the basement and blew straight up through the roof . . .

H: Very interesting; that is a danger, yes.

B: And carried the roof off – the blast did. Twenty-seven bombs have fallen round about my house in the country, all in the fields.

H: This house had been in the country, not in London?

B: No, my house was blown up in London. In the country not so. But my point is that bombs – I don't believe that one bomb in ten gets home.

H: Gets home – yes.

B: I think for every ten bombs that are thrown down only one does the real work. Do I make that clear?

H: Oh, I think less even.

B: So do I, so do I. I don't believe that bombing is a conclusion in war.

H: No, never. I wrote it here in this memorandum.

B: The Siegfried Line was no use there.

H: No use.

B: Those lines are no use.

H: Oh it had been of great importance; as long as we had to fight in Poland we . . .

B: The French never would have attacked you.

H: Oh yes, if there had been no Siegfried Line, they had attacked us.

B: Would they?

H: Oh yes; surely.

B: It seems rather degenerating, rather a little bit, the conversation. [He is referring to the interview transcript of Jonathan and Lord Simon he is reading.]

H: The submarine war had been, yes?

B: No, I have not got to submarines.

H: But I wrote about the submarines in this memorandum too. I think you, – there is plenty of time.

B: Later on?

H: Not for me, not for me. Surely, if you like to read, but you will see it in this memorandum. Have you a translator of whom you are personally confident?

B: Oh yes, certainly. I've got a boy that was in the British Embassy in Germany for a long time.

H: He's in your . . .

B: In my employ. He's my secretary. He was in Germany for a lifetime. He came back with me from Germany. I used to go to Germany quite often before Hitler came to power and I was in Berlin the day of Hitler's election. Of course, you may know, my newspapers always gave him a good hearing.

H: Yes, I know it.

B: Yes. We always ran a very good hearing for him. The English unfortunately, the English listened a bit, but not very much to the voices telling them to arm – there were many voices here saying, 'Arm!', but at the same time I was one of the principal voices saying 'Arm, Arm!', and at the same time, 'Hold out the hand of friendship to Germany.' Now the public would say, perhaps, that I was wrong to say hold out the hand of friendship to Germany, but that I was right to say arm, and arm at once.

H: I know you had seen with Hitler together a film concerning the last war and the Führer told me you had been very impressed and he himself just, a germ of ending by an understanding.

B: I saw him three times all told.

H: [Laughs] Oh, I know he likes you very much. Oh, he is very sorry we must fight one against the other, very sorry.

B: The whole thing is bloody.

H: Yes, the whole thing is bloody, but we can use our blood for better things; you can use your blood in your Colonies and for your Empire, and we can use our blood for the East. We need ground for our population.

B: Hm.

H: I thought I can come here and find a certain common sense. [Laughs] But I have been wrong, I know it.

B: Very difficult you know, to find common sense when war is on.

H: When it is on, I know.

B: War is not common sense.

H: Yes, surely you are right.

B: Once you get into the conflict of war – once you get into the blood and the guns and sacrifices, then reason goes.

H: Yes.

B: There is no longer any reason after that, none at all.

H: None at all, – no. But nevertheless I thought that some leading men would have common sense enough to say 'why continue to fight one against the other?' It is not necessary. I don't believe it is necessary.

B: Of course. The difficulty of those things is – the difficulty of that sort of thing is that when you make such a declaration, that you let down the fighting spirit of your own people.

H: Yes.

B: For the danger is that if one side tries to stop the fight, then that side may suffer terrible consequences through a failure of the willingness and desire of her people to continue the fight.

H: Yes.

B: There is the morale of the people that you've got to keep at a high pitch and a great altitude and a mighty strength all the time; and if you ever disturb the morale of your people, then you do something which is really dangerous, don't you?

H: Yes, but I don't believe that it is necessary to disturb the morale by that.

B: Hm.

H: In those times we have the wireless, we have the newspapers and we have the propaganda; we can tell people why it is better, and I am quite sure as well your people as our people would be very glad; our people did not like this war against England, and the present war today.

B: What does Ribbentrop do? Does he now run the foreign policy of the country?

H: Yes.

B: Is he of great importance with the other leaders like you and Goering and so on?

H: Yes, quite surely.

B: Of equal importance.

H: Yes.

B: Hmm. I know him quite well.

H: You know him, yes. I know. He is better than he is usually told in England.

B: Yes; he didn't get on very well here.

H: No. I know it. But it is wrong, I think.

B: Yes. He was wrong. Yes he was; I used to see him continually and talk with him a great deal. But he was wrong, you know.

H: He was wrong?

B: He was wrong, I think so, yes, here in England.

H: In England.

B: I thought so, yes.

H: I can't tell that.

B: No, I thought he was a bit uncompromising. Do you know what that means?

H: Uncompromising?

B: Hmm. I thought a bit. I admired him in many respects. He was a vital fellow.

H: Yes, surely.

B: He's done well, hasn't he, to have got to high places without having been in the movement from the beginning?

H: Yes.

B: I don't quite see how to go about anything at all really. I wish I could see what is going on. I wish I could penetrate it. I go seeking, seeking all the time, trying to find some way to penetrate the mists, and I can't manage to see through the gloom at all. Everywhere seems to be gloom. And there comes altogether a different and confusing picture, most confusing. It's hard to say what. The Russian campaign has gone on much longer than I expected.

H: Yes; as we expected too, I think so. I don't know it because I haven't been in Germany, but I think so and I think it had been – oh, the Russians had made their armament in all silence to be ready one day to start the war.

B: Hmm. That the Russians had got everything all ready in silence to start the war against Germany?

H: One day, yes.

B: Hmm, yes.

H: Germany, and that is to say the whole Europe, no States in Europe would, can give resistance if not Germany; one day they would be here at your coast in Belgium and so on.

B: Hmm.

H: We can't defeat that and even if we defeat them – in a few years they will be stronger than ever.

B: Perhaps there won't any longer be Bolsheviks. They may get a dictator.

H: Dictator! Oh, they are, they have a dictator.

B: Well they may get, however, a Royal dictator; they may set up a royalty.

H: Oh, I don't think so; oh no, I have not the impression. Otherwise they would not fight as well for Europe, Russia of today.

B: No, they couldn't fight so well?

H: No.

B: They fight well because the spirit of the people has been uplifted.

H: Yes, surely.

B: Hmm.

H: I am sure one day they will be a very great danger for your colonies – India, for example too; they have their frontier there, and they have a big army.

B: Hm.

[A guard interrupts to ask if they will have dinner.]

B: I must be ashamed of myself for having stayed so long.

H: Thank you; you'll come back?

B: Yes; I'll come back.

H: You promise.

B: You have my promise.

H: When will you come back? When will you go to Russia?

B: Pretty soon now, very, very, soon.

H: Very soon.

B: Yes.

H: And how long you will remain, you know it?

B: Not very long, just a little while. And you can congratulate me on my journey.

[H laughs; B chuckles]

The laughter faded as Beaverbrook collected his hat, bid Hess goodbye, and left the room with a copy of his memo advocating war on Russia. Although a senior member of the War Cabinet, Beaverbrook was aware that there were limits to his knowledge, and after meeting with Hess he suspected that his mental condition was the result of a secret narcotic regime. 'Max thinks he was probably given some kind of drugs by our people to make him talk,' wrote Robert Bruce Lockhart, head of the Political Intelligence Department of the Foreign Office in his diary. While the use of Evapan Sodium, a 'truth serum' was suggested by the War Office to 'pick whatever brains that gentleman may still possess', there was no evidence that it was administered.

Four weeks later Beaverbrook was dining with Stalin in the Kremlin and watching as he downed glass after glass of red Caucasian wine, while keeping by his elbow a bottle of champagne with one glass over the mouth. Although in his memoirs Beaverbrook referred to the interview transcription, it is believed to be more likely that it was Hess's memo which he handed over.

During a private meeting Stalin asked, 'Do you intend to make peace?" Beaverbrook enquired his reason for such a question. He said he concluded Britain meant to make peace because we kept Hess in our hands instead of shooting him. It was plain that Hess was the line of communication. Beaverbrook replied that Britain could not shoot Hess without a trial. Stalin then asked him why Hess had come to England. Beaverbrook replied, 'To persuade Britain to join Germany in making an attack on Russia.' He then produced the memorandum and handed it over. As he later recorded, 'Thereafter we got on well.'

12

The Black Art

The marbled Mayakovsky station in Moscow was Stalin's bunker against the bombs of Hitler's Blitzkrieg. It was here, hundreds of feet beneath a city under siege, that, on 6 November, on the Chairman of the State Defence Committee paced in his soft leather boots, puffed on his pipe, and announced that the Blitzkrieg had stalled, the Soviet Union was saved, and 'Hess's mission' to unite Britain and Germany in an anti-Bolshevik crusade had failed. Although almost four years of fighting still lay ahead, at a cost of millions of lives, Stalin knew Hitler had hoped to achieve a swift and decisive victory before the cruel Russian winter deployed her own Generals. He had failed. Of the four wartime leaders – Churchill, Hitler, Stalin and Roosevelt – it was Stalin who was the most obsessed about the true meaning behind the mission of Rudolf Hess. It can be argued that he, or more accurately his people, paid the highest price. Two years later Sir Archibald Clark Kerr, Britain's Ambassador to Moscow, explained to Winston Churchill that the reason for the Soviet Union's deep suspicion of the United Kingdom was the secrecy surrounding the Deputy Führer. How would Churchill have reacted if Ribbentrop had flown to Russia with the Prime Minister unaware of his intent? Hess, explained Kerr, was like a 'skeleton in the cupboard', whose jangling bones played on the nerves.

The man most anxious to amplify each 'rattle' was a Russian agent, codenamed Sonnchen, who sat opposite Frank Foley at the meetings of Section V, the Counter-Intelligence Department of MI6, at its headquarters in St Albans. Kim Philby had been recruited as a Soviet spy at Cambridge and served the worker's revolution by passing secrets to his NKVD handler, Anatoly Gorsky. On 14 May, three days after Hess parachuted down, Philby sent a report stating that Hess had been identified by 'Kirk Patrik' [*sic*], an official of the *zakoulok* or 'back alley' as Soviet Intelligence called the Foreign Office. The question of why Rudolf Hess had flown to Britain was of imperative importance to Stalin as he struggled to make sense of Germany's military build-up on the borders of the Soviet Union. What began in January 1941 as a trickle, had become a flood by May: Russia's partner in the non-aggression pact of 1939 now had between 105 and 107 divisions in position, according to Soviet Intelligence. The day after Philby's despatch arrived, Stalin examined an emergency plan drawn up by the Red Army which illustrated that they could neither adequately attack nor defend the nation. Stalin, unwilling to face the worst-case scenario that Hitler was preparing to tear up the non-aggression pact (as he had so many treaties before), began to pin his hopes on Hess. There had been rumours that any attack would be preceded by an Anglo-German agreement, but if Hess was being viewed as a rogue agent, not as an official emissary, could this not provide room for a Soviet-German negotiation?

Yet the fact remained that when Stalin first heard of Hess's flight he immediately suspected that he was acting as Hitler's emissary. At the time, Stalin was in the company of Krushchev who argued that Hess was undoubtedly on a 'secret mission from Hitler', to which Stalin replied, 'Yes, that's it. You understand correctly.' Stalin's suspicions about Britain stemmed from the Revolution when the British had intervened against the Communists and on the side of the White Army.

The flight of Rudolf Hess was interpreted in two ways by Stalin. The first was that Germany was anxious to strike a deal with Britain that would permit Germany a free hand in attacking Russia or, worse, a combined Anglo-German assault against Bolshevism. The second was that Hess, who was known to be virulently anti-Bolshevik, had split with other members of the German leadership who were keen to open negotiations with Russia. If Hess had fled, this meant that those anxious to do a deal with Russia had the upper hand, and the massed tanks on Russia's borders were a prelude to a deal rather than war. Stalin convinced himself it was the latter and felt he had supporting evidence.

The NKGB had reported to Stalin that Hess's arrival in Britain coincided with rumours of a meeting between the Russian leader and Hitler. The statement endorsed the idea that Hess was attempting to prevent a German-Soviet agreement. Stalin's view of Hess was as a hapless figure: when Hess had met Russian Foreign Minister Molotov in Berlin in November 1940, he was viewed as a barrier to rapprochement, but equally as an unimpressive character. 'Do you have a Party programme?' Molotov demanded of the Deputy Führer, quite aware they did not. 'Do you have Party rules? And do you have a Constitution?'

An NKVD report sent to the Kremlin from the Russian Embassy in Berlin on 14 November was also highly critical of Hess, and spiced with salacious rumours. The agents could find no one to praise his 'propaganda or administrative talents', though he was viewed as 'trustful'. As the officer said, 'Perhaps he has some extraordinary capabilities, but as it happens no one has yet detected them.' According to the report, Hess had once belonged to a 'group of "hots" (homosexuals) who nicknamed him "Black Bertha", a name by which he was referred to behind his back not only in Munich and Berlin, where he was also referred to as "she" and his wife as "he"'. The report concluded that Hess was 'an insignificant person in a most conspicuous position'.

When Hess landed in Scotland, a member of the Gestapo who was, in fact, a double-agent for the Soviet Union called 'Litseist', reported that the Deputy Führer was a lunatic who had spent four to seven months during the past two years in a sanatorium, and had been stripped of authority. He was 'a bitter opponent of the Soviet Union' and 'an enthusiastic supporter of England', who had now developed the idea that he was 'the new Christ' who would 'save the world'. It was this agent who had briefed his handlers that there was a split within the German leadership, and that any military action against Russia would only take place after the collapse of negotiations. A second double agent, 'Starshina', advanced another rumour that Hess was working with Goering on his mission.

However, Kobulov, the head of station in Berlin, decided to cover both possible avenues by reporting that Hess had departed 'in an excellent state and with the knowledge and at the suggestion of the German Government'. He explained how an agent, 'Frankfurter', had dined with a General who said the flight 'was not an escape but was done with Hitler's connivance; a mission with peace offers to England'. Yet while reporting all rumours, and other reports, Kobulov then came to the personal conclusion that Hess had acted on his own initiative with a view to ending war against Britain, thus freeing up more German troops for the East.

If these were the reports from Berlin, what was coming from London? It was certainly less decisive, and there was a problem: Stalin was suspicious that so many appeasers remained in the British Cabinet, ready – should circumstances prove suitable – to reach out an open palm towards Germany, and for this there was precedence. When Britain was at her most vulnerable after the fall of France, Lord Halifax had, on the advice of Sir Stafford Cripps in Moscow, told Ivan Maisky, the Russian Ambassador, that Britain's response to a peace deal by Hitler would depend on Russia's deals with Britain. As a result, Soviet Intelligence was constantly on watch for any signs of a British-German deal. In July 1940 they reported that Hitler was in talks with the Duke of Windsor – the former King Edward VIII: 'Edward is discussing with Hitler the possibility of the formation of a new English government and the conclusion of peace with Germany, on the condition of the creation of a military alliance against USSR.' In April 1941 there was anxious talk in Moscow of an Anglo-German pact. Maisky was persistently pestered to keep an eye on the appeasers.

After Hess arrived in Britain, Maisky met as quickly as possible with Rab Butler, Parliamentary Under-Secretary at the Foreign Office, who told him talks with Hess had not yet begun. Maisky then briefed the Kremlin on 15 May that 'a very strong anti-Soviet attitude' would run through the debriefings, and that Hess was against the Ribbentrop-Molotov Pact; but, he reported, Hess had come on his own initiative and had not yet leaked any secrets.

The silence from the British Government disturbed Maisky as much as it did his master back in Moscow, so he arranged a second meeting with Butler on 16 May, ostensibly to discuss the repatriation of Soviet sailors and vessels held in British ports. While Butler was not privy to any inside information, he told Maisky that he did not believe Hess had been acting on behalf of Hitler. Butler then said it might be possible that Hess was acting for a splinter group within the German hierarchy. Maisky reported Butler as saying that if Hess had 'the strange idea that he would find a mass of Quislings here, waiting only for Germany to stretch out its hand, then he is already or soon will be convinced of his mistake'. He also insisted that there would be no meeting between Hess and Churchill.

At a third meeting on 21 May Butler developed his own perceptions even further, saying that 'there was a quarrel between Hess and Hitler, as a result of which Hess decided to make his flight to England in the hope that here he would succeed in finding influential circles prepared to make peace with Germany.' Maisky reported to Stalin that the hopes were 'a fantasy'.

Meanwhile, Anatoly Gorsky, the Soviet spymaster who ran Philby, Burgess and Maclean, sent another report from Philby (who had got his information from Tom Dupree, the deputy chief of the press department of the Foreign Office) that Hess planned to appeal through Hamilton to the 'Cliveden set'. He was aware of

Hess's first meeting with Kirkpatrick but could not provide details of the peace proposals. As a result NKGB stations were instructed to find out what the peace proposals were, and whether they had been sanctioned by Hitler or were supported by those in the military in disagreement with Hitler's rule.

The report that was to sow the deepest doubt in Stalin's mind was sent by Philby on 22 May. The Russian leader was already confused by the correct report that Hess remained loyal to Hitler, and the false reports that he had already had meetings with Beaverbrook and Eden. So when Philby reported 'that the time for peace negotiations has not yet arrived, but that later in the course of the war Hess could become the centre of intrigues for a compromise peace and would therefore be useful for the peace party in England and for Hitler,' Stalin became convinced that Hess was an ace Churchill was keeping up his sleeve.

The Soviet Union's fears were to be deliberately manipulated by the British Government, who wished to achieve two specific goals. In May, Britain also believed the military build-up in the east was a negotiating tactic, and her first goal was to prevent a new agreement being struck between Hitler and Stalin. The second goal was to dispel the impression that Britain was deliberately attempting to manoeuvre Moscow into war.

The decision to use Hess as a wedge between Russia and Germany was made on the evening of 14-15 May 1941, when Churchill was finally dissuaded from making a full statement to Parliament and agreed to the idea, put forward by Eden and Lord Beaverbrook, that the Government should manipulate the information for propaganda and so change Soviet policy towards Germany. The Soviets' fascination with the Hess affair had already been reported to London by Cripps, who explained that Britain was blessed with a 'golden opportunity' to prey on Russia's fears or put them to bed. As Cripps explained:

> 1. Hess incident has no doubt intrigued the Soviet Government quite as much as anybody else and may well have aroused their old fears of a peaceable deal at their expense.
>
> 2. I am, of course, unaware to what extent, if at all, Hess is prepared to talk. But on the assumption that he is, I very much hope you will consider urgently the possibility of using his revelations to stiffen the Soviet resistance to German pressure either a) by increasing their fears of being left alone to face the music or b) by encouraging them to think that the music, if faced now and in company, will not be so formidable after all; or preferably by both, for the two things are not really incompatible.

The disinformation the British Government decided to spread was that the German leadership was now split over how to handle Russia. Hess was cast as 'one of the most fanatical of the Nazis', whose mission was to scupper any successful negotiations between Russia and Germany.

The reason Britain wished to act in such a manner was because of their understanding of the reason behind Germany's military build-up on Russia's border. British Intelligence interpreted it as a move to force Russia to agree further concessions, rather than as any precursor to invasion. The Joint Intelligence Committee said there were already indications that 'a new agreement between the two countries may be nearly complete'. Another report stated, 'Hitler and Stalin may have decided to conclude a far-reaching agreement, the basis of which is not yet clear, for political, economic, and even military collaboration.' War between the two nations would only occur, according to British Intelligence, if Russia failed to agree to Germany's demands. Among Britain's concerns was that a new Soviet-German agreement would threaten Britain's Middle-Eastern oil supplies.

As a result of these concerns, the Foreign Office and the secret service toyed with the idea of using Hess 'mendaciously' to prevent the Russians from agreeing to any deal. As Stalin had recently been lulled by Schulenburg, the German Ambassador, into believing reconciliation was possible, the flight of Rudolf Hess backed up his own assumption but also raised a new fear that Hess might actually succeed in uniting England and Germany.

On 16 May, a Foreign Office paper was prepared by Sir Orme Sargent, detailing the disinformation he was keen to promote:

'Hess considers himself the custodian of the true and original Nazi doctrine, the fundamental tenet of which is that Nazism is intended to save Germany and Europe from Bolshevism; Hitler has now been persuaded by the later adherents of the Party, who are mere opportunists, and by the Army, to try and reach a settlement with the Soviet Union to the extent of bringing her in as a full Axis partner; this was more than Hess could stand and hence his flight to this country.'

The seed of the idea which MI6 and the Foreign Office wished to see grow in Stalin's mind was that Hitler, by embarking on new negotiations, wished to draw Russia ever closer into Germany's domain with the eventual goal of toppling Stalin and replacing him with a puppet government. Yet Eden was concerned for two reasons, first that word would reach Germany, whom he wished to keep in the dark about what Hess may or may not have said, and secondly that the plan could backfire and actually push Russia closer to Germany. So he put the plan on hold.

The fact that the Hess debriefing was failing for the moment to produce any usable material meant it now made sense to use him in another manner. So it was decided to seep out snippets of misinformation via more low-key elements. On 23 May the Foreign Office agreed to a directive by MI6 'for the exploitation of the Hess incident through underground channels abroad'.

The directive, codenamed Venom, was to be dripped into the appropriate Soviet ears by Embassy staff in Stockholm, New York and Istanbul. The briefing paper read:

> The following is a directive on Hess designed for Russia only and to be spread through channels leading directly to Soviet. Hess's flight indicates a growing split in Party and nation over Hitler's policy of collaboration with Soviet. Nazi purists whom Hess led, hold as fundamental tenet of Nazi faith that Party's duty is to save Germany and indeed Europe from Bolshevism. Hence bitter resentment at what they consider Hitler's betrayal of Nazi faith. Although, therefore, Hitler may persevere with policy of collaboration with Soviet he will not long be able to carry with him the Party and still less the country. Sooner or later he will abandon it either willingly or under Party pressure. Therefore, in any pact with Soviet, Hitler will insist on immediate benefits in the form of raw materials, oil, political and military pressure by Soviet against Turkey, etc. while Soviet benefits will be such as require time to materialise, and before they have materialised Hitler will have repudiated his undertakings. In that event the last state of Soviet Government will be worse than first, for they will have broken with their friends in favour of Germany and given Germany valuable materials and allowed infiltration in the form of German technicians planted in Russia.
>
> Moreover, having lost friends with whom they might have jointly resisted German aggression, they will eventually have to face Germany single-handed. Thus flight of Hess is clear warning to Soviet to beware of Hitler's present offer of collaboration and friendship.

While Morton (Churchill's intelligence liaison officer) said of the memo, 'I don't myself find it very impressive,' he could see no reason to object. When Sargent read Morton's judgment on it, he wrote of his own text, 'I think this is rather good,' while Eden added that it was 'quite good' and that 'we want to start as many "whispers" as possible.' Meanwhile, Cadogan merrily declared that 'whispers can be much more irresponsible and even, without disadvantage, conflicting and confusing.'

As a result of the plan, Cripps was advised not to embark on his own brand of disinformation but to follow the new, and false, Government line: 'We are putting it about through covert channels that Hess's flight indicates growing split over Hitler's policy of collaboration with the Soviet Union and that, if pursued, [Hitler] will insist on short-term benefits knowing that he will be forced to abandon it and to break any promises which he may have made to the Soviet Union, so that in the end their last state will be worse than their first. They will have lost potential friends and made concessions and will be left to face Germany single-handed in a weakened state.'

The 'Whisper Campaign' took off. Anthony Eden invited a group of journalists into the Foreign Office and informed them that 'Hess was earnest about his mission, and that the mission indicated a split within the German leadership.' *The Times* reported the next day that Hess was trying to 'get a peace plan over', though they went a step further by stating that it had been authorised by Hitler himself.

Eden then misled Maisky by telling him that Hess had fled Germany because of a quarrel he had had, not with Hitler himself, but with several senior figures in his entourage such as Ribbentrop and Himmler. The Russian Ambassador was now struggling to make sense of the conflicting reports.

The whisper campaign was picked up by the NKVD, who reported in early June that the 'ruling circle' (Hitler, Von Ribbentrop, Himmler and chief of the armed forces, General Keitel) were planning a 'policy of Bismarck' (a reference to Otto von Bismarck, the Iron Chancellor who united the German states) in relation to Russia and that they were now stronger after the departure of Rudolf Hess. Stalin's view was that Hess's mission might herald the long sought-after negotiations with the Germans.

Meanwhile, Maisky decided to try and ride both horses without falling off. He was also frank, stating that it was difficult to 'sift the most probable from the mass of tales, reports, guesses, suppositions, rumours, etc, surrounding this strange, almost romantic story'. Two dinners in May, however, resulted in the unappetising notion for the Soviet Union of a possible deal between Britain and Germany against Russia. First, Maisky dined with Sidney and Beatrice Webb, the anti-capitalist socialists on 23 May, during which he tried to find out the politicians' view on a peace deal:

'[Webb] gave us what he believed to be the truth about the Hess affair. Hess had been quite frank about his mission; though he refused to say that it was with the assent of Hitler. He wanted to persuade the British Government to give way: the British and the Allies would be beaten in the war for the domination of Europe, though it would exhaust Germany in doing it. Germany must remain the dominating force in Europe; Great Britain must keep her Empire except for a few minor concessions in Africa. Then Germany and Great Britain could stop the spread of Bolshevism, which was a devil.'

The second dinner was with Lord Beaverbrook who insisted, 'Oh, of course Hess is an emissary of Hitler.' Beaverbrook then hyped up Hess's views, presenting them as Britain and Germany against the barbarism of Russia. Beaverbrook confided that 'Hess apparently thought he would only have to unfold his plan to make all those dukes run to the King, dump Churchill, and create a "reasonable government". Idiot!' Beaverbrook said Britain would consider peace with Germany on 'acceptable terms' but he felt it was unlikely such terms would be offered 'at this stage'. Maisky now believed Churchill would strike a deal with Hitler if the right proposal were made.

Russia and Germany were in the midst of what turned out to be false negotiations, but Russia was worried that if Britain learned of this then she would jump the gun and do a deal, through Hess, with Hitler. So on 5 June, when Maisky told Eden that there were no negotiations, Eden replied that, according to his information, 'serious negotiations' dealing with matters of 'tremendous significance' were already in motion. On the same day, Eden issued an official guideline that no other department was to speak about Hess but that the Foreign Office could and would continue to do so.

Five days later Maisky met Lloyd George who was dispirited and talking openly about a compromise peace. The former Prime Minister said 'acceptable terms' to Britain were the German possession of Danzig, Silesia, Austria and Alsace-Lorraine, and a role as 'protectorate' over some portions of Europe and Poland, with 'adjustments' made in Holland. However, he insisted 'the proposals produced by Hess were absolutely unacceptable.'

When Maisky learned that Lord Simon (whom he regarded as an arch appeaser) had met with Hess, the Russian was deeply troubled. He read into the event – and accordingly reported to Stalin – that while Churchill, Eden, and the Labour ministers were opposed to negotiation, other 'men like Simon' were not averse to sounding out the possibility of peace. The fact that Stafford Cripps was recalled to London around the time of Lord Simon's interview heightened the Russians' suspicions that a deal could soon be struck between Britain and Germany. However, Maisky interpreted from these puzzling pieces of information that a Cabinet struggle had taken place and Churchill had won. Yet Maisky's report failed to stop Stalin brooding on the idea of Hess being kept back as a bargaining chip.

The Political Intelligence Department at the Foreign Office was now concerned that no benefit was being derived from Hess, and was keen that as much anti-Bolshevik material be extracted as possible. The question was whether the Foreign Office should continue with the whisper campaign or tell Russia the genuine reason for Hess's visit, revealing what information they had. Eden and Cadogan were keen that the whispers should continue, while Duff Cooper argued that it should be presented to Cabinet for a ministerial discussion. Eden got his way and the whispers continued.

When, in June, Britain told Stalin that they had learned from the ULTRA decrypts from Bletchley Park that Germany was not preparing for negotiations but for war, Stalin dismissed the intelligence as just one more attempt to get him to go to war. On 14 June he issued a TASS communique denouncing 'rumours of war' as false and saying that German troop movements had 'nothing to do with Soviet-German relations'. Stalin expected Berlin to respond in agreement and was intimidated by their silence.

His answer came on the morning of 22 June 1941, when the German tanks rumbled across the Russian border. In Stalin's mind, an unbreakable link was soldered between Hess's flight to Britain and the beginning of Operation Barbarossa.

Three years later, in October 1944, after Churchill and Stalin had divided Europe into specific percentages, Stalin raised the subject of Hess with the British Prime Minister. Churchill wrote in his memoirs: 'Stalin then rather unexpectedly proposed a toast to the health of the British Intelligence Service which had inveigled Hess into coming to England. He could not have landed without being given signals. The Intelligence Service must have been behind it.'

The genesis of this belief was a report that Lavrenty Beria, Chief of the Soviet secret police, sent on 24 October 1942 to Stalin and Molotov, explaining that Hess had been lured in by the British secret service. Churchill was indignant and denied this, but Stalin said that British Intelligence simply did not tell him, just as the Russian Intelligence Service 'often did not inform the Soviet Government of its intentions and only did so after their work was accomplished'. As the historian Oleg Gorodetsky has written, 'The affair clearly had disastrous repercussion on Stalin's state of mind in the crucial month leading up to the German-Soviet war.'

Meanwhile, the British Enemy Propaganda Department wished to turn Hess into a magnet that would attract the German population away from Hitler. To do so, they could not portray him as a traitor, nor one who had seen the light of democratic values and adopted anti-Nazi ideas. Instead, he had to be viewed as 'the character they have long admired – as a loyal German; as the most normal, decent, restrained, likable family man amongst Nazi leaders, with a strong, simple sincerity . . .' 'By doing so, 'a Jekyll and Hyde contrast can be developed so that Hess becomes Dr Jekyll and Hitler becomes Mr Hyde:

'In using Hess to demoralise the enemy, our main objectives should be 1) to keep alive the interest, affection and confidence which the ordinary German feels towards Hess. 2) To draw from his actions a political moral for all Germans, calculated to produce an effect favourable to ourselves.'

The idea was for the propagandists to portray Hess as a leader who, from his unequalled vantage point, had seen where Germans were being led, and who acted out of a 'simple revulsion against the reign of violence and deceit'. On this point they had been assisted by the German authorities, who in their post-flight statements claimed Hess's mind had been unbalanced by his horror of destruction. As the report stated, 'The Germans have therefore given the departed Hess an exceptionally good character. It is only necessary to prove his sanity and to turn the message he is supposed to deliver to the British back onto the Germans to take advantage of their mistake in failing to discredit him.'

It was suggested that the best way to illustrate Hess's sanity was for the Deputy Führer to record a series of daily radio broadcasts in which he delivered the political message that 'Hitler has forsaken his vision of a happy Germany peopled by Germans' and had now condemned her youth to live abroad as oppressors. To achieve this effect, the report argued that Hess's secretly recorded conversations should be edited to collate any points that would back up the planned propaganda and be billed as 'Hess Speaks'.

Under the section headed *Leaflets*, was written:

'Pictures of Hess in England should be dropped in Germany. He should be photographed in civilian dress to symbolise his attitude of the advocate of peace. The following are some simple poses which would be understandable but disconcerting to his wide public amongst the youth and women of Germany: Hess with arms characteristically stiff and hands clasped in front of him, with the stare he usually devoted to the Führer this time directed at the Leader of Europe, Mr Churchill; Hess in civilian dress conversing in a comradely way with the Duke of Hamilton in Wing Commander's uniform; Hess stooping to address an English child in unblitzed surroundings; Hess in attitude of spiritual meditation or disillusioned indignation.' (Alexander Cadogan underlined Churchill's name and wrote 'Gosh!!!' in the margin of his copy.)

Another plan was to have the Duke of Hamilton deliver an address, a stirring piece of prose in which he took Hess and his 'murderous' gang to task, but this was quashed by the RAF's refusal to allow the Wing Commander, who was himself less than keen, to participate. For weeks, the Enemy Propaganda Department had been champing at the bit to unleash their inventiveness on an already bizarre situation. Yet they had been held back because the Government first wished to concentrate on running 'the Bolshevik hare'; then, after the German invasion of Russia rendered it redundant (the hare crushed under its treadmills), the Government was concerned lest any statements produced by EPD could be contradicted by any fresh position adopted once Hess had been fully debriefed, with the information properly weighted and considered.

The gambit of using Lord Simon to stage a negotiation had failed and so the Foreign Office chose to examine what benefits could be derived from a fresh propaganda campaign. As Sir Alexander Cadogan wrote, 'I have always contemplated that, after trying our "Dr Guthrie" gambit, we might have to consider what we could do about Hess in the matter of propaganda. The Guthrie conversation has, of itself, yielded nothing, and is likely to yield no more.'

And 10 Downing Street stated: 'I submit that the time has now come to cash in on this wind-fall. In my opinion, great value could accrue were an official statement and propaganda to be issued at once. The longer we wait the rottener the apple.'

Cadogan then arranged for Con O'Neill of S.O.1 to be given access to all the current Hess documents, including full transcriptions from which O'Neill drew up what Cadogan then described as 'a very good and very interesting plan'. In a typed, seven-page memorandum, O'Neill set out his argument that 'whispers' could continue to be used, but with the Bolshevik hare now quite dead, the best theme to play on was that 'Hess came because he knew Germany could not win the war' – a blatant lie, but permissible as a rumour. O'Neill, however, favoured open propaganda, using the press and the BBC, but for this avenue fresh facts were required, as well as a detailed Government statement. He asserted that 'The few facts already published have been sucked quite dry, and no more flesh can be got off these bones.' Speculation, he explained, can last five minutes but a new batch of facts would form a 'staple diet' for a week or a fortnight. He believed that either the Prime Minister or the Foreign Secretary should make a statement in the House of Commons that was most consistent with 'an effective propaganda policy and, as far as possible, with the truth'. The problem was that Hess's current position did not make for good propaganda. The line used for the past five weeks was consistent and followed four key points:

Hess is sane.

He has given important information on various subjects.

He is anxious for peace because he has lost his confidence in German victory.

He is not an idealist or a refugee, but a Nazi who has lost his nerve and his faith in Hitler.

'None of these is true,' O'Neill continued, 'but it is nevertheless important, if at all possible, to continue to follow this line and the additional glosses on [point] c. which we have in fact employed – namely that Hess has lost confidence in German victory because he is anxious about the USA, British bombing and Russia.'

O'Neill had prepared a draft statement for the Prime Minister and Foreign Secretary which bent the truth over the state of Hess's mental health, but as the civil servant argued, 'It may be repugnant and disagreeable to distort the truth. But if we are to use the case of Hess to inflict the maximum damage on the morale of the enemy, made specially vulnerable by this episode, I think we must do so.'

The target was the German people, with the Government's statement to be followed up with quotes from Hess, tailored for use in open propaganda. The statement would also detail his attempted suicide, but present it not as proof of insanity but as the 'despair of a blunderer ashamed of his stupidity'. In arguing for the retention of this paragraph O'Neill wrote, 'Finally, I think it would be desirable to announce this fact from the point of view of the public at home. They will be gratified to learn that Hess has hurt himself; and the fact that he has got to be in bed for four months should completely quench all idle speculation as to his whereabouts.'

Among O'Neill's other suggestions was that a letter Hess had written to his son detailing his flight should be broadcast in Germany; the manuscript should be photographed and reproduced in German leaflets: 'The handwriting is firm and normal, and gives no impression of insanity'; the most pessimistic passages of his recorded conversations should be edited and broadcast in Germany.

O'Neill was critical of the manner in which Hess was being debriefed:

> While I think a very high degree of skill has been shown in conducting conversations with him, the range of subjects that have been covered, at least in the reports that I have seen, is limited. Moreover, on one or two occasions his interlocutors have interrupted him just at a point where he threatened to become interesting e.g. on Blomberg and Ribbentrop. I suggest efforts should be made to engage him in further conversation on the

subject of his own work in Germany about which he seems ready to talk. On the subject of our propaganda to Germany, which does not seem to have been touched on, on the subject of the air war, about which as an ex-flying officer he must know a certain amount, even if it be only minor gossip, and on the subject of a few notorious episodes in Nazi history such as 30 June 1934, and the death of Von Fritsch.

I suggest further that advantage be taken of his convalescence to allow some of his English friends and acquaintances, such as he has, to visit him and engage him in general conversation. Such visitors need know nothing of arrangements for recording and should be asked to submit their own reports. The list of topics for conversation to be pursued by his present interlocutors or other visitors could be extended indefinitely.

Frank Foley was shown O'Neill's memo and was broadly supportive of it. He agreed that the suicide attempt should be revealed as, despite the most stringent security at Camp Z, it could possibly leak. He said Hess's conversations were packed ready for dispatch, with a detailed catalogue. He felt it was unlikely Hess would consent to a radio broadcast, and reserved his most robust wording for the criticism of him and his officers' interrogatory technique:

At present Hess is not communicative – he may improve. It is almost impossible to make spontaneous conversation with him, as all the officers here will testify – I doubt whether he would react usefully to visits of English friends, he would probably suspect them. He would most probably insist on the Duke of Hamilton coming first and refuse anyone else if that request was not granted.

'It does not seem to be realised by SO1 that, until 17 June when he was allowed *The Times*, topics of conversation were limited by the ban on news and by other considerations con-

> nected with the visit of the negotiator – since then he has been too preoccupied with his health. It is only fair to state that officers here have spent many patient hours with him without getting more than a grunt in reply to their attempts to converse with him on many subjects; this morning he again mentioned his fear of poisoning to the MO.

The nine-page public statement to be presented by Churchill or Eden to the House of Commons would have explained the letter from Albrecht Haushofer to the Duke of Hamilton; Hess's flight, and his denial of Hitler's involvement – 'and no good reason has been found for doubting this denial.' While remaining coy with the exact reason for his arrival, 'this much I can say: Hess came because he was anxious that the war should be stopped.' The statement falsely attributed to Hess 'equal concern in contemplation of Russia either as a possible friend or as a possible enemy'.

However, the statement was upfront on Hess's plan for peace with Britain: that Germany reign supreme over Europe, including Russia as far east as the Urals and Caspian Sea, with Britain retaining her Empire, minus 'of course, all former German colonies, including South-West Africa'. It also stated the Government's position on Hess's plan: 'I need not tell the House that H.M.G. have not given a second thought to the so-called peace proposals brought by Hess.' The statement then detailed Hess's ignorance of Britain – her politics and her people. He had expected to find a one-party state where the people were starving in the streets. Hess, the statement declared, was not only 'ignorant and credulous' but 'weak, incompetent and, indeed, contemptible'. The second lie was inserted into the next sentence: 'What can be more abject than the spectacle of a man who forgets even his duty of discretion and loyalty to that leader . . . For, Honourable Members will be interested to hear, Hess's discretion and loyalty have not been conspicuous since he arrived here. We are glad that this is so. But to what extent it is so, and in what particulars, the House will not expect me to divulge.'

In addressing Hess's health and mental character, the House was to be told, 'Yes, he is sane enough in the clinical sense,' but the statement went on to paint him as a grotesque, cursed with the 'stigmata of degeneration' that included malformed ears, receding lower jaw and a high-arched palate – the whole foul pen-portrait capped by the revelation that an x-ray had revealed him to be in possession of 'a small and narrow heart'. His suicide attempt was put down to the failure of his mission and his 'ignominious captivity', and when he was chastised for previously assuring his guards he would not try to kill himself 'he endeavoured to excuse his conduct by observing that had Field Marshal Goering been in his position, he would have committed suicide at a much earlier date.'

The statement ended, 'There for the moment I will leave this interesting history. We shall not forget it, nor will the people of Germany. Meanwhile, we shall continue to prosecute the war, fortified by this exhibition of the quality, anxiety and disunity of the leaders of our enemy.'

It was a speech destined never to be delivered. For while Cadogan praised O'Neill's proposed propaganda campaign he added, 'But I am doubtful whether we should do this.' He admitted that there was considerable demand for information on Hess in Britain and that the recent memo – of which he had been ignorant – alerting him to the concerns of American industrialists about the prospect of a 'negotiated peace', was a reason to get information out; but he added that a lot had happened since then, including the re-bombing of Germany.

He felt that on one hand the British Government's silence about Hess was effective in making the German Government 'thoroughly uncomfortable'. But he felt that he would prefer to keep propaganda moving forward through current means – whispers – 'rather than official statements'.

Cadogan wrote this on 28 June. The following day, in a handwritten minute Anthony Eden endorsed Cadogan's views, stating, 'I agree with Sir A. Cadogan. Mr O'Neill's is a very capable production and we are most indebted to him. It does, however, involve a statement by the Foreign Secretary (or the Prime Minister) that is admittedly wide of the truth. I should not be willing to make such a statement, despite its possible immediate advantage.'

Had he known of Eden's decision, Goebbels would have been delighted. The German propaganda minister was already surprised by Britain's failure to properly capitalize on the arrival of Rudolf Hess and had declared: 'We are dealing with dumb amateurs over there.' While Hitler mocked Britain for 'muffing their biggest political opportunity'.

13

The King and I

The crinkled brown leaves that now blanketed the lawns surrounding Mytchett Place were swirled away by the arrival of a letter that transformed a British autumn into a high summer in Germany. For a few brief moments, Hess was transported from the bedroom of a draughty English country house and the watchful eye of a uniformed guard, to a sun-dappled swimming pool where his son nervously ventured out with the assistance of water-wings; to the garden, where Ilse and her sister picked strawberries, and to the countryside around Harlaching where he had often walked with his dogs, Pursel and Tapsi. If the dogs, as reported, were homesick for their master, one can only imagine how Hess himself felt on receiving a letter from his young son which began, 'My dear Daddy,' and which explained that it was being typed by 'Mummy' in his old work room with Buz sitting on her lap. 'I would rather do it quite by myself, because I do love sitting over Mummy's typewriter. But Mummy said I am still too small for that, and if I did you wouldn't be able to read it after all.'

This first letter from home was bitter-sweet. Written on 9 August 1941, it was a message from the past when his young son could still look forward to visiting Granny and Grandpa. In the letter, Buz told how they had found a picture of him and that it now hung above his bed and was each evening bid 'Good night'. The envelope contained two new pictures of Buz and the letter ended with a hope that 'you haven't tummy ache Daddy dear'.

Hess replied on the day of receipt, 26 October, and enclosed a pencil drawing of his plane in the letter. 'My dear little Buz, Just think, the first letter which Daddy received from home was a letter from you . . .' He explained that, while it had been a long time since it was written, it had given him no less pleasure, and that by next summer he expected Buz to be swimming properly without a belt. 'You told me in your letter that Mummy sometimes opens the cupboard in the small work room. Has Mummy also fired the big gun? I am afraid she does not know how to load it – mummies cannot know such things, only daddies. But probably you showed her how it was done.'

He reminded his son of the day of his departure and how, just as he was saying *Auf Wiedersehen*, Buz had opened his eyes and asked, 'Where are you going, Daddy?' and he had replied, 'I cannot tell you, my son;' and when the boy asked why not, Hess explained that he would only tell him upon his return. He reiterated the promise to reveal everything when next they met but, unaware of when this would be, he offered him some advice. In his letter, Buz had talked of fighting with a little girl. Hess assured him that 'Buzileins' [his term for girls] would bring many unexpected and painful experiences, but that they were 'very lovable' and that he should not take them 'too tragically, or life itself – that is the best way to get on.'

Hess also enclosed a letter to Ilse, in which he expressed the hope that his mother had recovered from the shock of his father's death, and explained that in his own grief he had been reminded of two poems she was familiar with from which he quoted:

All ways in this world, both lovely and unfriendly, all roads lead to my door, was the first; the second, *And even if you leave your homeland, your home does not leave you.*

He ended the note by asking that she 'give my son a nice birthday table for me too.'

The joy brought by the letter from home quickly diminished as it served to remind him of his captivity. From his bedroom window he saw the construction of a small exercise ground, encircled in wire mesh, to which he would now be restricted. There would be no more roaming the gardens. He told Foley that he would not leave his room and go downstairs until it was enlarged and suitably altered. A couple of days later, Scott noted 'Z seemed very depressed, probably owing to the fact that he received another letter, this time from his son.' Yet it may also have galvanised Hess to seek a means of improving his current conditions, and finally clarifying whether his father was indeed dead. On the evening of 3 November he asked Foley if he knew the name and address of the Minister of the protecting power, as the Swiss were known. Foley said he did not, but would check. Hess asked if he knew whether there were telegraphic facilities between London and Berne, as he planned to ask the Swiss Minister to check on his father. Foley was suspicious that Hess was explaining what he wished to discuss with the Minister, and considered it a deliberate attempt to cover up an alternative plan. He assumed that if permission for the meeting with Swiss Minister were granted, then a verbatim record would be required, and asked that Lieutenant Colonel Kendrick ('Wallace') be permitted to come back and assist.

A letter had arrived from Hess's aunt, Emma Rothacker, in Zurich, in which she passed on family news and praised Ilse as a 'capable life-comrade', as well as assuring him that 'we think of you so much! You know that we think about you with love and confidence.' She said that she hoped he was being well looked after as 'the country in which you are is not low as concerns hygiene . . .' In reply Hess wrote of his father's death: 'Although it hurt me very much, I was glad that his sufferings were not long-drawn out. That would be terrible for him who had scarcely known illness in his life and was always active.' Fate, he said, had been hard on him for not allowing them to meet once last time. 'We do not understand why fate directs our paths in one way and another. On the whole this is especially applicable in this war. At the last minute, the immense danger with which

Bolshevism threatened Europe and our whole civilisation was stopped by fate.' He ended the letter with a forlorn postscript: 'It would be nice if you would write to me again.'

October was a difficult month. On Thursday the eighth, the papers had carried news of the death of Hess's father in Hindelang after a short illness. Foley decided it best to break the news himself and visited him that morning. Although Scott later reported that 'Foley informed Z of this but he appeared to be quite unmoved,' it was a false front, put up to deny the enemy an insight into his true feelings. Six days later he would write to his mother, 'I have waited a few days before writing to you in order to obtain at least a little inner detachment – I succeeded externally from the beginning.' He continued, 'My greatest sorrow is that I was not able to see father again and that he did not witness my return.' Hess said he was consoled by the news that part of the family was present, but his thoughts drifted back to the question of fate: 'I believe more than ever in the inevitableness of man's fate. Thus individual men at least are forced to an action which is of decisive necessity for the great events of the world.' Perhaps thinking also of himself, he added 'a few chosen ones are called upon to decide the aspect of centuries by perhaps a single deed. I have in mind the Führer, who decided to forestall the attack of the Bolshevists: the full significance of his decision will only be completely recognised in later ages.' He closed the letter, 'We must, therefore, submit to the death of Father as unavoidable fate, however painful we feel it.'

The final hours of the life of Rudolf Hess's father, Fritz, were detailed by Ilse in a letter addressed to 'my dear little husband', which he received on 13 January 1942. Although his father had cancer, and had endured a 'frightful' attack of shingles, he also had calcification of the coronary arteries and, as Ilse explained, 'It was a question above all of the general weakness of old age combined with great heart weakness.' Buzz had been by his grandfather's side until three hours before his death and 'showed his usual tenderness to anyone with bodily and mental ailments by sitting beside him and laying his fair head near him so that he could stroke it.' When Buzz went to bed, Ilse stayed with Hess's father 'until I felt the pulse stop and there was nothing left except a beautiful peaceful countenance, and we shall never forget the peace of the end.'

Hess's mother said in the final moments, 'I can now quite forget how bad and angry he has often been to me', a comment which Ilse took as a positive sign. She told her husband: 'So you see, old boy, what people are like and how quickly we are ready to forget the bad in each other and preserve the good in our hearts, aren't we?'

Hess had had a difficult relationship with his father, and Ilse tried to heal the breach. 'We shall remember him and so must you dear, by the Virginia creeper stiffly erect in the corner when there was sun, or hanging mournfully when there was driving rain – in the little green huntsman's hut with the glass hanging there – or at home tuning in the wireless and winding the clock which, owing to old age, would never go . . . on his chair on the veranda asleep over the newspaper – blustering or tender, angry or gentle, as he could be – and remember that at the end he wanted only me and Buz; you know, don't you, who it was he really wanted?'

It is interesting to note that MI9 (Military Intelligence) examined the letter carefully, after their suspicions were alerted by the way in which it was 'somewhat peculiarly couched' and which they finally put down to 'family style or jargon'.

When the cast was taken off Hess's leg he asked to celebrate with a bottle of champagne. The wine cellar was searched and a suitable vintage duly served with the evening meal. It was fortunate the news that soldiers had acted as sommeliers did not reach the ears of Will Thorne, the Member of Parliament for Plaistow, who had taken a particular interest in the lavishness of Hess's food, and raised a question in Parliament about its 'special and luxurious' quality. As a consequence of his question to the House, an investigation had been launched into Hess's diet. It was conducted by Colonel Boulnois, who arrived at Camp Z at four p.m. on the afternoon of 11 October to make an inspection. It proved a farcical affair. It had begun with Boulnois meeting Hess in his living room, after which the Colonel announced that he resented 'having to shake hands with a murderer', and ended with him falling into a ditch while inspecting the grounds.

In the intervening few hours Boulnois quizzed Colonel Scott on the cost of keeping Hess. In the midst of the conversation, which took place in Scott's office, the telephone rang. It was General Gepp, who wished to know if the messing subscription (the sum contributed by each officer) was two shillings and ninepence or three shillings and one penny. The line crackled with static as Scott had to repeat what he had told Boulnois minutes before: that while the sum for officers was two and ninepence, the figure for Hess ranged between three and seven shillings, with the added sums used to buy various extras such as syrup of figs, paint brushes etc. As Scott told Boulnois, 'We were unable to draw rations for Z as he had no ration card. In consequence, the officers and inside staff have to contribute a proportion of their rations for his maintenance.' Boulnois felt this was 'most unfair', an opinion which he conveyed to General Gepp when he took over the phone.

The next point was to satisfy the Colonel that a staff of ten officers was necessary: 'I had little difficulty explaining how we worked and, on seeing part 1 orders, he realised that a) we only have six duty officers b) four had to be in camp and two on 48 hours leave.' A tour of the camp then took place, and it was at Post B that the Colonel took a tumble. 'With the help of CSM Sgt Marden, Guardsman McLean and myself, he was raised to the surface. His tunic suffered somewhat, though not himself.' During a tour of the actual house, the Colonel visited the kitchens and interviewed the 'so-called cook and Sgt Waterhouse, who was questioned at great length as to the rations etc.' The day ended with Colonel Boulnois triggering the alarm and afterwards appearing 'extremely satisfied' when, four minutes and 12 seconds later, the cry went up, 'Defence manned.'

Yet Camp Z was not to hear the last of questions about the kitchen. In a fit of exasperation, Major Foley nailed down the definitive statement about Hess's culinary concern. In a minute marked MOST SECRET and headlined 'Jonathan's Food', he wrote the following:

> Statements have been made in the House about Jonathan's food. I have not read Hansard; the press reports lead me to think that the position has not been understood.
>
> The facts are:-
>
> 1. The Officers' Mess at Z. Camp is made up of 10 Officers and 4 other ranks (3 sergeants and one cook), plus Jonathan. These fifteen individuals draw fourteen rations, i.e. Jonathan does not draw rations.
>
>   He is fed on 1/14th (one fourteenth) of a ration from each of the 14 serving soldiers. There is, therefore, no cost to the country for Jonathan's food as the 14 members of the armed forces would draw their rations in any case.
> 2. The actual basic rations per head drawn are:-
>   Meat 6 oz. daily (including fat and/or bone) net weight 4 oz.
>   Sugar 2 oz. daily
>   Tea 2/7 oz. daily
>   Jam 1 ½ oz. daily
>   Bacon 1 ¼ oz. three times a week
>   Margarine 1 ½ oz. three times a week
>   And other small items.
> 3. Each officer in this mess pays 2s. 9d per day messing, with which extras, outside the issue ration, are bought. Jonathan shares in these extras i.e. the officers supplement his food

out of their pockets as he is treated as a member of the officers' mess as far as his food is concerned.

4. The F.O. allows 3s 0d. a day for Jonathan, that sum is used in principle to pay for his messing. In practice it is spent on his special requirements i.e. barley water, medicinal tea, Dettol, razor blades, soap, etc.
5. It was reported in the press that we were given canned salmon and offal as an issue. That is not correct.
6. I feel you will be interested and amused to know that we are keeping Jonathan in food. The curious position arose logically owing to the fact that it was considered desirable in the public interest not to divulge to the BASC, and other persons concerned with feeding, that Jonathan was in this camp.

The Camp Z diary, kept by Scott, stated 9 October:

Major Foley showed me the translation of Z's official request also a copy of a letter he, Major Foley, has written as a covering letter to Z's request.

In this he strongly criticises this camp in view of its position, unsuitability as regards exercise for Z, and asks for a ruling as to the status of Z. If he is to be considered a P.O.W. then it seems that the convention would be contravened in that this camp is surrounded by military objectives. In short, he recommends careful consideration being given to the possibility of moving Z to a quieter neighbourhood where there would bc greater facilities for his exercise, and the relaxation of the very close confinement which, owing to the position of this camp, is essential for his security.

Foley's report read:

I beg to submit an English translation of a Statement of Evidence and Protest which Jonathan proposes to hand to Dr Livingstone [cover name for Lord Beaverbrook] when he makes his second visit as promised:

1. When Jonathan told me he was writing it I volunteered to do a translation, as I thought it both proper you should know the contents in advance and preferable they should not become known to an outside translator.
2. Originally, Jonathan authorised me to send a copy to 'London'. He withdrew his permission the next day; I agreed to respect his wishes. He is not aware, therefore, that you have a copy. That explains why the German text is not attached.
3. You will observe that the greater part is a repetition of the document which he thought was sent to Mr Loftus MP. There is an important addition which may require consideration e.g. the Protest.
4. People who speak to Jonathan, but who have not been in constant touch with him or who have not read the documents, are inclined to think he is normal. Dr Livingstone told me he had not noticed any trace of insanity. Only the initiated would notice a slight trace of a mind not fully balanced in his recorded conversation with that gentleman.
5. This document will, I think, convince even the sceptical and unpractised lay mind, or anyone who may have thought that Jonathan suffered a deep mental depression of a temporary or ephemeral nature only.

It is not simply the case that no one will ever convince him that he was not given in the past an obnoxious drug to cause insanity. His incapacity to reason logically; his habit of distorting conversations, and of attributing his own statements to others when, consciously or unconsciously, it suits his purpose; his conviction that not only distinguished doctors and surgeons but even a most eminent statesman tolerated, even if they did not actively assist in, the foul work of the 'active agents'; his commiseration of his own alleged frailty, whereas he eats as well and as much as the average person in England, and sleeps more than most; his refusal to believe that his position in Germany has changed; his habit of muttering to himself and of staring for five to ten minutes at the corner of the ceiling; numerous other idiosyncrasies, incline one to conclude that a return to general normality is a doubtful probability. The medical view is, I believe, that a person suffering from paranoia never recovers.

Jonathan is asking the government to accept his word and to order that he be treated with little, if any, restraint, as a sane and normal person of privileged and ministerial standing who came to this country for its own salvation.

He demands the right to spend money and to by-pass the Camp Commandant, both as regards the persons he would commission to buy and the articles bought. His object is, no doubt, to make certain his medicines and foods are not adulterated before they reach him. He advertises his paranoia and simultaneously demands the abolition of restrictions which apply not only to a sufferer, but also to a normal prisoner of war.

Foley then went on to detail his concerns about the current set-up at Camp Z following Hess's suicide attempt:

When he leaves his sick-room, his position will be one of some difficulty. His exercising ground has been considerably reduced (30 x 60 yards); there is no distant view or outlook. It is true that the lattice work over his windows will be removed, but armour-plate glass will be substituted in windows which will only partly open; the fireplaces will be screened and locked.

His "cage" remains. The well of the house has been wired from the ceiling to the door of the lower sitting room, the French window of which will be his only exit to the exercising ground. Anything which might serve as a lethal weapon will be removed.

He demands to be allowed to move freely and unaccompanied between his room and the perimeter, but he will never be left alone day or night. The security constructional work is crude: it will be a constant reminder to him that he is considered a mental case or a potential suicide. It is not of the discreet variety one associates with a mental home. He will be a mental case in a house which is partly military, and coarsely equipped as a mental home.

I am aware that many considerations arise relative to security from attack from outside, etc, but I fear that the plans which are shortly to be put into execution in this house will have a most deleterious and disturbing effect on his mind. They will probably increase instead of decreasing his urge to destroy himself. I venture to think that from the political point of view it is in our interest to keep him as sane as possible. This case is not one which concerns the medical services only. That is my justification for writing of matters which might appear to be the sole concern of the doctors. Perhaps it would be expedient to use this document of Protest as an excuse to review the whole problem.

With regard to S.I.S., I cannot think of any way in which he can be of further use to your organisation unless it is decided to give him a companion whom he would trust and to whom he would open up. To be of any real use, the individual would have to be a man of rank and of good political education.

If a prisoner of war were chosen, the question of the location of this house might have to be considered as, apparently, it is too near a military target to conform to the Geneva Convention. Has the status of Jonathan been defined? Is he a prisoner of war or a prisoner of State? I suppose he has no right to assume, as he does, that he is a Reichsminister and a Parliamentarian, as the Führer appears to have disowned him.

There was one highlight for Foley. On Tuesday 4 November, they purchased a new pair of shoes for Hess at a cost of 37 shillings and sixpence. The shopping trip to Aldershot involved not one but three officers – Foley, Dicks and Captain Percival – though one imagines the opportunity to escape Camp Z, however briefly, would have been difficult to resist (especially given the proximity to a decent pub). Their choice of a stout brogue met with Hess's approval. 'Z was so pleased that he got out of bed, half dressed, and then tried them on and expressed his pleasure and appreciation.' Meanwhile, Scott turned his attention to improving the Camp's camouflage. A plane had recently been sent up to take aerial photographs, which revealed that the old slit trench on the lower lawn showed up with striking clarity.

While Foley and Hess continued to meet daily, progress was slow. On 6 November, Hess asked him to translate into English the lengthy memo, *Germany-England from the Point of View of the War Against the Soviet Union*, which he had previously passed on to Lord Beaverbrook. Foley was already aware of the contents, which contained no new intelligence. Instead he decided to use the anniversary of the Bierkeller Putsch on 8 November as a topic of conversation, with the goal of discovering more about Hess's adjutants. Hess denied any knowledge of a Hans or Fritz Koch, instead launching into another explanation of Hitler's genius. As Foley wrote:

> He has invariably professed total faith in his [Hitler's] universal genius: architect, statesman, productions chief, strategist etc. He told me yesterday that Hitler had a greater knowledge and better grasp of strategy than any member of the German General Staff.
>
> When Hitler produced his plan for the attack in France, the Generals thought it was impossible to execute and would result in disaster: they sent a deputation to Hitler and propounded their own plan to him; they were thinking in terms of static warfare or of a frontal attack by attrition tactics on the Maginot Line. Hitler listened to them according to his custom but refused to change his mind. The Generals then approached him, Jonathan,

> and tried to persuade him to influence the Führer. He declined to accede to their wishes. He knew Hitler was a greater general than any of them.

Foley pointed out that, 'The evidence one has collected leaves no doubt that Jonathan is absolutely and entirely devoted to the Führer; that he would not participate in any intrigue against him; that he considers him infallible in matters of state and of war; that he knows the war against Russia is right because the Führer ordered it; that he is certain this country is doomed because Hitler has said he will smash it. It is blind, unreasoning belief, which is not amenable to any argument.'

On Armistice Day, at the eleventh hour of the eleventh day of the eleventh month, the entire camp fell silent for two minutes to remember the dead of the First World War, and those who had already fallen in the Second. In the early morning Foley had toured the camp with a collection can and distributed poppies.

When the masseuse who had been treating Hess's injured leg for the past three months was finally withdrawn, Lieutenant Colonel Scott voiced the concern that 'it may be interpreted by Z as further persecution', but he also had other concerns on his mind. Hess asked to see Captain Percival, primarily about securing a shampoo and haircut, but went on to talk about the news he had learned, either through radio or in *The Times*, that Hitler had renamed the hospital that previously carried Hess's name. Hitler, he explained, must be very angry with him and would now be unlikely to receive him. (In fact, Hitler had stated that Hess should be shot as a traitor.) The fact that his name had been stripped from a hospital, combined with a recent broadcast by Winston Churchill in which the Prime Minister had referred to him as the author of 'useful information', had opened his eyes to the reality that he was likely to be considered an enemy of his own people.

He now viewed the security in a new light – instead of too high, it was now too low. He told Percival that there was not enough wire for his protection and that 'There should be some laurel bushes in front of his windows which might be used as cover for a sniper' (Hess obviously envisaged the foliage would obscure any attempts to take a shot at him). In the Camp Z diary, Scott noted that recent events had 'shaken him [Hess] and opened his eyes as to his personal safety and the possibility that there may be enemies who are out for his blood'. Hess asked that evening if Captain Percival would dine with him, and would have been concerned to know that Colonel Scott was investigating a security breach: one of the Coldstream Guards had been discovered by MI5 to have been talking at length about Camp Z and its occupant.

After retiring Hess settled down at his desk to pen a long letter to the only man who could help him now: King George VI.

> Your Majesty,
>
> After my arrival in Scotland last May I addressed myself to Your Majesty through the Duke of Hamilton. I placed myself under your protection, appealing to your chivalry and to the chivalry of the whole English people.
>
> I know that my appeal was not in vain. You gave instructions that were to guarantee my safety and my health. Officers of the Bodyguard were posted in my quarters with this task. These officers are noticeably concerned to carry out Your Majesty's instructions regarding my treatment.
>
> In spite of this I have cause for serious complaints. These I have recorded in a Statement of Facts and a Protest to the British Government. I enclose them herewith.
>
> In an appeal for the protection promised by Your Majesty I turn to you because I do not trust the British Government to see that the guilty are punished and my treatment fundamentally altered. This lack of trust springs from my experiences to date,

and from the following circumstance for which Major Foley, a senior officer in my quarters, was responsible.

The Prime Minister has personally made all decisions about my treatment. He has to be asked even about details. My complaints were answered by the assertion that they arose solely from auto-suggestion and psychosis. I am firmly convinced that the Government will try, in the case of Your Majesty also, to use the same assertion to prevent the redress of my grievances.

I ask, therefore, that a Commission, independent of the Government and responsible only to you, should be set up to investigate my complaints and my letter of protest.

In order to ensure an entirely impartial finding, it would be essential that this Commission should have the power, in the King's name, to free the witnesses called by me from their obligations of secrecy, and to cross-examine them.

Statements from witnesses would, in my opinion, only be valid as evidence if they were made orally before the Commission charged by His Majesty the King. For I am quite convinced that the witnesses, of necessity, put on paper, or have put on paper, statements intended for me which, for reasons of State, do not correspond with the truth.

I ask further that the Duke of Hamilton should be chairman of the Commission, or at any rate a member of it. For the Duke of Hamilton is the Englishman to whom I entrusted myself after landing in Scotland, and who possesses my confidence today just as much as on the first day.

I am prepared to give an undertaking not to reveal the finding of the Commission. I shall also quite understand if, in view of the seriousness of my charges, the findings are, for reasons of State, withheld from me. (Out of consideration for England I am giving to the bearer of this letter no indication of its contents.)

My object in thus approaching the final and highest authority in Great Britain is not to establish the truth of my charges. On this point I am perfectly clear without having to establish it.

I have in mind: 1. that Your Majesty should know how a man was treated who, of his own free will, came to England to render a service to our two peoples, and then placed himself under your protection; 2. that a continuance of the existing methods of treatment should be made impossible.

I count, too, on an end being put to the innumerable petty annoyances to which I am almost daily subjected, without their performance being perceptible in each individual case.

The whole shows this as a most sinister scheme for tormenting a man, and perhaps damaging his health for the rest of his life, without those who are entrusted with his protection being aware of it or believing it. For these, too, would be prejudiced in advance against my complaints by the suggestion that I suffer from a psychosis. This very process was enacted on the occasion of the visit of the Lord Chancellor, Simon.

For the treatment so far accorded to me there can, in my view, be only two possible explanations:

a) People desire to exert pressure on me on account of the alleged treatment of prisoners in German Concentration Camps. This is confirmed by the statement of Second Lieutenant Atkinson Clark that I should be treated here like the Gestapo treat prisoners in Germany. (See page 7 of the attached Protest). On this matter I have expressed my views in Appendix 1 to the letter of Protest.
b) People hope to bring me to such a state that I shall be ready, simply in order to secure my release from the miserable position in which I find myself, to convey one day to the Führer, either in person or in writing, English peace proposals of such a nature that, in the ordinary course, I should never be prepared to transmit. As regards this, I make the following statement. Every attempt to exert such pressure on me would have the opposite effect to which people hoped. If I were really so lacking in character as to put forward on

purely egotistical grounds proposals that would be unacceptable to Germany, I am absolutely certain that the results would be purely negative, and the proposals would naturally be rejected. At the same time it would have made it impossible for me, at some later stage, to convey possibly acceptable proposals to the Führer, and for me to advocate their acceptance. The Führer would neither listen to me again, nor would he pay any attention to any further letters from me. This was his own attitude towards other personages in similar circumstances of imprisonment, and nothing could persuade him otherwise.

Never would I have thought it possible that in England I could be subjected to the horrors disclosed by the spiritual and physical tortures which I have described in my letter of Protest. I came to England relying on the fairness of the English. As a former airman I know that this is often, and often shown towards an opponent. How much more could I expect fairness towards myself, who did not come as an opponent. For I came with my life in my hand and without arms to England in order to try to bring to an end the antagonism between our two countries. I still believe today in the fairness of the English people, for I am convinced that the treatment accorded to me is not in accordance with their wishes. I have no doubt that it is only a few subordinates who are responsible for it.

I rely on the fairness of Your Majesty.

Rudolf Hess

PS. As I have no relatives or friends in England who could visit me during my illness, I ask Your Majesty to give instructions that the Duke of Hamilton should be allowed to visit me. I am naturally prepared, if necessary, to give an undertaking to avoid all political discussion with him.

As an example I quote the following:

1) As a result of months of lying in bed and reading in this position, my eyes have got bad. They grow tired after short periods of reading or writing and headaches follow. On October 13th, therefore, I asked for spectacles. On the 31st of October, this is to say, after half a month, I was told that it would be several weeks more before I could be given the spectacles. Reading and writing are my only occupations during what is now nearly six months of illness. The wireless that was at least placed at my disposal after three months of lying in bed has recently been subject to frequent 'inexplicable' disturbances. I have therefore the choice of either damaging my eyes further or giving myself up until the arrival of my spectacles, this is for several weeks, to a nerve-destroying inaction. I feel certain that, in view of my very unusual circumstances, it would have been possible through good-will to procure spectacles for me in less than 'some weeks', particularly as it was, according to the oculist, a question of spectacles for all day use.
2) From time to time I suffer from stomach pains. These are relieved by warmth. As the weight of hot-water bottles is too great on account of the pain, I have for months past asked again and again for an electrically heated cushion. I have always been told, in answer, that through the war such a thing was unobtainable in England. In the meantime I saw, on the first page of *The Times* of November 6th, an advertisement in which an English Company, Warmglow Company, were offering heated cushions. According to this, they could be obtained without difficulty, and were only withheld from me so that my suffering could be increased.

The accuracy of the above facts can easily be proved by anyone deputed to do so. From these cases can conclusions be drawn as to the accuracy of other facts which I have produced.

> The person deputed must, however, if he is to find out the truth, come himself in order to question, for instance, the nurses.

On Wednesday 19 November Hess was questioned by Foley on Germany's Secret Weapon. 'Z, on being questioned about Germany's Secret Weapon, said he knew there was one but he had no idea what it was but that Hitler would not use it except as a last resort.'

When the decision was made to fit bullet-proof glass in the windows of Hess's living quarters – a considerable upgrade in defence against the sniper's bullet when compared to the laurel bush he himself had suggested – Foley neither expected, nor received, any sign of gratitude. The work required that Hess be moved to another room for a number of hours, a decision which upset him greatly, but Foley was in no mood to tolerate any Nazi histrionics. When Hess told him that he had clearly been moved to provide an opportunity to read his private diary, Foley told him sharply to 'cease talking nonsense and not be insulting'. As was often the way when confronted by a stern response, Hess attempted to wriggle around his insinuation by pointing out that if Foley had wished access to his diary, such underhand conduct would be permissible in times of war. 'Such conduct on my part would not be different in wartime from that of one soldier killing another in the field of battle. He brought up one of his favourite old tags, which seems in his mind to be the guiding principle of all Englishmen: right or wrong, my country.'

Foley pointed out the absurdity of Hess's philosophy, at which point Hess cleared Foley of any participation in the clandestine operation now being carried out in his living room. Hess pointed out that the glazier was, no doubt unknown to anyone in Camp Z, a secret agent sent down from London to riffle through his papers. As Foley noted in brackets in the day's report: '(The old glazier would be greatly surprised if he knew he had joined the ranks of those nefarious secret agents.)'

Hess was increasingly concerned at the lack of response from the Swiss Minister and, on 20 November, lodged a formal complaint with Foley about the decision not to forward on his letters. Foley said he personally did not know why the Minister had not come, or even whether he would come, but Hess could not know that his letters had not been delivered. 'He replied that he "knew" they had been stopped. He had special infallible sources of knowledge . . . I gathered that he was referring to his gift of second sight! It is always a bad sign when that comes to the surface.'

Hess went on to say that he was sure the reason the British Government had not delivered his letters was that they were afraid of what he would divulge to the Minister about his appalling treatment at their hands. However, he would make a deal if the Government promised to deliver his letter, and give his word of honour not to mention the subjects of his protest dated 18.9.41. Foley felt that his demand was couched in such terms that C would find it difficult to believe that Foley had quoted him correctly, so he asked that Hess prepare a written statement.

The result was a memo, headed Rudolf Hess to Major Foley, and where the address would usually appear in a letter, Hess wrote 'Here.' The memo read:

> In confirmation of to-day's conversation:
>
> 1. I give my word that during the visit in the near future of the Swiss Minister or Chargé d'Affaires, I will not complain either by word of mouth or in writing, nor in any way mention the complex subject of my protest to the British Government dated 18.9.41.
> 2. A condition for my giving my word according to paragraph 1 above is: The British Government will give me via Major Foley the guarantee that my future letters will immediately be delivered to the Swiss legation.

3. With reference to paragraph 2, I envisage the following: I will leave the British Government fourteen days' time to fulfil the demands set out in my memorandum of protest dated 18.9.41. If they are not fulfilled within the period of time, I reserve myself the right to complain to the Swiss Minister or Chargé d'affaires about them – with the exception of the paragraph entitled 'Punishment of the Guilty'. I continue to consider that latter point to be a matter to be settled between the British Government and myself.

20.11.41
Rudolf Hess

This was the enclosed letter Hess sent:

'I hereby request the visit of H.E. the Swiss Minister or, in his absence, of the Swiss Chargé d'Affaires in England, in his capacity of Representative of the Protecting Power of German Reich Nationals in England.

'I should be grateful if the Legation seal and wax could be brought for the purpose of executing an official document.'

He followed this with another note to Foley on 25 November in which he 'herewith begs' for written confirmation that his letter of the 20th to the Swiss legation was delivered.

On Friday 28 November, Scott's Camp Z diary records, 'The doctor took Z's trousers back to the tailor because he didn't want them turned up at the bottom!'

The season of Advent began with a distinct lack of goodwill towards one man at Camp Z. Hess, once again, was becoming increasingly difficult and had still to yield solid actionable intelligence. He spent most days in bed, and despite having made a full recovery from his broken leg, refused to come downstairs. He said he would remain inviolate whilst he was held captive at the camp, where the only exercise area now available was a wire mesh cage unfit for an animal. Instead, as Scott noted, 'He asks that he may be transferred to Scotland where he could roam over the moors and indulge in his favourite pastime of cycling.' He had also introduced a new weapon into his arsenal of phobias, complaints and medical conditions, both real and imagined: amnesia. When questioned, he would often state that he could not remember and the cloud of confusion was widening over more of his life.

His fear of being poisoned had also returned, and for once Colonel Scott was in agreement with Hess. Despite the best efforts of the camp chef, toiling amid the heat and steam of the house's black and white tiled kitchen, the quality of the food served had deteriorated considerably. The problem was that the base at Pirbright, from which supplies were sent, appeared to be cherry-picking the best cuts for themselves. As Scott noted on 1 December, 'His feeling that he is being poisoned is not altogether to be wondered at, as the food that Pirbright has been providing for us lately as near as touch poisoned us all.' The next day, when one more bad bit of beef was served in the Mess, Scott snapped: 'Went over to Pirbright with the contemptible piece of meat they sent us yesterday.'

To Hess it was clear that the mental torture inflicted upon him by his captors during the summer had returned. A particular poison was being secretly administered, producing recognisable symptoms: sharp, stabbing headaches, an inability to concentrate, and now a loss of memory. However, the latter symptom he could use to his advantage, for a man cannot tell what he does not remember. Thoughts of suicide had also returned. He had previously promised the medical officer that he would make no attempt on his life if he were allowed the privilege of using a knife and fork and a drinking glass. On 8 December he withdrew his word and actively sought the means to kill himself.

Scott wrote that, 'He actually asked the medical officer and myself to give him the facilities to take his life once and for all and to discontinue the torture. He begged us this afternoon to arrange for the Swiss Chargé d'Affaires to visit him today, so that the persecution by poisoning might cease. When I explained that it would be impossible for that gentleman to come today, he begged even more insistently that he should come tomorrow. In order to calm him I said I would convey his wish to London. In my opinion, which is only that of a layman, he is in a worse state today than he was when he tried to kill himself.'

As it happened, the Swiss legation had received all three of Hess's letters, dated 3, 6 and 20 of November, with the delay in replying caused by the Minister's absence from England on business. Upon his return, the Minister drafted a reply and visited the Foreign Office to ascertain if a visit (which the British Government was not bound to permit) was indeed possible. This was to be a delicate operation, which both sides kept secret. The Minister was concerned about the possibility of Hess asking to speak to him alone, since the convention was not quite clear on this point. He said that if Hess asked him to pass a message on to the German Government, he would first be obliged to ask the consent of the British Government, but if Hess was to make a statement to him strictly for his own personal information, he would agree to receive it and keep it to himself. Another point of concern was Hess's desire to make a codicil to his will. If he was in an unbalanced state of mind, would it be legally valid? The Foreign Office said it would look into the matter but that it struck them as a matter of German, rather than English, law. (The Prisoner of War department pointed out that Article 19 of the fourth Hague Convention required that all facilities should be made to permit prisoners of war to transmit legal documents such as wills or powers of attorney: 'We ought therefore to provide the necessary facilities to enable Hess to sign the proposed codicil if he wishes to do so.')

At nine a.m. on Friday 12 December, a government car pulled up in Park Lane, outside the Dorchester Hotel which was the current residence of Walther Thurnheer, the Swiss Chargé d'Affaires, and the car arrived with its passenger at Mytchett Place at 10.15 a.m. The Minister began his visit to Camp Z by meeting briefly with Captain Johnston and Major Dicks, who had returned specifically for the occasion, after which he was shown upstairs where Hess greeted him while in bed and wearing a pair of freshly laundered pyjamas.

Among the list of complaints Hess discussed with the Minister was the infrequency of his mail; he could not believe that only two letters had been sent from his family. Then there was the matter of his spectacles, which had taken six weeks from request to delivery.

Hess had prepared a new will, relating solely to his family's affairs and with the main provision that Ilse receive a regular monthly income of 500 marks tax free. If he should die while still in Britain, he did not wish the will to be sent on to Germany, but to be retained in the Minister's safe. He specifically asked that his government not be told about the existence of the will's codicil in case they thought he entertained thoughts of suicide. He made no mention of his previous suicide attempt and, in general conversation, indicated he was still convinced of ultimate German victory. He asked the Minister to lend him German-language books and to get him a seal, bearing his initials, RH, for securing papers.

Although Hess was most anxious to confirm the news reports of his father's death, he asked that instead of contacting his wife or mother, the Minister speak to his aunt in Zurich. The Minister said he would contact a colleague in the Ministry of Foreign Affairs in Berne to contact his aunt. Hess then settled down at his desk and spent one hour writing another letter to the King while his visitor waited patiently in the living room.

The postscript to this letter read:

> Yesterday I at last received the spectacles, but my eyes have in the meantime been seriously damaged. I can now only read for

minutes at a time. In addition, there has come a peculiar failing of memory and increasing nervousness. These cannot be attributed only to the absence of the spectacles. They began shortly after I asked for the Swiss Minister to visit me. They have come, of that I have no doubt, because something or other has been put into my food and my medicines which produces the above effects. The object in this case is quite clear to me. My nerves are to be brought to a condition in which it appears conceivable that all my complaints can be attributed solely to illness of the nerves, that is to say, that they are nothing but imagination.

It can therefore be taken for certain that the enormity of the treatment so far accorded to me, and of my consequent complaints, will reduce my credibility to nil. I therefore beg you not to give the particular contents of this letter to the Government until the safety of my person has been assured. Above all, I beg you to remove with all speed the possibility of more of the harmful stuff being put into my food and medicine. I beg you to have my house occupied without warning in order to confiscate the doctor's 'preparations'. Proof will probably be found in them. If possible please send the Duke of Hamilton at the same time, for I cherish a deep mistrust of people unknown to me, as a result of my experiences.

It is the greatest wonder that I have not yet gone mad, but there is need of haste. I cannot hold out much longer. As far as I am concerned, it is certain that the man who gave the relevant orders is mad.

Once completed and placed in an envelope, the Minister called in Foley. Together, they applied seven wax seals to the envelope, five British and two Swiss, while Hess watched intently. Hess then handed the sealed envelope to the Minister, along with a set of written instructions as to what to do with it – hand the letter directly into the open palm of King George VI. When he explained that he did not have the right to an audience with His Majesty, an accommodation was reached. If the Minister could not reach the King, the letter was to be passed on to the Duke of Hamilton, and if he in turn was unwilling or unable to comply, then it should be handed personally to Sir Alexander Cadogan. Action was to be taken within ten days and if, after this time, there was no success, the Minister was to open the letter himself and note the contents. In ten days' time the Minister was to return to Mytchett Place and report on what course of action he had taken. Thurnheer later noted that, for all he was being addressed by a man in his bed, Hess was 'conscious of his own dignity, treating everyone with whom he came into contact as subordinates, and being very full of his own importance as a Reich minister'.

Hess was 'particularly anxious that his family should not have any inkling that his health is anything but good'. He discussed his fear of being poisoned, complained of intestinal trouble, memory loss and broken nerves, and the drugs mixed in with his food to prevent rational conversation with him. Yet when the Minister asked him if he had any real cause for complaint, he said no, but wished to know how best to contact him if he had.

After leaving Hess's room at 12.40 p.m., the Minister went downstairs to lunch with Foley, who set him straight on the issue of new glasses. At the moment in Britain there was a three-month waiting list for a new pair of spectacles; Hess secured his in six weeks through Foley putting the prescription in his own name and telling the optician that the matter was urgent as he was being dispatched overseas on active service.

Although Hess had made no mention of his attempted suicide, Foley briefed the Minister and explained the structural changes that had been made to prevent a repetition. The Minister asked the medical officer for a short report on Hess's condition, which he was allowed to read, but which Foley said should then be passed onto him via the Foreign Office.

The letter to King George VI was a heavy weight in the Minister's hands. As he thought the letter to contain peace proposals between

Germany and Britain, he – as strictly neutral – was profoundly anxious not to have to open it himself. When he returned to the Foreign Office to brief them on his visit, he explained his plight: an audience with the King was impossible and Sir Alexander Cadogan was abroad, so the only hope was the Duke of Hamilton, who he was then told had no wish to become further involved in a matter that had tarnished his name and caused considerable embarrassment. A compromise was reached with the Foreign Office, who arranged for the Swiss emissary to meet with Sir Alexander Hardinge, private secretary to the King.

As a Foreign Office memo stated: 'The Minister was very favourably impressed with the Camp Commandant and by Major Foley and seemed to think that we were really treating J very well. J had given him one or two examples of harsh treatment on our part, but the Minister evidently realised that J suffered from a number of delusions and he seemed quite prepared to believe that the letter's allegations were untrue.'

Christmas at Camp Z was marked by tinsel on barbed wire, paper streamers, and a fir tree in the hall decorated with what glittery baubles could be collectively sourced. The radio played the recent hits: Billie Holiday's 'God Bless The Child' and Horace Heidt's 'I Don't Want To Set The World On Fire', as well as the usual classic carols. After Lieutenant Colonel Scott's visit to Pirbright to discuss the quality of meat supplies, he was assured a reasonable seasonal bird, which was served to the officers on Christmas Eve. A plate of festive fare – goose or turkey, roast potatoes and stuffing – was sent to Hess's room where he dined alone. 'No officer went up to Z . . . he cannot be said to have got the Christmas spirit.'

Hess had attempted to steel himself against the depressive nature of his circumstances by writing to his family on 23 November and pointing out that, as he did not know how long his letters took to reach them, he 'must calculate that it is high time for me to write a few lines for Christmas'. He began by reminiscing on Christmases past, where his accommodation was considerably poorer. 'Once upon a time I spent several Christmases in the field. I "celebrated" one of them in a goat hutch in Roumania; it was so small that I could not stand and could not lie out. The Christmas tree consisted of one single candle – and we were very glad that we had at least some light. But it was terribly cold; one could not heat the hutch.' His Christmases in France were 'a few degrees more friendly and more comfortable, according to the slightly higher degree of civilisation in that country.

'One knew that it was war, and one accepted these Christmas festivities as the inevitable accompaniment of the hard time and looked forward to keeping the next Christmas in peace at home. At present there is indisputable war again. I shall look upon the next Christmas in the same way. With thoughts of the millions who will have to spend Christmas this year as I did in those days in Roumania.'

The fact that he was now a prisoner of war brought Hess closer to those soldiers freezing on the Russian Front, bogged down on the outskirts of Stalingrad. He explained that he would not have been 'quite happy' if he celebrated the holiday in a 'warm and comfortable' home, with his only sacrifice being to deliver a speech to the troops on the wireless as the 'Speaker from Home'. In his present circumstance, he said, 'I shall have the feeling that I am, in my way, bearing my part of discomfort and that, far from home, I carry within me martial thoughts and feelings.' He said he would be thinking of family, friends and neighbours, and wished to be remembered to them, but adding,'I believe that it is psychologically favourable that I am not at home while a number of families will not be able to have one or several members of the family at home, or will have to do without them for ever.' He continued, 'Do not imagine that I shall pine away here in melancholy.'

Yet that is exactly what he did. The Camp Z diary records that,

'Z in a state of despair today [Christmas Day] and begged the doctor to lunch and dine with him, which he did.'

His despair might have been lessened had he received the Christmas letter from his aunt, which did not reach him till March, and in which she had said, 'At Christmastide all our thoughts hastened to you with old love and affection.' She had hoped that he would not spend the day in solitude but would have an opportunity to 'know some of the English Christmas celebrations, which are similar to our German customs, and that having to be so far from home was not too hard for you.' The joy and happiness of Christmas past was absent for adults; as she explained, 'only when young children are there, who are not yet able to grasp the difficulty of the times, is there cheerfulness and joy'. Instead, the festive season was marked 'in a holy German manner'. Germany was under a blanket of snow, which made Goebbels' order for the mass collection of skis for troops fighting in Russia more painful, particularly for Ilse who, before handing her own pair over, embarked on one final run only to fall and break her shinbone.

The New Year brings its own reflections to all, and for Hess the contrast between 31 December 1940, when he was Deputy Führer of the Third Reich and his plans for peace still pulsed with hope, and today, when they were as ashes and he a captive who had wilfully piloted himself into prison, was stark.

On the final day of the year, he turned to his mother: 'At the end of this year, which is so fateful for Germany, Europe and the world, and also for our family, I send you all my greetings and wishes.' He wrote that, as her seventy-fifth birthday approached, he knew how sad the day would be without her husband by her side. 'But I do know the strength in your soul, which is anchored in a knowledge of a higher power. It will help you to bear your fate.' He promised, propelled either by hope or delusion, that upon his return they would celebrate her birthday together; 'by then father's death will be distanced. We will honour him then in his way.'

The dry kindling for what hope Hess still possessed, remained with King George VI. For Major Foley, however, any hope of unlocking the mind of Rudolf Hess had faded.

14

Departure

The quarters of Rudolf Hess at Mytchett Place had, by January 1942, taken on the sickly, musty air of its occupant, who had not left his two rooms since he so athletically leapt the first-floor banister six months before. Although he had recovered sufficient mobility to allow him to walk on crutches, he refused to embark on the six steps that separated him from the bathroom. He clung, instead, to the use of a bedpan, and to the bed-baths administered sullenly by the six RAMC orderlies who tended to him in two-man shifts round the clock. The wireless, within reach on his bedside table, brought him depressing news that the German army was bogged down in Russia, with Hitler's plan for a lightning victory collapsing in the winter snow. He was almost relieved when the 11 p.m. broadcast from Berlin news was over and the room was once again filled with big-band show tunes. When motivated he read, the Swiss ambassador having delivered the works of Goethe, or he spent time with pad and pencil, designing the various homes in which he would settle after the war. His baronial home in Scotland would have a dining room for 170 people.

For Foley, the end of his assignment was drawing near and he felt frustration and a sense of failure. Yet each day he persisted in his attempts to persuade Hess to talk. 'It is almost impossible to induce him to speak of politics, the war, and personalities. One notices an unmistakable dread of betraying German interests and the Führer.' A conversation they had on 20 January over lunch in

Hess's room was notable in that he asked Foley his views on the progress of the war in Russia, and admitted that it was a source of depression for him. 'He added there could no longer be any doubt that the Führer had not reckoned with the necessity of having to fight in the open in the Russian winter, and it was plain that the Germans were not fighting on the terrain they say they had prepared.' He said that it was clear the Russians were stronger in men and material than the army had been led to believe – a fault he laid at the feet of the German secret service.

Germany, Hess told Foley, had given Russia a *Prinz Eugen*-style heavy cruiser as a means of seducing them to supply urgently required goods. 'I tried to draw him on that point,' noted Foley, 'but he refused to say more than that the cruiser would be frozen in by now in any case.' It was, at least, one point of which Foley had been unaware, and he passed it on to C, commenting, 'I do not know if you were aware of this barter transaction? It was the first time I had heard of it. Perhaps it indicates that at that time Hitler did not envisage war with Russia, although he may have considered it to be a kind of soporific for her.'

Three days previously, General Field Marshal Walter von Reichenau, commander of the 6th Army in Russia and the first prominent German army officer to embrace Nazism, had died of a stroke. In October, Reichenau had issued an order demanding the mass execution of captured Jews, who were to be treated as Partisans: 'The soldier must learn fully to appreciate the necessity for the severe but just retribution that must be meted out to the subhuman species of Jewry . . .' Yet, like Hess, Reichenau made exceptions. His sister-in-law hid her Jewish lover in her Berlin apartment, which Reichenau frequently visited when in town to partake of a few glasses of Turk's Blood – a mixture of Burgundy and champagne – though he pointed out that even he could not protect her if the Gestapo found out.

Foley was interested to find out if Hess thought Reichenau's sudden death might be the result of foul play, a suggestion Hess immediately disregarded. He was not surprised that Reichenau had suffered a stroke, given the family history for corpulence. Hess said that the General once told him that his family 'inclines to immense fatness' and once, when Hess enquired about why Reichenau was so vigorous in his pursuit of energetic sports, he replied, 'You should see my brothers and sisters!'

In December, Hitler had sacked Walther von Brauchitsch as Commander-in-Chief and tried to foist Reichenau into his place, but other military leaders rejected the choice. Thus, Hitler appointed himself instead. 'Jonathan thinks the Führer may have made changes in commands but discounts, with contempt, statements which have appeared in the press that there may have been a fronde [dissidence] in the army among the Generals.'

While trying to mine Hess's fractured mind, Foley had to listen to his persistent complaints: 'He complains in general that he suffers from indigestion, lack of sleep, bad memory, lack of power to concentrate, headaches, tired and watering eyes; that the glasses we bought for him after a thorough examination by an eye specialist do not suit him; that he cannot remember the German words of English words he understands; that his wireless reception is disturbed.'

In spite of Foley's cajoling, and his insistence that his mental and physical debility was a result of a lack of exercise, Hess said he would not leave the room until either a) he was released at the end of the war or b) certain alterations were made to the recent security changes. Foley believed that if the door to the prisoner's 'cage' was unlocked it might appease him and, given the presence of a guard armed with both Tommy gun and revolver, would not result in a diminution of safety and security.

'He has been told that the door and guard are to protect him from outside attack but he fails to see the logic of locking the door from the outside. I take the view that it is to everyone's advantage if he can be kept as sane and normal as possible or he will be plotting to destroy himself again.'

Noise, as always, was an issue: 'Jonathan complains constantly of the noise in this house. It is true that this house has all the qualities of a huge drum and that one cannot expect soldiers to move with the silence of trained female domestic staff. Then again, guardsmen like all the world to know when they are giving orders.' (On 14 January Hess made a meticulous note of how many times he heard the downstairs door bang; then, in the evening, after delivering a tirade about this deliberate disturbance he made a point of repeatedly slamming his own door so violently that it woke the doctor.) Over lunch, Foley noted the paradox that Hess, while fearful of being poisoned, retained an appetite 'so excellent that it is a constant source of wonder and amusement to us all'.

There had been a brief break in the clouds surrounding Hess's paranoid fears. On the afternoon of 15 January he had invited Foley to meet with him. Foley was aware that such invitations were often the result of a long period of contemplation by Hess who, on this occasion told him that he wished 'to begin again'; that, instead of succumbing to his fears, he wanted assistance in conquering them. Foley noted that, 'He does not accuse the hidden hand, which is unknown also to me, of wanting to poison him to death, but only to incapacitate him in mind and body.' Foley was hopeful at the sudden change and offered his usual assurances. Hess then took a step further: he said he would drink a cup of cocoa, but not from the Bournville tin he kept under close observation in his room, but from a cup prepared in the kitchen from ordinary army rations. 'He also said he would eat alone and dispense with the companionship of an officer who is really a taster. These steps seemed to indicate definite progress as he had never at any time spoken so frankly about himself to anyone.' Foley reported the progress to the medical officer, who made a note in his diary.

It was to be an early and exceedingly brief spring.

The night of that meeting, Hess slept badly. He suffered indigestion and emerged the next day disturbed and depressed, admitting he dreaded his food and the new cocoa so thoroughly that he asked the medical officer not only to dine with him, but to prepare the cocoa by his side. When Foley next shared a meal with him, he explained to him 'How disappointed the MO and I were that he had broken his good resolution so soon,' but 'he was obviously in a bad way and fairly incoherent.'

Foley was aware that for months Hess had been hiding away samples of food and pills in his drawer. He had not let on that he knew but, one afternoon, Hess said he no longer wished to keep the samples secret. He had collected them with the idea of having them analysed in Germany after the war. He then opened the drawer and showed Foley various biscuits, Ryvita, cocoa, sugar, and an assortment of pills.

At this, Foley decided to take drastic action and offered to consume the contents of the drawer in front of Hess as proof of their benign nature. Hess could have interpreted this as a devious attempt to dispose of the evidence, with Foley then swiftly departing to have his stomach pumped of the assorted poisons. Instead, he was surprised and moved by a gesture he considered nothing less than heroic.

'I offered to consume the tablets, and swallowed them then and there to his utter amazement, although he was not able to say whether they were sleeping draughts or laxatives. I also ate some of his Ryvita and made cocoa in his presence with his secreted cocoa and sugar, and persuaded him to share it with me.'

The image this conjures is startling: a British Army Major in full uniform, sharing a mug of cocoa with a pyjama-clad Rudolf Hess on a cold winter's afternoon. Hess turned to Foley and said, 'I must admit that I have made a mistake.' Then, Foley noted, 'in a pathetic kind of way', Hess added, 'I must be suffering from a psychosis.'

The spell was broken. He was not the heroic victim of an evil conspiracy by a clique in the British Government to dull his mind and prevent his peace plans from being heard. There was an enemy:

not the one he had thought, but himself. The ideas, thoughts and beliefs that sprouted up in the night were partisans acting for paranoia. The weight of the revelation must have radically altered Hess's countenance, for Foley was quick to banish the idea of psychosis as quickly as possible lest it deepen his depression. He did so by means of a joke.

'I replied that I had no knowledge of medical terminology, and tried to get him away from that dangerous idea by telling him that it would probably be true to say that he was labouring under a false idea, which he had acquired from Dr. Goebbels, about the wickedness of the English. He is always amused when one has a gentle dig at Joseph Goebbels!'

However, when Foley reported these developments, there was little faith among his superiors in a lasting change. Loxley wrote: 'I'd venture a small bet that Jonathan will be full of suspicions again at a distant date.' Cadogan added, 'Yes. Meanwhile Major Foley is full of an extraordinary mixture of medicants.'

In the evening, over dinner, Hess told Captain Johnston that he had been mistaken in his fears, then asked the medical orderly to throw away the supplies he had so carefully gathered. The knowledge that he had been acting in response to a 'false idea' prompted him to review his recent actions, and he wrote again to the King:

> Your Majesty,
>
> On December 12th I handed to the Swiss Minister a sealed letter to Your Majesty written in German, dated November 3rd, 1941. I had attached, as an annexe to it, the British translation of a Protest addressed to the British Government, of September 5th 1941. I assume that it has by now reached your hands.
>
> During this time Major Foley, whom I mentioned in my letters, has consumed before my eyes some of the food and tablets which I assumed to contain some harmful substance. In view of this, I am driven to the conviction that the probability is that my

protests in this respect are the result of an autosuggestion resulting from my imprisonment.

In these circumstances I do not hesitate to withdraw, with an expression of regret, the complaints made in my letter against a number of named culprits, provided that the enquiry which Your Majesty will have surely ordered does not reveal any guilt.

My withdrawal could not of course cover the incidents which do not admit of explanation through the working of autosuggestion. In this respect I put in the forefront the incident described in Point 8 of my Protest [the catheter incident], when Mr Dicks attempted an attack on me against my will and by use of force, and sought, in company with the young guards officer who was present, to insult me.

(Signed)
Rudolf Hess.

On 24 January Foley reported, 'J told me yesterday, and repeated today, that he was writing again to the King in order to withdraw the statements he had made about us and to acknowledge that the trouble is within him. This change in mood would appear to be the result of my swallowing his poisoned medicines and foods, one wonders how long it will last.'

On 26 January Scott noted in the Camp Z diary, 'Herr Hess has now written another letter to the King, sending it direct this time instead of via the Swiss Minister. Herr Hess sealed the letter himself and we have no knowledge of its contents. But from remarks made by him to the camp officials it would appear that its object is to withdraw the charges of ill-treatment contained in his original letter. While this, if true, is satisfactory, he is subject to such abrupt mental changes that it would not be at all surprising if he swung back any day to his earlier attitude.'

Even as Scott was writing those words, Hess was upstairs engaged in a furious row with an orderly over his radio, which was emitting atmospheric static. He had interpreted this as proof that it had been tampered with, and calm descended only after Foley had agreed to take it away and conduct a thorough check of its internal components.

Hess had been informed by letter from the Swiss Minister that he planned to pass Hess's letter on to the King's private secretary if this met with his approval, which it did. From the hands of Sir Alexander Hardinge it was passed into those of King George VI who, around 12 January, cracked open the seven wax seals and read of, among other points, Hess's failure to be provided with a hot cushion. Hess's highest hope would have been that, upon reading his plea, His Majesty would immediately command his rescue. New troops would sweep into Camp Z, banishing the brutes, releasing him from his cage, and escorting him to Buckingham Palace. There, from across Britain's great estates, would have gathered the landed gentry who comprised the Peace Party, and who would usher out the premiership of Winston Churchill and usher in a Prime Minister who valued a lasting accord between London and Berlin.

It was, needless to say, not to be. On 12 January Sir Alexander Hardinge sent a letter to Sir Alexander Cadogan: 'The Swiss Minister brought me the communication to the King from Hess. It was opened by His Majesty personally, and by his command I send it to you herewith, together with a translation which I have made rather hurriedly, and I hope more, rather than less, accurately! Hess has evidently got the persecution mania, and I do not imagine that there is anything that can be done about it.'

Upon reading the letter, Cadogan appended a handwritten aside: 'Incredible stuff. I hope that prisoners in German Concentration Camps have "electrically heated cushions".'

On 22 January Cadogan wrote to Hardinge: 'I take it from the last sentence of your letter that you hold the same view [as the King]? But in order that there may be no misunderstanding, I should be grateful if you would confirm that the King does not wish the Secretary of State to pursue the matter further. I gathered from the King himself on Wednesday that he thought there was nothing to be done, but I should be glad to be assured that this is so.'

Later on Sir Alexander Hardinge spoke to Cadogan and it was agreed that the King need take no further action, and that if any questions were raised by Hess or anyone else, the reply would be 'that he [the King] took the usual constitutional course of referring this matter to the responsible minister'. The King was no doubt relieved to receive Hess's letter of 24 January withdrawing his accusations.

On 30 January, the Camp diary records: 'X ray van arrived to take a final photograph of Z's fracture. As it arrived with only 60 feet of cable it had to be backed up to the camouflage gate and the cables taken in through the window. Z, finding himself the centre of attention, became quite cheerful but relapsed into gloom soon after.'

Hess told the medical officer, who visited daily at 10.30 a.m., that he would like to see Foley at 12 noon, as he wished to make a formal statement in German – a method he adopted on formal occasions.

Foley reported on this in a memo: 'One is prepared for anything in this peculiar case, but I must confess that Hess's complete incapability to understand British mentality, and his lack of logic, again surprised me. He told me that he had decided to ask the British Government to give him a gun "for self defence so that he could shoot himself". He realised that if he died a violent death the British Government would be accused, or at least suspected, of murder, and in order to cover them he would invite the Swiss Minister to visit him and would make a formal application in his presence so that he could testify that the gun was given to him for self defence at his own request.

'I suggested that the British Government was very short of guns at present and I doubted whether the terms of reference of the representative of the Protecting Power would allow him to play.'

At the bottom of Foley's memo, AC – Alexander Cadogan – added in pencil, 'I have a pair of sporting guns (which I never surrendered to the Home Guard). I feel inclined to send them to Jonathan by registered post. The man's a pest and I don't think the world will come to an end if he insists – preferably swiftly – in killing himself . . . poor Foley [when is he] going to be unchained from this . . . nightmare?'

Change was coming to Camp Z. Lieutenant Colonel Scott was departing, and the security was being transferred from the Scots Guards to the Pioneers. On their arrival, Scott said they were dressed in 'quite filthy' rags and sent back 23 out of the 130-strong deployment as unusable. It was around this time that the press finally arrived. The search for Rudolf Hess had become one of the great games of British journalism during the Second World War, with hungry editors sending reporters to roam the country in search of his secret location. On 2 February, R.R. Foster of the *Daily Herald* got closer than most, right up to the front gates of Camp Z, where he told the duty guard that he was making enquiries about a 'certain incident which had taken place at this camp five weeks ago'. This was a reference – five months out of date – to Hess's suicide attempt, rumours of which had begun to circulate in Fleet Street. Aware that Hess was under the control of the Foreign Office, Foster asked the guard who granted permission to enter: the War Office or the Foreign Office? The guard stated it was nothing to do with the Foreign Office, then listened as 'he put forward the usual moan that he would have to face an infuriated editor if he returned empty-handed and made every effort, without success, to glean any knowledge of this camp.' Two days later, the *Daily Herald* dispatched a Mr E.L. Calcraft, who was similarly rebuffed.

With the change of arrangements at Camp Z, Major Foley was now anxious to depart. He recommended that he remain until the middle of February to allow the new officers and men to bed in, and for him to have 'a chance of studying them', but he felt he could now be better deployed elsewhere. 'I rather feel that I am no longer able to produce anything of value for the war effort and that I am wasting my time.

'Finally, after constant observation of Jonathan you may care to hear my opinion of Jonathan's mentality, although it is only that of a layman. It is that I think he is incurable, that although there will be recurring periods of comparative sanity he will gradually deteriorate.'

In early February, Hess wrote two letters. The first to his wife, the second to his former secretary, Hildegard Fath, ahead of her birthday:

> 6 February
> My dear little mummy,
>
> I wonder where you are these winter days? On the Burgli in the snow? Buz and Buzilein perfecting their skiing – I presume their skis had not to be surrendered? I assume grandmother is at Hindeland as before and takes her walks diligently, with plenty of company I hope, like Frau Binder. That she was able with all her energy to do two hours is a great feat at her age. I cannot admire it sufficiently. You wrote about it in a letter which, it is true, was written a long time ago, but finally arrived.
>
> Please make copies of your letters that I may at least read them at a later date and as a souvenir for times to come. When Buz is a man these letters will mean a lot to him. A letter of more recent date came from Zurich from Aunty E.
>
> I learned that 'Herr von Scholz' had been given the 'Ritterkreuz'. I must openly admit that I had not esteemed him highly enough before! But it is better than the other way round. Please give him my best wishes.
>
> How are the other acquaintances, especially those of the inner circle? The adjutants Rudi, Platzer and the rest? How are Spatzen,

and Michserl who must be a little woman already? Greetings to them all and to their families from me. How are you yourself? Are your pains – or is it one pain – better?

If not, I beg of you, do something about it and do not wait till the war is over.

My best wishes are always with you, Buz, Grandmother and all of you! Aunty E. has written to say what a great help you are to all. I am grateful to you.

5 February
Letter by Hess to Miss Hildegard Fath
Dear Freiburg,

My best heartfelt wishes for your birthday. I wish you the fulfilment of your hopes and wishes, especially good health to you and yours.

I can imagine with what anxiety you and the remainder of the Risse family think of the father of the family and of the so young soldiers during the hard fights in the East. I hope that your mother is well.

What are you doing without your 'bread giver'? Do you help at Karlaching, work in the Brown House, in the Chancery of the Party – or are you employed in the Liaison Staff? There are more possibilities of work today than ever before for those who are willing to work. The daily telephone conversations at noon and in the evenings from Berlin to Munich are no longer part of your duty since my flight.

Please look after old Winkler for me. Besides the fact that I am fond of him, I am interested in the complete execution of the trial cure as an experiment. If he wants financial help Conti will surely assist as he is just as interested. If necessary, his assistance will go as far as repaying sums which have already been advanced for this purpose. If my mother wants to do a cure this year, please place the necessary means at her disposal in my name from my funds.

When you visit in Innsbrucker Street greet father, mother and daughter. I assume that my Miss Nichterl has well recovered.

Best wishes, your 'bread giver'.

PS Greetings also to Gretl and Inge if they are in Berlin. I have written direct to Karlaching but twofold greetings are welcome.

Hess added the following to this letter:

In the folder which I gave Pintsch before my flight there are:-

1. A minute on the relevant dream of the General.

2. The horoscope made by Schulte – Strathaus.

3. The prophecy which Grete Sutter gave me at Christmas a year ago.

Please copy them all and deposit them under seal at a notary's who must certify the date on which they were deposited. I am interested in the matter from the scientific point of view. Greetings to the General, Stratgehause and Pintsch, also to Grete Sutter in this connection.

While the letters are polite, controlled, and refer to previous events, Hess was falling apart again, as the orderly's night report on 5 February indicates:

'Was very miserable & occupied in his own thoughts until 23.00 hrs. 01.50 hrs he awoke & began groaning with exclamations of "Ah-ah, Oh-oh, it is terrible" [complaining] of pains in the low region of the abdomen, and it apparently became very acute in about five minutes. Tossing & turning in bed, rubbing the affected part with constant groans. Was persuaded to try the [hot water] bottle but with no results. At 02.15 hrs he leapt out of bed and began frantically pacing up & down, making a terrific noise with his feet and groaning. Kept curling up with the supposed pain, then asked for the Medical Officer. Immediately the MO was sent for he said the pains ceased & then returned to bed and appeared much quieter on the arrival of the MO.'

Years later, Hess wrote:

> On the 4th of February, 1942, Nurse Sergeant Everett brought me dessert. Unfortunately, the glass dish had been broken and another one had not been available. I asked whether there was any possibility that there were glass splinters in the dessert. Everett replied that this was impossible because the dish had been damaged before filling it. On the strength of my previous experiences, I nevertheless investigated the contents. Everett became very nervous and tried to prevent me from it. There were glass splinters in the dessert. Afterwards, I received the apologies of the cook, and it was added that the crack in the dish had been called to my attention before. The mistake had merely been that the filling of the dish took place after it had been damaged. This glass dish, as all other dishes in which I was given poisoned food, bore the monogram of the King of England. [This is the cipher G.R. (Georgius Rex) with which all British War Department property is marked.]

When Rees visited Hess on 21 February he found him gaunt, pallid, deep in depression and 'with it a distinct loss of memory'. He said he did not remember receiving any letters from his wife or the visit in December of the Swiss Ambassador. 'This may be due to the increasing mental deterioration or it may be just a phase from which he will emerge . . . His memory was very much at fault.' Rees was concerned enough by his patient's appearance to arrange for Lieutenant Colonel Evan Bedford, a distinguished consultant physician, to examine him, but he could find nothing wrong.

In February, Hess's memory loss made questioning him even more futile. It was also suspicious, since it is rare for amnesia and paranoia to settle on the same person. On 27 February, Foley reported: 'I saw Jonathan in the early evening and found him in a very depressed mental and physical state. Although he had slept many hours he could not, or at least did not, stop yawning. His mind seemed inactive, and incapable of following simple conversation on actual topics.' Foley knew Hess had read about the RAF bombardment of the German battle cruiser, the *Gneisenau*, at Kiel docks, but when questioned about it, he professed ignorance. Once again Foley tried to shake him out of his despondency: 'I decided to shock him and told him that we would not allow his health to deteriorate and that he would have to decide to come downstairs and take some fresh air. After some slight hesitation he agreed to come down next day.'

There was a new wardrobe of civilian clothes for Hess to choose from. In January the Foreign Office had agreed to the release of 82 clothing coupons so that he could be provided with an overcoat, a pair of grey flannel trousers, two shirts, four collars, two pairs of long underwear, three vests, two pairs of socks, one scarf, one sports jacket, and a tie. Yet when Foley arrived to fetch him for their walk at two o'clock the next day, he discovered Hess had gone back to bed, complaining of feeling tired. Foley told him he had one hour to dress, and 'He was dressed at 1515 and left his room for the first time since his attempted suicide.'

Of Hess's memory Foley wrote:

> His loss of memory is puzzling. One does not know whether it is genuine or simulated. According to medical experience, paranoiacs do not usually suffer from loss of memory. The nurses and I find it difficult to believe that he is such a consummate actor that he is able consistently to pretend he has forgotten things which should have impressed themselves strongly on his memory. The MO has an open mind. There are innumerable instances. When I told him that Col. Bedford RAMC, who had given him a very thorough overhaul, had reported that there was nothing wrong with his physical health, he professed complete ignorance of that doctor's visit. On Sunday he told us he did not remember exercising the previous day. Last night he asked for a sedative

> and was offered a small dose of Luminal. He asked the nurse what Luminal was as he had never heard of the drug before!!
>
> For many weeks now he has either been incapable of intelligent conversation on any subject, or he has made up his mind not only to simulate loss of memory, but to behave as if one's words were not registering in his brain. In fact there is no longer any response to anything one says to him: he takes no interest in his surroundings; he is practically a one-syllable man.

Of the two prisoners at Camp Z, Major Frank Foley was the first to be released. For the past few months he had made no contribution to the war effort, or so he felt, and was anxious for more challenging work. MI6 had now found itself entwined in a bitter turf war with MI5, and the intelligence services of each of the three armed forces, over the network charged with running double agents, known as the Double-Cross System. Foley was appointed to represent MI6 on a new committee charged with untangling the current logjam. On the morning of Sunday 23 March, Foley met Hess in his room to break the news of his imminent departure. As Foley walked into the room, he was aware that under the floorboards lay a hoard of glucose tablets hidden by Hess, who planned to present them to the Swiss Minister during his forthcoming visit. Foley saw little point in letting Hess know, instead saying how sorry he was to have noticed that his meal-time suspicions had returned.

'Hess smiled and said that one thing was certain: either he or we were suffering from a psychosis, but he felt certain that it was not him.' He then said that he had difficulty understanding how it was possible that Foley and his fellow officers could administer poison, as he had always found them 'to be decent men'.

When Foley told Hess he was leaving, he added that he could return to visit him if he so desired. As he moved towards the door, Hess astonished him by saying that he too would be leaving soon. He explained that he intended to ask the Swiss Minister to arrange his removal to another place 'where there would be no noise, no mosquitoes, no machine gun fire, no cage etc'. He said he was sure his request would be granted, smiled as the major departed, and returned to his book.

As Hess had not received a reply from the King, he wrote again to the Swiss Ambassador requesting a second visit. On 28 March he received a letter from Thurnheer explaining that he hoped to visit within a fortnight. When this deadline passed in mid-April, Hess concluded that the authorities were deliberately delaying Thurnheer's arrival so that it would coincide with his next mental collapse, allowing the British authority to dismiss his allegations of abuse as ravings. So as to hasten the Ambassador's arrival, Hess began to play his role: 'I pretended to become more nervous from day to day; after I had reached the climax, the envoy comes.'

During this period, Hess rolled around stricken with phantom pains, jumped in and out of bed and, as Corporal Everett noted, continued 'trying the tempers of staff, while he himself is in a very nasty temper'. On 6 April he told Private Dawkins that 'the Jews are trying to kill him and if he stays much longer he will finish up in a madhouse.' The next day Lance-Corporal Everatt heard him insist 'someone of the Jewish faith is trying to bring about his end.' Hess then sent a second letter to Thurnheer asking him to 'accelerate your visit'.

The visit was set for 18 April. In the morning Hess took a brief walk in the gardens. He refused both breakfast and lunch, lest these meals be used as a vehicle for more poison. While Foley agreed to collect the Swiss Ambassador and drive him down to Camp Z, Rees visited Hess, whom he found once again in bed 'but very talkative and quite different to his state at my last visit when he was very depressed and shut away'. Hess did complain of a violent headache, 'the worst I have ever had in my life' but, as usual, refused the aspirin Rees offered.

Thurnheer arrived at 3.20 p.m. and did not depart until seven o'clock. He brought more books from his library, and apologies that he had been unable to hand Hess's letter directly to the King, but told him that it had been accepted on the King's behalf by his private secretary, Sir Alexander Hardinge. Thurnheer was surprised to find Hess still in bed, but Hess explained this was due to stomach cramps. The Minister then settled down to listen, while Hess told him that 'everybody was trying either to poison him or rob him of his memory.' The same pattern of paranoid thoughts unfolded as Hess stated that doors were banged 123 times in 30 minutes; that his sleep was disturbed by deliberate coughing fits from the orderlies, and how the incessant noise would mysteriously stop as soon as he accepted a Luminal tablet or consumed a poisoned meal. Much of their time together was spent meticulously wrapping and labelling a whole new set of samples that Hess had secretly accrued, and which he hoped the envoy could get scientifically studied – which, Hess believed, would reveal a well-known Mexican poison.

Thurnheer's own report stated:

> The prisoner then asked me to send this report to the German Government at once so that they can inflict reprisals on the British generals, in return for which he promises to ensure that Switzerland is treated in the New Europe in accordance with whatever desires she may put forward. I tell Mr Hess that I regret I cannot meet his requests. My mission here is one of trust: I had been allowed in to him without any checks . . . Taking his hand to create an impression of utter reliability and decency, I add that while I deeply value the promise of special treatment for Switzerland, I can assure him that such promises can have no bearing on my attitudes. Rudolf Hess responds that he did go a bit too far . . . and I should put it down to his desperate plight. But in the present case a crime is being committed and, that being so, he would go further if he were me . . .
>
> I tell him it is his duty to keep fit, because if Germany wins the war then he must be there to share in her reconstruction.

None of these remarks seems to impress him as he is obsessed with one idea, that they are trying to destroy him by noise outside and indoors and by medication. He asks whether I cannot at least send his report direct to the highest judges in Britain? I remind him that the legislature and executive are separate, and that I can only forward the report through the Foreign Office, which Rudolf Hess refuses.

Rees assured the War Office in his report that, as regards Thurnheer, 'There was no question whatever in his mind, of course, of the mental derangement.'

The cost and inconvenience of maintaining Hess at Mytchett Place was growing, but with no benefit to Britain. Cadogan wrote: 'Jonathan's value to us as a source of information and as material for propaganda is now zero; and the problem of his housing [should] be considered on grounds of security and convenience. But it would clearly be impossible to let him return to Germany; we must therefore avoid putting ourselves in a position in which we should have some difficulty in avoiding his return.'

The various reports collated on Hess's psychological condition had been studied by Colonel Bedford of the RAMC, who briefed the War Office that the correct location for Hess was a medical institution, but such an act would make him suitable to be sent back to Germany.

'As it has been ruled that Z is a Prisoner of War, there would appear to be no doubt . . . that a Mixed Medical Commission would pass him as eligible for repatriation. It would be a mistake to certify him. If he were moved to an Asylum, in his saner moments he would realise his position and might demand examination by a Mixed Medical Commission,' briefed General Gepp of the War Office on 4 March.

Yet, from a security point of view, the current location remained unsuitable, with Camp Z in an 'A.1' invasion area. The War Office advocated a move to Talgarth Asylum, situated in a sparsely populated part of South Wales. Colonel Rees, who had also inspected Dumfries Asylum in Scotland as a possible home, had recently completed an inspection of Talgarth, and agreed with the recommendation. However, the Foreign Office was concerned that, as Talgarth was a facility for the exclusive use of the mentally ill: 'If, therefore, we send our friend there, even though he be given separate accommodation, it would probably become extremely difficult to refuse to repatriate him if ever he asked to be sent back to Germany.' Instead, it was suggested that a smaller hospital for general patients, but one capable of providing the necessary facilities for Hess, be sought.

Maindiff Court appeared to be the perfect solution. A brand new building, opened in June 1939 as an admissions facility for the County Mental Hospital, it had been taken over three months later as a War Emergency Hospital for injured military personnel. Although equipped for the treatment of the deranged, it currently housed no mental patients, but one ATS officer, four other officers, and 40 patients of other ranks. 'It is very well tree'd and secluded and not overlooked,' stated Colonel Gepp. Instead of the 102 men currently guarding Hess, the figure could be reduced to just six mental orderlies, a guard of three officers, and 20 other ranks.

The proposal was approved on 19 May, on condition that the padded cell which was adjacent to Hess's new quarters be 'unpadded, or some expedient devised to explain to him why the door must remain permanently locked'. Anthony Eden briefed Winston Churchill: 'Arrangements can be made to provide quarters for "Jonathan" completely secluded from the rest of the place and giving satisfactory security.' On the first anniversary of Hess's arrival, Cadogan had come to a firm conclusion: 'By now, it's pretty clear that Hess's escapade was a mad venture on his own, and that the German authorities knew nothing about it beforehand.'

*

On the morning of 26 June 1942, in the company of the new Camp Commandant, Lieutenant Colonel C.E. Wilson, an armed guard, and one medical orderly, Rudolf Hess departed Camp Z with whatever secrets he held, firmly intact. Five days previously he had written a letter to General Dr Karl Haushofer in which he said, 'There is no denying that I have failed. So in that respect I've no cause for self-recrimination. At any rate, I was at the helm. But you know as well as I do that the compass that we set our course by is influenced by forces that are of unerring effect even though we know nothing of them.'

The letter contained the following lines:

Let the waves crash and thunder,
Life and death denote your realm.
Whether soar aloft or fall asunder,
Never take your hand off helm.

Epilogue

One afternoon at Mytchett Place, Rudolf Hess had written to General Dr Karl Haushofer and pondered the question of when they would meet again. Four years were to pass before fate and the Allies' pursuit of justice brought about their reunion. It was not a happy event for either man. When Hess had pencilled his note, he was in a spacious room overlooking beech trees, and was still confident of a German victory and triumphant return, however deluded that may have appeared. By November 1945 Germany lay in ruins. Adolf Hitler had taken a cyanide capsule and left his body to be burned outside his bunker in Berlin. The war was over and Germany had lost.

Rudolf Hess had arrived in Nuremberg on the evening of 10 October to be tried, along with other ranking Nazi officers, for war crimes. Among his possessions were carefully wrapped packages and parcels containing scraps of food, pieces of cake, and an assortment of pills – all testament, in his mind at least, to the tortures of Camp Z. For the past three years, Hess had suffered intermittent bouts of amnesia and had returned to Germany in a mental fog that now conveniently obscured large swaths of his life and career.

In a bid either to jolt his memory back into gear or reveal the lie under which Hess now laboured, the authorities arranged for him to be reintroduced to leading figures of his past. However, it was not possible for him to meet with young Albrecht Haushofer.

He had become involved with the Resistance and went on the run following the failed assassination attempt on Hitler's life by Count Klaus Schenk von Stauffenberg on 20 July 1944. He had been hidden in a chalet in the Bavarian Alps by a family friend but was found in December and taken to the Gestapo Headquarters at Prince Albrechtstrasse Prison. Himmler had wished to keep him alive in case he could assist in any future negotiations with the Allies.

But when Himmler developed a more effective contact, Count Folke Bernadotte of the Swedish Red Cross, whom he asked to contact the Western Allies on his behalf (Himmler's offer of co-operation with Britain and America, but not Russia, was rejected by Churchill and Roosevelt), Haushofer was rendered surplus to requirements.

In the early hours of 23 April 1945, Haushofer, along with 15 other prisoners, was marched outside and shot. When his body was found, scraps of paper containing poems were clenched in his hand, one of them entitled 'Guilt':

I lightly carry what the judge calls my guilt
Guilt in planning and caring
I would feel guilty had I not from inner duty
Planned for the people's future
But I am guilty other than you think:
I should have sooner seen my duty
I should have sharper condemned evil
I have too long delayed my judgment.
I now accuse myself
I have long betrayed my conscience
I have lied to myself and to others.
I soon foresaw the evil's frightful path;
I have warned,
But my warnings were too feeble.
I know today wherein lies my guilt.

The father and son who had assisted Hess on his mission had borne the brunt of its failure, which had fractured the family. Karl Haushofer was bitter towards his son who, he believed, endangered the whole family in his attempt to flee; while his son marked him from the grave in his poem, 'The Father', which captured his feelings that his father had failed to grasp the grim consequence of his geopolitical ideas and teachings:

He once had it in his power,
To cast the demon back into the dark
My father broke the seal
But failed to see the evil
He let the demon escape into the world.

The July plot had led to Karl Haushofer's short period of imprisonment in the Dachau concentration camp. After the Allied victory, he faced the possibility of a trial for his involvement in the Third Reich, but the American prosecutors eventually decided his role had been simply academic. It was while Haushofer was under investigation that he was brought before Rudolf Hess in a small room at the Nuremberg gaol. Hess stared straight through him and insisted he did not recognise his mentor, the man who had helped his plans take flight. On 11 March 1946, Karl Haushofer and his wife, Martha, took a walk in the woods near their home, and in a hollow by a stream and under a willow tree, they took poison. Martha also hanged herself, but Karl lacked the strength and was found slumped on the ground.

Haushofer was not the only person Hess did not recognise. On 16 November, he was confronted by his two former secretaries, Ingeborg Sperr and Hildegard Fath. It was arranged that Hess was sitting with his back to the door when Fath was brought in. At first he appeared to recognise her, but then showed no emotion and denied any knowledge of her. When she spoke of his family and showed pictures of his son, he brushed her off. Afterwards, when Sperr was brought in, Hess was already prepared and again denied her. During the interview he said, 'I do not remember', at which point Sperr produced a picture and said, 'Here, maybe this will help you to remember,' but Hess waved her away with the words, 'I do not want any help!' When introduced to old comrades such as Goering, he again failed to recognise them.

Meanwhile, the physical examination found him to be in good health, if a little underweight, while psychiatrically he was described as 'alert and responsive'. He appeared to want to help but repeatedly answered questions with 'I do not know. I cannot remember,' and when first admitted to the prison he was unable to state his date of birth or birthplace etc. for the basic history that was then required. Among the psychiatric tests Hess underwent under the guidance of Major Ellis Kelly was the Rorschach Ink Blot test and, on 16 October, a report on his psychiatric status was passed to Justice Jackson.

It explained that the Rorschach test 'was significant in that, while it revealed marked neurotic reactions, it did not indicate any evidence of an active psychotic process. The findings from this test indicate that Hess suffers from a true psycho-neurosis, primarily of the hysterical type which is grafted upon a basic paranoid personality. In other words, fundamentally, Rudolf Hess is an introverted, shy, withdrawn personality, who basically is suspicious of his environment and projects upon his surroundings concepts developing within himself. This paranoid projection is emphasised in his suspiciousness, his desire to have everything "just so", and is shown in the Rorschach Test by certain types of bizarre responses. These responses, however, are not sufficiently deviate to indicate a really active paranoid process at present, but indicate the possibility of a psychotic episode.'

The general feeling was that Hess was suffering from an hysterical amnesic reaction, but it was also obvious that a large portion of the 'total' amnesia was 'deliberately assumed'. While he blocked every attempt to penetrate his mental process by stating, 'I cannot remember', there was a pattern of inconsistency in his behaviour. One day he was able to remember events of three days past, while the next day events of that morning were lost. He claimed he could not read the indictment against him because by the time he reached the end he had forgotten the beginning; yet at night he lay in bed reading lengthy books, while his stomach cramps involved him rocking back and forth in pain but able, in a split second, to calmly discuss how painful they were.

It was suggested by Major Kelly that he be given sodium amytal or pentothal in an attempt to differentiate the qualities of his amnesia, as well as to determine how much was real and how much was being deliberately blocked, but this was refused by the American authorities. The Foreign Office had also refused on the same grounds – that there had been a small number of occasions when the drugs had 'untoward results'. As Justice Jackson later explained, 'We felt that if he should be struck by lightning a month afterwards it would still be charged that something that we had done had caused his death; and we did not desire to impose any such treatment upon him.'

On 30 October, the parcels Hess had brought with him were opened in his presence. The food, chocolate, bread, condiments, sugar etc. had notes, detailing the alleged poison present, attached to each parcel. When shown the parcels, he smiled 'in his usual superficial fashion' and denied any knowledge of them, though he admitted recognising his own handwriting. On 8 November, at the suggestion of one of the members of the court, he was shown a collection of newsreels of himself with other leading Nazis, at the peak of their power. He knew he would be scrutinised and prepared himself, but his hands tensed visibly during certain sequences. Afterwards, he said that he would never have recognised himself in the newsreels as it had been so long since he looked in a mirror.

The question posed by the Judges who would supervise the trial was whether or not Hess was fit to stand trial. Mr Justice Jackson,

US Chief of Counsel, felt there should be a thorough examination in two phases: the first before the trial to assess fitness to plead etc., and the second after sentencing, when a team of psychiatrists, psychologists and sociologists from each of the Allied countries could study the convicted men and produce a report so as to assist in the understanding of Nazi mentality.

On 5 November, Hess was found by Dr Gustave Gilbert, the prison psychologist at Nuremberg, to have a 'high average class' of intelligence.

Phase 1 took place on 8 November 1945, when Dr Rees was asked by the British War Crimes Executive in London to go to Nuremberg. Each of the four governing nations, Britain, America, Russia and France, were asked to compile a three-man team – psychologist, physician and neurologist. Dr Rees was accompanied by Lord Moran, Churchill's personal physician, and Dr George Riddoch, a senior British neurologist. Each team would examine Hess, both collectively and individually, before pronouncing judgment on his mental health.

One week later, on 14 November, the collective panel conducted a group interview with Hess. He was seated at one side of a large square table, handcuffed to an American guard, and surrounded on each side by members of the commission. Since Dr Rees had an established relationship with Hess, he entered the room last in order to allow the commission to scrutinise the prisoner's reaction. There was deemed to be not a flicker of recognition as Hess greeted the doctor courteously and shook his hand. Rees then embarked on a series of questions about Hess's time in England, but was again met with a mask of ignorance. It was, however, noted that after three minutes of answering questions in English, Hess asked if he might answer in German through an interpreter – a switch that was seen as a means of allowing him more time to formulate the safest possible response.

The Russians, with the assistance of Colonel Schroeder from Chicago, persistently hit Hess with a series of difficult questions, but nothing elicited a response that found either for or against the claim of amnesia. One interesting point was that Hess said he could remember a fair amount about the Führer: as it was noted, 'It almost seemed that Hitler, like God, had in some curious way escaped the oblivion of most men and events in Hess's past life.' All except one medical man agreed that the amnesia was hysterical and would break down during the trial, while one member of the commission argued that Hess was unfit to stand trial.

The British report read as follows:

> The undersigned, having seen and examined Rudolf Hess, have come to the following conclusion:
>
> 1. There are no relevant physical abnormalities.
>
> 2. His mental state is of a mixed type. He is an unstable man, and what is technically called a psychopathic personality. The evidence of his illness in the past four years, as presented by one of us who had had him under his care in England, indicates that he has had a delusion of poisoning, and other similar paranoid ideas.
>
> Partly as a reaction to the failure of his mission, these abnormalities got worse, and led to suicidal attempts.
>
> In addition, he had a marked hysterical tendency, which has led to the development of various symptoms, notably a loss of memory, which lasted from November 1943 to June 1944, and began [again] in February 1945 and lasted till the present. The amnesic symptom will eventually clear when circumstances change.
>
> 3. At the moment he is not insane in the strict sense. His loss of memory will not entirely interfere with his comprehension of the proceedings, but it will interfere with his ability to make his defence, and to understand the details of the past, which arise in evidence.
>
> 4. We recommend that further evidence should be obtained by narco-analysis and that if the Court decides to proceed with

> the Trial, the question afterwards be reviewed on psychiatric grounds.
>
> (Signed) Moran,
> J.R. Rees, George Riddoch.

The Russian report, which was more lengthy, stated, 'The loss of memory by Hess is not the result of some kind of mental disease but represents hysterical amnesia, the basis of which is a subconscious inclination toward self-defence as well as a deliberate and conscious tendency toward it. Such behaviour often terminates when the hysterical person is faced with an unavoidable necessity of conducting himself correctly. Therefore, the amnesia of Hess may end upon his being brought to trial.'

On 30 November 1945, the Tribunal at Nuremberg considered the question of whether Rudolf Hess was fit to stand trial. The prosecution, supported by the psychiatric reports, argued that he was fit. The defence, Dr Rohrscheidt, argued that Hess was unfit, but the matter was finally settled when Hess himself rose to speak. The previous day, he had been confronted by Colonel Burton C. Andrus, the American commandant of the prison, who said that he was a fraud, which was 'not a very manly thing to do'. Andrus then stated that Hess had a duty to himself, his family and the German people to state the truth. It is not known if this was the final prompt, or a concern that the court would judge him insane, but when Hess spoke it was to startle the courtroom:

> Mr President, I would like to say this: At the beginning of the trial of this afternoon's proceedings I gave my defence counsel a note that I am of the opinion that these proceedings could be shortened if one would allow me to speak myself. What I say is as follows:
>
> In order to anticipate any possibility of my being declared incapable of pleading, although I am willing to take part in the

rest of the proceedings with the rest of them, I would like to give the Tribunal the following declaration, although I originally intended not to make this declaration until a later point in the proceedings: My memory is again in order. The reasons why I simulated loss of memory was tactical. In fact, it is only that my capacity for concentration is slightly reduced. But in consequence of that, my capacity to follow the trial, my capacity to defend myself, to put questions to witnesses or even to answer questions, these, my capacities, are not influenced by that.

I emphasise the fact that I bear the full responsibility for everything that I have done, or signed as signatory or co-signatory. My attitude, in principle, is that the Tribunal is not competent – is not affected by the statement I have just made. Hitherto in conversations with my official defence counsel I have maintained my loss of memory. He was, therefore, in good faith when he asserted I lost my memory.

Once returned to his cell that evening, Hess was elated at the success of his deception and deeply proud of his acting abilities, particularly at having fooled Herman Goering. In a conversation with Major Kelly, he said the sternest test was watching the newsreel footage, and that he had felt certain afterwards that his emotional response had been detected. The reason for his behaviour was simple – after suffering a genuine bout of amnesia, he said he noticed that this had excused him from questioning. Thus, he had decided to extend it as a means of avoiding interrogation, as well as in the hope that it would lead to his repatriation on the grounds of insanity, as the Geneva convention required.

However, Hess told the court, when he arrived in Nuremberg he thought it wise to maintain the memory loss; this allowed him to watch how matters played out and prevented the interrogators from obtaining any information about him which could be of use to the prosecution. He pointed out that he might not have seen his papers again if they had not been used as a means to test his amnesia. During the conversation with Major Kelly he was aloof, and when told he was underweight he explained that it did not matter because, after the trial, he would be back at home with his family who would be sure to feed him up. He added that if he was executed it did not matter if a fat man or a thin fell through the trap door.

The reaction of his former comrades to his deceit differed from person to person. Goering was amazed, upset, and resentful that he had been fooled. Ribbentrop was dumbfounded, at first unable to speak and then said only, 'Hess. You mean Hess? The Hess we have here? He said that?' In a state of agitation he added, 'But Hess did not know me. I looked at him. I talked to him. Obviously he did not know me. It is just not possible. Nobody could fool me like that.'

The question of Rudolf Hess's sanity cannot be conclusively answered. The collective opinion of the psychologists who studied his behaviour at Nuremberg was that he was not insane in the legal sense, in which an individual is incapable of distinguishing right from wrong or is unaware of the consequences of his actions. Yet it was clear that he was psychologically disturbed, which raised the further question of extent. Even the amnesia that he may or may not have suffered is difficult to tease out with any certainty, given Hess's claim that the matter was one of pretence. However, according to Dr Gustave Gilbert, Hess's *claim* of a pretence was a pretence in *fact*. Gilbert believed that the amnesia was genuine, but broke up when he told Hess on the morning of his competency hearing that he might be in danger of being declared 'incompetent'. If so, he would have been excluded from the proceedings, which would have been a blow to his ego. During the lengthy trial Hess giggled, played with his fingers, and irritated Goering to such an extent that he asked to be seated elsewhere (his request was denied). The disintegration of Hess's behaviour was mirrored by his memory when the amnesia returned to the point where he was unable to retain information for more than a few hours. He fretted to Gilbert that nobody would now believe him, as he had repeatedly cried wolf.

In the final chapter of *The Case of Rudolf Hess*, Dr J.R. Rees conducts a 'general review of the case' in which he draws on the ground work prepared by Dr H.V. Dicks. Following his work with Hess, Dicks conducted a thorough study of the psychology of German prisoners of war between 1942 and 1945 in order to tease out personality traits common to those who held strong Nazi beliefs. Dicks detected a strong correlation between fanaticism and the willing acceptance of a strong father during childhood. The Prussian tradition of discipline, ruthless force and domination had been accepted by the rest of Germany, which Dicks viewed as more impressionable and soft-skinned, in much the same way as a 'hard shell slips over a snail'.

The review stated: 'The German is stirred by the sense of might and order, of belonging to a mighty national organism about which he has created a legend of invincibility; it helps him personally to feel stronger . . . The greater the father figure to whom he can subordinate himself, the more manly and noble it is to submit to such a figure.'

Nevertheless, Dicks and Rees argued that there remained a residue of hate felt by every man to the tyrannical father figure and that this had taken the form of a 'Romantic Revolt' – an unconscious act in which the German identified himself with a hero who rescues, primarily, his mother 'and so his homeland, or his German soul, from the tyrannical oppressor'. In the past this fuelled the nation's romantic literature, poetry and music, but over the past fifteen years the Nazis had redirected this hatred against the regime's principle scapegoats: the Jews and the Bolsheviks.

This was the backdrop against which they dissected the psyche of Rudolf Hess. The hypochondria he suffered was dismissed as a well-established symptom found among the German elite: 'No country in the world has so many small and delectable spas where the insightless, greedy, over-driving *Herrenvolk* can take their psychosomatic distresses, their functional "heart and nerve" disorders, and place them in the hands of witch doctors abounding at these places, and wash away their guilt in passive submission to purificatory rituals of countless varieties of healing waters, nature cures and regimented ordeal by fasting.'

Rees and Dicks had detected within Hess a repressed hatred of his father: 'In this situation is the making of an unconscious passive homosexual disposition, which, in turn, is widely held by psychiatrists to play an important part in later paranoid attitudes.' This, in their view, was compounded by Hess's close relationship with his mother:

> In Hess this split appears to have become unusually marked. We note the antithesis of the street-fighter and the sentimentalist who fishes a wasp out of the jam-pot; the tough mountaineer and the health faddist; the storm-troop leader and the dog-like devotee and follower.
>
> The personal roots of Hess's outstanding sense of inner weakness and contamination can be derived from his unrecognised, repressed passive streak – as it were, the mother in him – and from his persistent adolescent auto-eroticism. Every psychiatrist will know the reactions which such immaturities are apt to engender in sensitive individuals. Both passivity and masturbation may lead to frantic efforts at ascetic self control, over-assertion of strength and masculinity, and intolerance of weakness due to the haunting dread of being morally bad and inferior.

It was stated that the psychotic notion of division of personality, one part ill and weak and poisoned, which could be joined to the other part incorporating the adolescent hero fantasy, was 'most likely based on masturbation guilt'. The review stated, 'We recall here the Parsifal story in which Amfortas the King, by his sin, has become incurable and the Holy Grail dim, to be saved by the "Pure

Fool" Parsifal. The appeal of this theme to Germans, in Wagner's lush rendering, is well known.'

On the question of why Hess embarked on his mission, the review suggested that, 'It is possible that he took flight from Germany because the idealised fantasy relationship towards Hitler as the perfect ideal father figure had become threatened. We have stressed earlier the paranoid individual's need to keep in good relations with at least one person. It may well be that, at Haushofer's mystic suggestion, he now chose as his new 'good figure' the gallant Duke of Hamilton as British aristocrat and sportsman, and somehow representative of the King, instead of the tarnished Hitler.'

In terms of diagnosis, Hess's history and behaviour pointed to paranoid schizophrenia:

> In this account of Hess as we saw him and as his life story has revealed him, he appears as a self-centred, shy, shut-in 'aoristic' personality, submissive but antagonistic to his father in early life, more devoted to his mother and what she stood for, suffering from guilt and an unsettled employment problem, given to an unstable alternation between heroic aggressive and doggedly industrious; submissive patterns of living, caught in the swirling political currents of his country, with whose fate he becomes emotionally identified and whose extreme forms of irrationalities he is driven to adopt by his craving for devotion and fantasies of glory. He basks briefly but uneasily in the early sunshine of Nazi success, but his haunting sense of inadequacy and inner conflict destroy his influence in a position of power far beyond his capacity – perhaps a little to his credit in the setting in which he was expected to live his life.

Prior to the end of the trial Hess maintained a strict distance between himself and the guard and visitors. He would stand rather than sit down during interviews. He refused to shake hands. When a guard handed him a dollar bill on which he had collected the signatures of the other prisoners and asked him to apply his own, Hess smiled, stepped back from the bar, bowed, then tore the bill into shreds which he then threw out of the window, declaring that 'Our German signatures are precious.'

His delusional beliefs were still firmly present. He said of his fear of poisoning, 'Even now, at times these ideas come over me. I will look at a piece of bread or a bit of food and suddenly I feel sure that it has been poisoned. I try to talk myself out of this belief, but usually solve the problem by simply putting the food away. Occasionally, however, I force myself to eat it and then invariably have an attack of stomach cramps or feelings of giddiness which merely confirms my idea.'

He said of his flight, 'I have the satisfaction of knowing that I tried to do something to end the war.'

But when confronted by the overwhelming evidence of the Holocaust, Hess said of Hitler, 'I suppose every genius has a demon in him – you can't blame him – it is just in him.'

In his final statement before the court he said, 'I was permitted to work for many years of my life under the greatest son whom my country has brought forth in its thousand-year history. Even if I could, I would not want to erase this period from my existence. I am happy to know that I have done my duty to my people. I do not regret anything. If I were to begin all over again, I would act just as I have acted, even if I knew that in the end I should meet a fiery death at the stake.'

Rudolf Hess, who was to consider himself the last standard bearer of the Nazi Party, was found guilty of Charge 1: 'Participation in a common plan or conspiracy for the accomplishment of a crime against peace,' and of Charge 2: 'Planning, initiating and waging wars of aggression and other crimes against peace.' He was found innocent of charges three and four, 'war crimes' and 'crimes against humanity'.

The Soviet judge demanded the death penalty, but the British,

French and American judges disagreed and he was instead sentenced to life imprisonment.

One of the final words should go to Winston Churchill:

'Reflecting upon the whole of this story, I am glad not to be responsible for the way in which Hess has been and is being treated. Whatever may be the moral guilt of a German who stood near Hitler, Hess had, in my view, atoned for this by his completely devoted and fanatic deed of lunatic benevolence. He came to us of his own free will, and, though without authority, had something of the quality of an envoy. He was a medical and not a criminal case and should be so regarded.'

Churchill's sentiment was shared by Hess's fellow companion at Camp Z. Frank Foley had retired from MI6 in 1949 and returned to his garden in Stourbridge, to his wife Kay, daughter Ursula and his old spaniel Johnny. Each Christmas he received a canned turkey from New York, sent by a Jewish doctor who had been the recipient of one of Foley's illicit visas. Foley died of a heart attack on 8 May 1958, and a year later a grove of 2,200 pines was planted in his memory at Kibbutz Havel, outside Jerusalem, each tree paid for by a person saved from the concentration camps by the British agent.

A year prior to his death, Foley wrote to a friend about Rudolf Hess: 'He was a nasty piece of ignorance, but he was not as cruel as some of those who are now free. He was quite mad and, in my mind, incapable of pleading. He should be freed, but I suppose is forgotten.'

After 42 years' imprisonment in Spandau Prison in Berlin, 21 as its solitary inmate, Rudolf Hess hanged himself, using an electrical extension cord in the summerhouse of the prison garden in 1987. He was 93 years old.

Acknowledgements

I would like to thank the staff at the public records office at Kew Gardens in London and at the House of Lords for assisting so superbly in my research. I would also like to thank my agent, Eddie Bell at Bell-Lomax and at Quercus, my editor, Richard Milner. Michael Smith, the author of *Foley: The Spy Who Saved 10,000 Jews* was a great assistance and provided me with pictures of Frank Foley. Today Mytchett Place is in the private hands of a research company and I would like to thank their staff for generously allowing me to visit and for giving me a guided tour of the house and its extensive grounds. I was also assisted by Peter Starling at the Army Medical Services Museum who provided me with microfilm copies of the reports by the RAMC staff who guarded Rudolf Hess. For extra assistance I'd like to thank Eben Harrell and Peggy Roberts.

For providing shelter and friendship in London, I'd like to thank Gerri Peev and her husband, Wayne.

For support over the past year I'd like to thank my mother-in-law, Sarah Anderson and my parents, Margaret and Frank.

I can never stop thanking my patient, understanding and loving wife, Lori for all she has done for me over the years. I hope to spend the rest of my life making it up to her.

Index

Adams, Major Vyvyan 171, 172–3
Ali, Rashid 141
Allason, Thomas 4
Andrus, Colonel Burton C. 314
Anglo-American Declaration 200–1
Anti-Comintern Pact 56
Ark Royal 70
Armistice 8, 19, 21, 25, 119, 141
Armistice Day 268
Atkinson-Clark, Lieutenant 166, 195, 271
Atrocities White Paper 184, 185
Auslands Organisation 75

Baker, Richard Arnold *see* Barnes, Captain
Barbarossa, Operation 56–7, 207, 247
Barnes, Captain 8, 11, 64, 65, 74, 93, 112, 166
  Hess' accusations 195
  Lord Simon meeting 113
  lunch with Hess 170
Battaglia, Roman 45
Battle of Britain 26, 51
Bayley, R. R. 5
Beaverbrook, Lord 53, 206, 207–34, 240, 264
  dinner with Maisky 245
  letters 204–5
Beck, Jozef 117, 220–1
Bedford, Lieutenant Colonel Evan 299, 300, 304
Belgium 118, 132
Bentley Priory 42–3
Berchtesgaden 39, 55, 62, 149
Beria, Lavrenty 247
Bernadotte, Count Folke 308
Best, Officer 179
Bevin, Ernest 172
Bismarck 70–2, 88, 194
Bismarck, Otto von 244
Blackford, Group Captain D. L. 34, 35
Bletchley Park 246–7
Blomberg, Werner von 190

Blumenthal, Werner Gaunt von
 see Barnes, Captain
Boer War 119, 134, 185, 198, 199
Bolshevism 198, 212, 214, 216, 232, 237
Bormann, Martin 25, 55, 56, 59, 61–2
Boulnois, Colonel 261–2
Boyle, Air Commodore 35
Bracken, Brendan 48
Brauchitsch, Walther von 288
British Expeditionary Force 224–5
Bruckmann, Elsa 205
Bruckmann, Hugo 205
Butler, Rab 239

'C' *see* Menzies, Sir Stewart 'C'
Cadogan, Sir Alexander 3, 33, 34, 47, 77, 81, 249–50, 255, 293–5, 304, 305
 diary 156–7
 Hess' letters to King 281, 282
 Hess' suicide attempt 164
 and Loftus 191–2
 Lord Simon's meeting 70
 The Times 174
 Whisper Campaign 243, 246
Calcraft, E. L. 295
Campbell, Mr 170–1
Chamberlain, Neville 26, 34, 116, 217, 219–20
Cheviot Hills 43
Chiang Kai-shek 180
Christianity 180
Christmas 282–4
Churchill, Winston 12, 26–7, 28, 50–3, 54, 178, 268, 321
 and Beaverbrook 207
 and Beck 220–1
 Duke of Hamilton meeting 47–8
 faux negotiation 69–70
 Hess meeting transcripts 149
 Hess' suicide attempt 164
 Murmansk 94
 note from Morton 192
 reports 104–5, 186
 rumours about Hess 172
 Russia and Germany 240
 and Stalin 235, 247
Ciano, Galeazzo 60
Clausewitz, Carl Philipp Gottlieb von 22
Cliveden Set 173, 239
clothing 300
Coates, Colonel Norman 2, 3, 7, 9, 74, 182, 192
Coldstream Guards 9, 64, 152, 269
Colville, Jock 47
concentration camps 183–4, 185, 186, 199, 271
 Boer War 119, 134, 185, 198, 199
Cook, Colonel Hinchley 182
Cooper, Duff 53, 54, 246
Copenhagen 118
Cot, Pierre 116
Crete 125–6, 226
Cripps, Sir Stafford 238,

240–1, 244, 246
Cumbrae Islands 43
Czechoslovakia 49, 116–17, 119

Dahlerus, Birger 26
Daily Herald 295
Dale, Professor H. H. 68–9
Danzig 26, 117, 178, 246
Davidson, Major General F. H. N. 88
Dawkins, Private 302
Denmark 29, 118
Dicks, Major Henry Victor 77, 78, 93–110, 112, 147, 151, 153, 158, 168–9
  catheter 165–6, 193, 196, 292
  Hess' accusations 167–9, 192–3, 195, 196–7
  Hess' distrust 167, 192–3, 199
  Hess' suicide attempt 160–2
  illustrated paper 174
  meeting with Swiss Minister 279
  Mytchett Place's atmosphere 93
  replacement 181, 189
  report 106–10
  review 317–19
  shoe purchase 267
  Soviet invasion 175
Dietrich, Dr Otto 57
Ditchley Park 47–8
Dollan, Sir Patrick 172
Donald, Major Graham 45
Dorsetshire 71
Double-Cross System 301
Dumfries Asylum 305
Dungavel Castle 42, 43–4
Dunkirk 26
Dupree, Tom 239

Eden, Anthony 48, 49, 51, 52–3, 240, 242, 243, 244, 245–6
  faux negotiation 69–70
  and Loftus 191–2
  Maindiff Court 305
  propaganda 255
  psychoanalysts 77–8
Edward VII, King 49, 115
Edward VIII *see* Windsor, Duke of
Elser, Georg 179
England's Foreign Policy under Edward VII 49
Evapan Sodium 233
Everatt, Lance-Corporal 166, 174–5, 299, 302

Farrar, 115
Fath, Hildegard 203, 296, 297–8, 309–10
'Final Solution' 26
Fisher, Lord 120
Fleming, Peter 47
Flying Visit 47
Foley, Kay 36, 184, 321
Foley, Major Frank 8–9, 64, 65, 74–6, 100, 103–4, 170, 285, 286–7
  Armistice Day 268

Foley, Major Frank (*cont.*)
Beaverbrook meeting 204–5, 206
Bismarck sinking 71
conversation with Hess 81–6
departure 295–6, 301–2
and Dr Graham 15
exercise ground 258, 265
Germany's secret weapon 274
Hess' accusations 195, 196, 197
Hess' broadcast 182–3
Hess' document 199
Hess' father's death 259
Hess' letters 182
Hess' poisoning fears 289–91, 292
Hess' statement 294–5
Hess' suicide attempt 162, 180–1
introductions 11
Jews 8, 184–5, 321
'Jonathan's food' 262–3
letter to Laird 200
Lisbon trip 36
and Loftus 187, 190–2
Lord Simon meeting 112–13
and Major Dicks 94–5
noise complaints 289
O'Neill's memo 252
psychological abuse 194
radio 293
Reichenau's death 287–8
reports 106, 156, 186–7, 263–8, 299–301
security 274–5, 288
spectacles 281
suicide concerns 102
Swiss Minister 275–6
The Times 166, 173–4
wine 111
Ford, Henry 37
Foreign Relations Committee 116
the Fortress bomber 227
Foster, R. R. 295
France 26, 87, 117, 221, 228, 238, 267, 283
Alsace-Lorraine 115
armistice 25
BEF 122–3, 224–5
WWI 49
'Frankfurter' 238
Freikorps 19
Friedenthal, Hans 184
Fritsch, Werner von 190

Gauleiters 59
Geneva Convention 94–5, 266
George VI, King 6–7, 16, 26–7, 80, 194–5
Hess' letters 101, 269–74, 279–81, 291–2, 293–4, 303
lunch with Hamilton 54
Gepp, General 261, 304, 305
Gestapo 178–9, 271
Gilbert, Dr Gustave 312, 316, 317
Gladstone, William 144, 198
Gneisenau 300
Goebbels, Joseph 22, 24, 57, 59, 60, 62, 255, 284
Goering, Hermann 26, 36–7,

56, 57, 59, 123, 139, 178, 189, 254
Blomberg's wedding 190
Hitler succession 25
jokes 188
Nuremberg 310, 315, 316
Goethe, Johann Wolfgang von 101, 102, 159, 286
Gorodetsky, Oleg 247
Gorsky, Anatoly 236, 239
Graham, Dr Gibson 14–15, 72, 74, 78
assessment of Hess 65–8
Bismarck sinking 71
Hess' accusations 195
Hess' suicide concerns 68
leaves 100
psychological abuse 194
Greece 143, 226
Greenwood, Arthur 172
Greim, Robert von 44
Guthrie, Dr *see* Simon, Lord

Hague Convention 278
Hahn, Otto 85
Halifax, Lord 26, 34, 36–7, 238
Hamilton, Duke of 11, 12, 16, 29–34, 37, 73, 80, 148
Beaverbrook's meeting with Hess 208
'good figure' 319
Hess' arrival 45–9
Hess' documents 194–5, 197–8
Hess interview 50–1
Hess' letters 101, 270, 272, 280, 281, 282
Hess' memo 182
Hess' talks with Loftus 191
Hess' uniform 157
home 12, 38, 43
lunch with the king 54
Olympics 15, 28, 45, 46, 54
propaganda 249
Hamilton, General Sir Ian 28, 180
Hardinge, Sir Alexander 282, 293–4, 303
Hart, Liddell 105
Hassell, Ulrich von 61
Haushofer, Albrecht 27–9, 30–5, 39, 253, 307–9
card 46
letters to Hamilton 48
report 62
Haushofer, Professor Karl 15–16, 20, 22, 27–8, 29–30, 37–8, 39
card 46
dream 66, 67, 81, 188, 199
letter to 306, 307
Nuremberg 309
Haw-Haw, Lord 178
Hedin, Sven 65
Heligoland Bight 132
Henderson, Sir Neville 176
Hess, Alfred (brother) 17, 31–2
Hess, Fritz (father) 17
death 258–60, 279, 284
hatred of 318
Hess, Ilse (née Prohl - wife) 20–1, 22, 39, 96, 189, 258
Hess' will 279

Hess, Ilse (*cont.*)
letters to 39, 101–2, 154, 159–60, 199, 203, 257, 259–60, 282–3, 296–7
marriage 22
skis 284
Hess, Klara (mother) 17, 259, 260, 284, 318
Hess, Wolf Rudiger 'Buz' (son) 39, 96, 160, 189, 296
grandfather's death 259–60
letters from 256–7, 258
letters to 41–2, 101–2, 257
Heydrich, Reinhard 62
Himmler, Heinrich 60, 61–2, 153, 169, 188, 244, 308
Final Solution 26
Fritsch accusation 190
Hindenburg, 24
Hitler, Adolf 255, 319
admiration of England 177
assassination attempt 178–9
and Beaverbrook 229
blames Britain for war 49
Blomberg's wedding 190
bombing raids 120
Czechoslovakia 116–17
death 307
Henderson's memoirs 176
Hess' admiration 267–8
Hess' personality 107–8
Holocaust 320
Jews 180
knowledge of Hess' mission 136, 137
Landsberg Prison 17, 22
letters to 39, 55–6, 59, 154, 158–9
Life Magazine 187
Naval Treaty 115–16
noise 179
pact with Russia 179–80
peace with Britain 26–9, 36
peace terms 46–7, 135–6, 137–41
Poland 117
post WWI 115
reaction to Hess' mission 55–63
Russia 241–4
Soviet invasion 175, 188, 198, 286, 287
Sterneckerbrau 21
U-boats 129, 131–2
Hoare, Sir Samuel 31
Holland 118, 120, 142, 246
Hollest, George 4–5
Hollest, John 4
homeopathy 25
Hoover, Herbert 170–1
Hopkinson, Mr 33
Horn, Hauptmann Alfred 45–6, 47
Hubbard, Lieutenant 102, 192
Hungary 185
Hunter, General 9, 10–11

Illustrated London News 174
India 119, 233
Iraq 141–2
Italy 140–1, 144

Jackson, Justice 310, 311–12

Japan 180, 216–17
Japanese Islands 146
Jeffreys, Sgt. 7
Jerome, Jerome K. 51
Jews 180, 287, 302
  concentration camps 183–4, 185, 199
  Foley's help 184–5, 321
  Hess' false beliefs 183, 185
  Holocaust 320
Johnston, Captain Munro K. 181, 189, 197, 201, 206, 279, 291
Joyce, William (Lord Haw Haw) 178
Jung, Dr Carl 77–8

Kaden, Helmut 39
Keitel, General 244
Kellogg, Dr 151
Kelly, Major Ellis 310, 311, 315, 316
Kendrick, Thomas *see* Wallace, Colonel
Kerr, Sir Archibald Clark 235
Kerr, Philip 31
Khrushchev, Nikita 236
Kiel speech 24
King George V 71
Kirkpatrick, Ivone 11, 12, 48–9, 50–2
  Atrocities White Paper 184
  Irish visit 170
  meeting with Hess 112–13, 114, 119, 125–6, 131, 133–4, 137–40, 144, 146
Kleist, Peter 26
Kobulov, Amiak 'Zakhar' 238
Kristalnacht 184

Laird, Stephen 200
Landsberg Prison 17, 22
Lascelles, Viscount 27
Lawrence of Arabia 118–19
Lebensraum 17
Ley, Robert 60
Life Magazine 187
Lindbergh, Charles 37
Lipski, Jozef 117
'Litseist' 237–8
Livingstone, Dr *see* Beaverbrook, Lord
Lloyd George, David 115, 132, 246
Lockhart, Robert Bruce 233
Loftus, Second Lieutenant M. 187–9, 190–1, 192, 197, 199, 200, 203
Luftwaffe 38, 83–4
luminal 155, 156, 301
Lundedorff, General Erich 21
Lutjens, Admiral 70

Mackenzie, Dr *see* Kirkpatrick, Ivone
McLean, David 45
McLean, Guardsman 261
Maginot Line 118, 268
Maindiff Court 305
Maisky, Ivan 238, 239, 244–6
Malone, Second Lieutenant William 12, 72–4, 102, 153–6, 163–4, 176–7, 178–80, 195

Malone (*cont.*)
alternative duties 151
final visit 189–90
Hess' poisoning fears 153–4, 163, 193
Hess' suicide attempt 163–4
Poland 190
Marden, CSM Sgt 261
Mass, Herr 75
Mayakovsky station 235
medicine 78
Dale's report 68–9
luminal 155, 156, 301
Veganin tablets 193
Mein Kampf 17, 188
Menzies, Sir Stewart 'C' 12, 15, 37, 51, 81, 162, 287
Foley's report 156
Hess' suicide attempt 164
illustrated paper 174
reports 106, 186
merchant navy 133
Messerschmitt, Willy 38, 39, 79, 123, 137
"Midget" U-boats 85
Ministerial Council for the Defence of the Reich 25
Mitford, Unity 176, 177
Mixed Medical Commission 304
Molotov, V. M. 25, 237, 247
Moran, Lord 312
Morrison, Herbert 172
Morton, Major Desmond 192, 243
Mosley, Sir Oswald 177
Mueller, Heinrich 56, 62
Munich Agreement 116
Murray, George James 5
Murray, Major J. B. 162–3, 165, 167, 169–70, 192
Mussolini, Benito 56, 60
Mytchett Place 2, 4–7, 10–306
atmosphere 93
Hess leaves 306

Namier, Professor 77
Napoleon Bonaparte 97
National Socialist German Workers' Party (NSDAP) 21–3, 58
Naval Treaty 115–16
Nazi Party 24, 60
newspapers 210–11
media outside Camp z 295
see also The Times
Nicolson, Harold 52, 53
Night of the Long Knives 23
noise complaints 73, 80, 105, 110, 147, 289, 303–4
Norway 117–18, 132, 142, 221
Nuremberg Rally 24, 25
Nuremberg Trials 307, 309, 311–16, 319–21

Olympic Games 15, 28, 45, 46, 54
O'Neill, Con 250–5

'peace party' 26–8, 148, 240, 293
Percival, Captain 267, 268–9
Percy, Lord Eustace 34
Philby, Kim 236, 239, 240

Picture Post 174
Pintsch, Karlheinz 39, 55, 199
Pioneers 295
poisoning fears 98, 103, 105–6, 146–7, 152–4, 167, 169–70, 277, 289–92
  Hess' report 192–3
  letter to King 280
  Nuremberg trials 320
  Swiss Minister's visit 301, 302–3
  truth serum 233, 311
Poland 117, 178, 181–2, 190, 228, 246
Powitzer, Gunther 184
Prohl, Ilse (wife) *see* Hess, Ilse (wife)
propaganda 91, 178, 223–4, 240, 247–55

radio 205–6, 273, 286, 292–3
rations 128
Ratzel, Friedrich 22
Reade, Lieutenant 113
Rees, Colonel John Rawlings 78–81, 153, 156, 189, 299, 302, 304, 305, 312
  background 77
  Hess' accusations 195
  Hess' mental state 168–9
  Hess' suicide attempt 164–5, 180–1
  Hess' trust 167
  report 202–3
  review 317–19
Reichenau, General Field Marshal Walter von 287–8
Reichsleiters 59
Reid, Margaret 9, 36
religion 177, 180
Ribbentrop, Joachim von 57, 180, 188, 231–2, 235, 244, 316
  Duke of Windsor's abduction 27
  Mussolini's appeasement 56, 60
  Russia 26
Riddoch, Dr George 312
Rigby, Major 165
Robb, Sir Frank S. 6
Roberts, Maxwell 30
Roberts, Violet 29–30, 31
Robertson, Major T. A. 34, 35
Rodney 71
Rohm, Ernst 23
Rohrscheidt, Dr 314
Roman Catholicism 177
Romilly, Giles 221–2
Roosevelt, President 149
Rorschach test 310
Rosbaud, Paul 84–5
Rosenberg, Alfred 39
Rothacker, Emma (aunt) 258–9, 279, 284
Rotterdam 120
Rudolf Hess Academy for Modern German Medicine 25
Ruge, General 9
Russia 26, 50, 112, 140, 198, 235–47, 249, 253, 287

Russia (*cont.*)
  Beaverbrook's meeting with Hess 207, 212–16, 218, 232–3
  Beaverbrook's trip 233–4
  German invasion 56–7, 175, 188
  German pact 179–80
  snow 284, 286

Salisbury, Lord 144, 145, 198
Salonika 226
Sands, Captain Hastings David 5
Sargent, Sir Orme 242, 243
Schellenberg, Walter 63
Schmidt, Paul 60
Schroeder, Colonel 312–13
Schulenburg, Friedrich Werner von der 242
Scots Guards 64, 152
Scott, Lieutenant Colonel Malcolm 2–3, 7, 11, 64, 74, 167, 193, 268
  Bismarck sinking 71, 72
  camouflage 267
  cost of keeping Hess 261
  defences 197
  diary 99–100, 166, 170, 197, 263, 276, 292
  escape contingency 203
  food 277, 282
  Hess' accusations 195
  Hess after meeting 150, 151
  Hess' improvement 189
  Hess' letters 258
  Hess' meeting with Simon 112
  Hess' suicide attempt 162, 164, 180–1
  leaves Camp Z 295
  and Loftus 192
  and Major Dicks 94
  responsibility 202
  security 269
  suicide concerns 102, 277–8
sdeithwerter 104
Sebottendorff, Baron Rudolf von 19
Semmelbauer, Doctor 75
shoes 266–7
Sicherheitsdienst (SD) 63
Siegfried Line 124, 228
Silverman, Sydney 171–2, 173
Simon, Lord 104, 111, 112–49, 153, 156, 190, 195, 217, 219, 249, 271
  Churchill meeting 156–7
  Eden meeting 69–70
  Hess' suicide attempt 164
  Maisky's concerns 246
Sinclair, Sir Archibald 48
Smith, Adjutant 151–3, 154, 163
Smuts, General 146
South-West Africa 146
Spandau Prison 321
Spartacus League 19
spectacles 273, 279–80, 281, 288
Speer, Albert 55
Sperr, Ingeborg 309–10
splitting the atom 85

SS (*Schutzstaffel*) 24, 90
Stalin, Joseph 233–4, 241–2, 244, 246–7
Hess' mission 235, 236–7
religion 180
'Starshina' 238
Stauffenberg, Count Klaus Schenk von 308
Steiner, Rudolf 98–9
Stevens, Officer 179
Stoer, Willi 38
Storm troopers (*Sturmabteilung* (SA)) 21, 22, 23–4
Strassmann, Fritz 85
suicide
attempt 158–64, 170, 180–1, 188, 193, 201, 211, 295
concerns 79, 81, 102, 201–2, 264–5, 279
Spandau Prison 321
Summers, Group Captain F. G. 34
Sussman, Toni 77–8
Sutton, Officer 7
Swinton, Lieutenant Colonel 2, 7, 9–10
Swiss Minister *see* Thurnheer, Walther

Talgarth Asylum 305
TASS communique 247
The Tatler 174
Tavistock Institute 77
Thorne, Will 260–1
Thule Society 19
Thurnheer, Walther (Swiss Minister) 258, 275–6, 278–82, 291–2, 293, 294, 301–4
The Times 166, 168, 173–4, 186, 200–1, 211, 219–20, 244
Tower of London 54
Tree, Ronald 47
truth serum 233, 311
Twelfth International Homeopaths' Congress 25

U-boats 81–2, 83, 85, 127–8, 129–34, 191, 198
Udet, General Ernst 38, 56, 137
ULTRA decrypts 246–7
United States 64–5, 134, 198
Anglo-American Declaration 200–1
rumours about Hess 170–1

Veganin tablets 193
Venom directive 242–3
Versailles Treaty 19, 21, 113, 115, 117, 119, 200
Volkischer Beobachter 37

Wagner, Adolf 60–1
Wallace, Colonel 7–8, 11, 64, 68, 74, 104, 170
Hess' accusations 195, 196
Hess' document 199
Hess' poisoning fears 105–6
suicide concerns 102
Swiss Minister 258
Waterhouse, Sergeant 166, 261–2

Wavell, Archibald 137
Webb, Sidney and Beatrice 245
Wehrmacht 60
Weizsaecker, Ernst von 61
'Whisper Campaign' 243–4, 246
will 278, 279
Williams, John Leigh 4, 5
Willis, Mary Leigh 4
Wilson, Lieutenant Colonel C. E. 306
Winant, J. G. 170
Winch, Henry 9–10
Windsor, Duke of 27, 177, 238
Wood, General 116
World War I 18–19, 49, 115, 128, 225

'XX' Committee 34

Yugoslavia 225–6